REORDERING THE PLANET:

constructing alternative world futures

Louis René Beres and Harry R. Targ
purdue university

ALLYN AND BACON, INC.,   BOSTON

To Valerie

and

To Rebecca Michelle and all the other
children who must find a better world

Contents

Foreword

"The most striking feature of the world we live in is that most of its inhabitants . . . are cut off from the future. Life has no validity unless it can project itself toward the future, can ripen and progress." These words of Albert Camus are even more valid today than when they were written in 1946. And they apply not only to each of us as individuals, but as well to our collective modes of existence.

With the help of Apollo Vision we are beginning to experience the unity and the jeopardy of our shared voyage through space on planet earth. World War II ended with atomic explosions, and kindled the apocalyptic imagination of men with prospects of a nuclear wasteland. Although this danger remains present, the locus of anxiety has recently shifted to fears of ecological collapse. These fears are accentuated by a variety of more specific concerns arising from population pressure, environmental decay, resource depletion, energy shortages, widespread alienation and oppression, and the fragility of the international economy. This awesome agenda of challenge is as yet unmatched by strategies for response. We remain cut off from the future, most of all in relation to the political destiny of the planet. To be blunt, we know that a new world order is necessary, but few of us are yet convinced that it is possible.

In such a situation formulas for action are not likely to be constructive unless preceded by genuine understanding. The need for understanding is particularly acute with respect to the international political system. For centuries men of good will have associated the most grandiose failures of social and political life with the war system. But good will and reason do not provide keys to understanding the role of war in human affairs much less inform us about how to do something about it. The line of argument that leads from the present impasse straight to the future utopia, with no intervening opposition from present power-wielders, is sheer phantasy, the dream of a rationalist every bit as irrelevant to the politics of change as the most grandiose, mystical vision of the kingdom of heaven. Linear thinking does not begin to comprehend the complexity of social and political reality and cannot serve as a source of either precept or insight into the future of the planet.

Professors Louis René Beres and Harry Targ have written a pathbreaking book addressed to these central world order challenges. Their inquiry, although animated by good will, seeks genuine understanding, even if their search tends to uncover questions rather than answers. In essence, Beres and Targ are crusaders for a whole new approach to international relations as a subject of disciplined study by political scientists. Reflecting the best work in recent social science, these authors provide a framework for inquiry that is rigorous, systemic, futuristic, comparative, multi-disciplinary, and normative. These six attributes of their approach provide the ingredients for a creative orientation toward the world order crisis of our time, which is the essential precondition for constructive response. We can no longer indulge either the luxury or the vice of reducing the study of international politics to shifting configurations of power and national aspiration. We need, as Beres and Targ realize, to call the whole state system into question. Beyond this, we need to appreciate that it is, in any event, disintegrating before our eyes.

This book helps us consider alternative forms of world order and orients us toward the selection of transition tactics appropriate for whatever world order goals are chosen. Such an inquiry equips us to participate in the central drama of human history by becoming citizens of the future as well as citizens of a particular state. In the last analysis, Beres and Targ propose a new orientation for the political man who would act constructively in these last, fateful decades of the century.

Beres and Targ do not tantalize their readers by setting forth a quick fix elaborated in world order rhetoric. Furthermore, they do not succumb to the traditional reformist dream of political unification or world government, nor do they give way to the opposite, fashionable seduction of wishing power away and entrusting the political order to communal energies mysteriously endowed, while eschewing power, with the capacity to dissolve existing power structures. Instead, their preferred orientation is appropriately dialectical, and aptly sensitive to the contemporary needs for centralization of authority to manage tasks of planetary coordination and of decentralization to overcome a growing sense of alienation arising from the decline of meaningful participatory roles at all levels of social organization. Beres and Targ are abstract thinkers who display solicitude for concrete individuals, they are as concerned with the dehumanizing personal effects of alienation as with the harmful social effects of war, poverty, ecological decay. Such a dual awareness, with its tension between opposite organizing tendencies, is a new, creative emphasis in world order literature, exhibiting an overall realization that the future of world order depends as much on what happens within sovereign states, even possibly at local community levels, as it does on the grand contours of geopolitics.

For many reasons, then, it is important to read Beres and Targ carefully, adopt their kind of approach, and spread their message. A central part of this particular message is, of course, its medium. We do need a new kind of educational experience, not just a reoriented course in international relations but entire academic programs and curricula devoted to world order studies. It remains an open question whether universities with their emphasis on specialization of inquiry with its consequent fragmentation and technicalization of knowledge can evolve conditions for the sort of integrative inquiry that is necessary if our students are to be prepared adequately for the challenges and opportunities that await them in the world.

We live at an exciting, dangerous, decisive moment in history. We need desperately to encourage young people to grasp the world order challenge and join in the work of fashioning a response, but such an urgency is not well served by counseling action without adequate prior preparation in thought and feeling. The history of world order reformist movements is largely a story of impotence and shattered expectations. Beres and Targ are building the sort of intellectual foundations that may endow the movement for world order reform, within a decade or so, with a presently unimaginable potency; that is, if their kind of thinking takes hold, not only here, but in other critical parts of our planet.

Richard A. Falk

Acknowledgments

If this book should lead students to the conceptualization and investigation of alternative world futures, it will be because we have had our efforts enriched by a variety of individuals and institutions. Above all, we are grateful to each other for the exciting and fertile partnership of ideas that has yielded this work. Although each of us has taken primary responsibility for one part of the book (Targ, Part I; Beres, Part II), ours has been a fully joint venture, a continuously pleasant and productive exercise in cooperative scholarship.

But this is not to ignore the contributions of others. In this connection, Professor Targ wishes to express his deep intellectual and emotional debt to several persons: to Harold Guetzkow, who made a lasting impression as a teacher and scholar of international relations; to Lee F. Anderson, Paul Kress, and Paul Smoker, who influenced his early growth as a graduate student; to Peter Knauss, who showed him that what *is* is not always what *should be*; to John Sloan, who stimulated some of the ideas in Part I; to William T. McClure, who demonstrated the integration of intellect and compassion; to Michael Stohl, who provided insightful critical reactions to an early draft of Part I; and to T. Kermit Scott and Robert Perrucci, who have been a continuing source of personal friendship and intellectual stimulation. The author cannot adequately express the debt he owes his loving parents, Genevieve and Irving Targ, who first instilled in him the value of education and offered him the psychic support needed to pursue his goals. Lastly, Professor Targ must thank Dena Targ, who has always felt he could succeed. She has provided the love and the independent intellectual insight that dramatically affected the author and his work on this book.

Professor Beres also wishes to acknowledge the helpful influence of several people. In this connection, the decisive impact of Richard A. Falk, whose leading role in the Institute for World Order's World Order Models Project is only the latest manifestation of an extraordinary record of scholarly accomplishments, is unmistakable. The author's debt to Professor Falk extends to his recent years of graduate study at Princeton, where the idea of thinking creatively and systematically about alternative world futures first began to develop.

Professor Beres also wishes to express a formative intellectual debt to another Princeton teacher, Oran R. Young. It was through the sympathetic and careful guidance of Professor Young that the author first became aware of a variety of substantive and epistemological underpinnings of international relations study. These are reflected throughout the second part of this book. The author would also add a special note of thanks to Princeton University itself.

This brings us to the author's dear parents, who started it all, and to his remarkable wife, who has kept it going. Indeed, it is to these three other Bereses, Sigmund, Margret, and Valerie, that the author owes his most profound debt of gratitude. Theirs has been a uniquely appropriate manner of influence, a living example of the kind of selflessness and cooperative harmony which must ultimately come to prevail between actors in world politics.

The authors also share several debts in common. Of the many friends and colleagues with whom we have chatted at conventions and professional meetings, a few deserve special mention: Mr. A. Michael Washburn, who over the past two years has been the guiding force of the Institute for World Order's University Program, a program that has provided us with a continuing source of ideas and productive interactions. Norman Walbek and Howard Stone of Union College were also especially helpful.

At Purdue, special thanks are due to our colleague William T. McClure for his very helpful comments on an earlier draft of the manuscript, and to the large number of our students who have sustained our interest in the subject of this book and reaffirmed our confidence in its attractiveness and importance. We would also like to acknowledge the secretarial services of Trudy Brown who typed the original manuscript, and of Dotty Eberle, who typed the revised version. Dotty's efficiency and lively intelligence has been most welcome. We wish to thank our research assistants, Bruce Goldberg, Larry Plumb, and Dennis Reece, for their particular contribution to our efforts. Finally, we would like to express our appreciation to Mr. Robert Patterson, Senior Editor, for his interest in our work, and to Ms. Harriett Posner for her skillful and scrupulous editing of the manuscript.

Several years hence, we hope to be able to say that all of the above, in one way or another, have played a part in *reordering the planet*.

All of the manuscript's shortcomings, of course, we must claim as our own.

Louis René Beres
Harry R. Targ
Purdue University

In the end, we still depend upon creatures of our own making.

Goethe, *Faust*

Introduction

As its title suggests, this book is ambitiously conceived. Its realm of concern is no less expansive than the very planet which we inhabit. Even the scope of its recommendations, also coextensive with the dimensions of our endangered Earth, far exceeds what is generally expected of modern social scholarship. Indeed, given the awareness that man's life support systems are closely bound up with extra-terrestrial conditions, it may not be unreasonable to suggest that its scope is broader still.

But this is not an apology! So long as we find ourselves in disagreement with the contention of Voltaire's Dr. Pangloss that this is already the best of all possible worlds, we must set out to "construct" other ones. And recognizing the increasing interrelatedness of principal planetary dangers such as war, population pressure, resource shortages, and environmental deterioration, nothing less than a holistic or world-system perspective can be equal to the task. Our concern for the future, then, will be full-blown; our vision of the world will be as big as the multitude of problems that now confront us with terrible urgency.

The first part of this book is concerned both with alternative world futures per se, and with the future of alternative world futures *study*. With respect to the second concern, it recommends that the study of global alternatives become an ongoing scholarly enterprise. As to the first concern, it is argued that alternative systems must fulfill a variety of human needs more satisfactorily

1

than does today's world of competing actors. This leads us to a detailed examination of three particular kinds of alternative futures that have regularly occupied men's dreams and scholars' thoughts. The part concludes with some tentative proposals for building organic communities in a functionally integrated world.

PART I: THE CHAPTERS

Chapter one discusses the role of international relations scholars as students of alternative futures. Emphasis is placed upon normative theory and the creation of models which can satisfy human needs without a necessary commitment to the current multistate world. Chapter two examines a variety of social-critical theories of the modern state and tries to show how criticisms of the United States may become relevant to many societies of the future, both national and global. Five kinds of theory are discussed. Chapter three offers a discussion of selected international relations theories from a social-critical perspective. Each of these theories provides a platform from which the adequacy of the contemporary world system is evaluated and challenged.

Chapter four analyzes a variety of utopian schemes and anarchist visions as they pertain to alternative futures. This literature is divided into microcosmic and macrocosmic models: the former emphasize self-sufficient community while the latter emphasize federations of communities in national, regional, or world commonwealths.

Drawing on materials from the European Economic Community and other regional experiments, chapter five investigates recent developments in integration theory. This discussion explores the kinds of political and economic processes necessary for integrative success and the implications of integration efforts for human needs. Chapter six analyzes world order visions based upon centralized political institutions, networks of organizations for functional cooperation, or homogeneous universal culture.

Chapter seven, which represents the conclusion to Part I, analyzes the many alternative future schemes discussed in the preceding chapters. The summary and analysis include an investigation of various notions of organicism, raising questions about the feasibility of building organic order at local and planetary levels. Finally, after considering the strengths and weaknesses of various possibilities, an integrated community/planetary scheme is speculated upon.

The second part of this book is more narrowly conceived than the first. While the chapters comprising Part I offer a wide variety of insights and analyses concerning alternative world futures, Part II has a more specific focus. *Substantively*, its conception of world order is confined to power management or war avoidance. *Methodologically*, it offers an elucidation of one particular way in which students may learn to render world order studies more systematic. This means applying to world order studies the same strict canons of inquiry which are now routinely applied to other scientific disciplines.

In conformity with this precept, it is recommended that the selection of world order models for investigation be informed by considerations beyond mere inventiveness. Inquiry must begin with suggested explanations of the particular world order problem in question, and models must be selected accordingly. Thus, whatever models are chosen for investigation must be constructed so as to permit the examination of particular hypotheses. Different hypotheses will tutor the description of world system models in terms of different dimensions. Each of the four chapters following chapter eight in Part II is based upon one principal system-describing dimension and a variety of the kinds of hypotheses that lead us there. These chapters are preceded by one on the dynamics of power management in the existing system of world order—the system our studies seek to improve.

PART II: THE CHAPTERS

Chapter eight describes the dynamics of war avoidance in the existing system of world order. Hence, it offers a look at the basic contours of the system we seek to replace. Chapter nine examines the world order features of several systems conceptualized along an *actor* dimension (i.e., systems described in terms of the kinds of actors in world politics). One of these systems, a system that is uniformly republican as to type of actor, derives from the Kantian hypothesis linking peace to the creation of republican institutions in every state. Some other systems examined in this category are informed by hypotheses connecting peace to (1) status quo rather than revolutionary or modernizing actors, and (2) various kinds of "behavioral" transformations (changes in the conditions of actor behavior).

Perhaps the greatest number of hypotheses concerned with world order problems lead to an examination of systems described in terms of a *process* dimension (i.e., systems described in terms of alternative patterns or processes of power management). Chapter ten examines the power management features of systems that are conceived for the purpose of investigating the world government hypothesis (balance of power, collective security, world government). Linking war to the decentralized nature of the world system, this hypothesis typically rests upon the argument that the actors in world politics are unable to coexist peacefully without a suitable authority above them. As in the case of individual men living outside the civil state, the absence of such authority in the world system constitutes anarchy, and anarchy breeds war. The required remedy is tentatively explained to be an alteration in the form of a world federation or world state.

Several hypotheses suggesting connections between nuclear weapons and world order lead to the examination of systems described along a *context* dimension (i.e., systems described in terms of the weapons technology background of world politics). Chapter eleven considers the power management features of systems that derive from the best known of these hypotheses. This hypothesis links the proliferation of nuclear weapons to increasing global instability. With the continuing spread of nuclear weapons, it is observed, the secure existence of actors in world politics becomes more and more precarious, more and more like the presumably dangerous condition wherein individuals coexist without an authority above them. This chapter also examines the relationship between nuclear weapons and the reliability of alliance commitments. More exactly, it seeks to determine how these weapons influence the ability of alliances to assist state actors in protecting themselves.

Of the several hypotheses leading to the examination of world systems described in terms of *structure* (i.e., systems described in terms of the prevailing distribution of global power), the most prominent are those centering on the bipolar-multipolar debate. Pursuant to the propositions of leading international relations scholars like Kenneth Waltz, Karl Deutsch, and J. David Singer, chapter twelve examines the power management features of both types of configuration. And pursuant to several less widely known hypotheses, it also considers more complex conceptualizations of the world system in terms of structure.

In sum, Part II of this book offers the student of alternative world futures a unique set of guidelines for making the investigation of war avoidance more systematic. As detailed in the conclusion to this part, these guidelines concern the manner in which system models are created and explored. Hypotheses are organized according to four principal categories of explanatory variables (actor, process, context, structure), and models are described in terms of these categories. The subsequent investigation of these models, it is recommended, must conform to the basic requirements of sound logical analysis. Finally, the student is reminded that he is involved in a decidedly *personal* kind of activity, that however broad and diverse the universe with which he is concerned, it is his own private preferences and judgments which must ultimately inform the shape of his "preferred world."

Taken as a whole, Parts I and II present a variety of issues, themes, theories, and methods concerning diverse paths to a more desirable world future. We begin with a multidimensional concern for human need fulfillment and then narrow our focus to the quest for security and war avoidance. We reflect upon certain classical perspectives on alternative world futures and then move to augment them with recommendations for more systematic kinds of inquiry. It is our firm belief that Parts I and II of this book must be considered *together*, that an awareness of their interdependence must precede a full and productive commitment to the study of alternative world futures.

PART I

Historical and
Contemporary Models
of Alternative World Futures

Chapter 1
Normative Theory,
Alternative Futures,
and Academic Discourse

INTRODUCTION[1]

The last ten years have been characterized by a great deal of tension, protest, and violence throughout the world. In our own country, a growing cluster of social problems has stimulated the emergence of newly important political forces. Most notable of these "forces" are the black, young, and poor people of America. Dissatisfied with what they have perceived as an unholy alliance of systemic racism at home and barbarous jingoism in Southeast Asia, these people now seem to regard war and discrimination in terms of a common institutional orientation. Still other sectors of American society have expressed concern for such broadly conceived issues as the destruction of our environment and the "quality of life" in general. Whatever the locus of discontent, the American malaise is increasingly being described in *systemic* terms. These relate specific problems to existing institutions and patterns of interaction.

With certain historic and cultural variations, the rest of the industrialized world has been witnessing similar kinds of problems. For the "third world" of Asia, Africa, and Latin America, however, very different issues seem to occasion violence and disorder. Here, modernization, anxiety about neo-colonial influences, and continuing political instability have yielded a seemingly indissoluble compound of poverty, militarism, and authoritarian rule.

Campus upheavals have been an important consequence of domestic and international crises in various parts of the world. Students and faculty have begun to question the "relevance" of their studies to such crises. It is widely believed that university teaching and scholarship are too often detached from problems of the "real world." Further, the university is sometimes viewed as playing a primary role in supporting existing structures and processes.

While students have been expressing concern on the campus, their enthusiasm for reform has not always been matched by careful scholarship. In the first place, their dissatisfaction has not often led to theoretically sound investigations. Despite an increasingly insistent demand for "system change," there has been scant attention paid to the dynamic forces that lead to such change or to those forces that inhibit it. In the second place, although many students have become political activists, few have taken the time to reflect dispassionately about alternative strategies for change. All too often, they have committed themselves to action based upon incompletely examined ideas and hypotheses. Finally, and most important to this book, students have not yet given systematic consideration to the kinds of alternative future orders they may wish to create. As with older generations whose call for world federalism rested more upon passion and desperation than upon careful analysis, current demands for "power to the people," socialism, and political decentralization are presently unconvincing. From the standpoint of rigorous academic inquiry, the connection between such measures and the ills they are designed to alleviate has yet to be sustained. In short, students are acting without a thorough enough understanding of the system they are challenging or the kind of future they intend to bring into being.

In the context of the contemporary crisis, the study of international politics is taking on new and broader interests. Traditionally, students of international politics often have been counseled to avoid value-laden inquiry and the kind of prescriptions that ensue. This orientation is changing quickly and dramatically. In response to the peculiar urgency of planetary danger, more and more consideration is being given to problems of system change and alternative world futures.

It is the purpose of this book to examine and systematize the study of these issues. The first several chapters will scrutinize many of the alternative future schemes which now exist. These range from plans emphasizing community organization to ones that recommend total-system or worldwide organization of one kind or another. In this connection, it is assumed that any thorough consideration of alternative world futures must look critically at the *whole* tradition of speculation and prescription about the future *at all levels of social organization*. Part II of this book will expand upon the different ways in which alternative systems of world order may be examined with particular reference to war avoidance, the planet's most urgent problem. This part will advise students on how they may rigorously test hypotheses about the futures they prefer.

THE QUESTION OF HUMAN NEEDS

A consideration that must precede critical analyses of alternative world futures is the kind of value standards that guide their evaluation. A commitment to communities, to regional international organizations, or to world order perspectives presumes certain underlying value premises or preferences. These values must be articulated *in advance* so that students of alternative world futures can systematically analyze each proposal in terms of its expected desirability.

Psychologists and political theorists have argued for centuries about the nature of man. Their theories have grappled with the problem of whether there are any qualities intrinsic to man's constitution. Some have debated whether man has any basic needs that must be fulfilled to maintain his human character. Without scientifically or philosophically concluding the debate, it is possible to posit a set of needs or values that humane societies ought to be fulfilling. These human needs can serve as a checklist to evaluate models of new social orders.

One useful postulation of human needs is found in the works of Abraham Maslow.[2] Maslow, a psychologist, defines a series of hierarchically ordered needs that he contends are basic to man cross-culturally. First, man seeks food, sex, and shelter, then security. After these are provided, man pursues love or a sense of belonging, then self-esteem, and finally, self-actualization. Maslow says that as each need is fulfilled, man seeks to satisfy the next order of needs. The first group may be referred to as "self-preservation" needs. The needs for love and sense of belonging can be called "community" needs. Finally self-esteem and self-actualization can be viewed as "self-determination" needs. Such needs can be related ordinally to economics, politics, and psychology. In this sense, a satisfactory alternative future must fulfill three requirements: the economic quest for human welfare, the political quest for meaningful participation in decision-making with others, and the psychological quest for the good life as manifested in feelings of freedom and the sense of self-worth and creativity.

Further, it is conceivable that various models maximize certain needs or values at the expense of others. It may be that man will be forced to choose between models that maximize certain values and not others. We may begin by seeking alternative world futures that provide for all man's needs only to discover that some needs will not be totally satisfied if others are accounted for. If that be the case, then the student of alternative world futures will be forced to rank order those values that are most critical. For example, the models discussed below may be able to maximize creativity, spontaneity, or involvement in political decision-making at the expense of intercommunal peace and stability. World order models may maximize stability and peace at the expense of cultural and political autonomy at the local level. These are empirical questions that should guide the analyses of alternative world futures.

Finally, it should be stressed that the Maslow argument is not the last word on the question of human needs nor is his notion of a hierarchy necessarily convincing. The value of such a conceptualization is that it provides a base from which we can speculate about and systematically study some of the possibilities that alternative futures may provide. Other checklists might also be used, but the rhetoric of political action in the postwar period repeatedly refers to one or another of the needs mentioned.[3] Consequently, the list is closely tied to apparent political demands. It also serves as a productive guide for evaluating various social orders.

ON POSTULATING ALTERNATIVE WORLD FUTURES

The postulation of alternative world futures at the community, national, or international levels has been viewed with scorn in the post-World War II period. Academic work and political discourse typically assume the perpetuation of "what is," while considerations of "what ought to be" are generally viewed as hopelessly romantic. However, commentators on the utopian tradition, such as Mulford Q. Sibley and Martin Buber,[4] argue that the human condition always leads man to dream and speculate about a more desirable social and political milieu. To have such visions is integral to being a conscious human being.

Because of the extraordinary problems plaguing the world today, it seems critical at this point in human history to begin thinking again about various alternatives. Political action is surely hopeless if citizens or subjects do not have coherent conceptions of visions they wish to accomplish by their personal and collective action. With this in mind, students of politics can apply their knowledge to the study of alternative world futures. The social sciences can create a new utilitarian discipline based upon the integration of empirical theory, the "what is," with normative theory, the "what ought to be." The scholarly examination of alternative world futures must not replace lay participation, but it can provide several system models from which citizens can choose.

In essence, the creation of alternative future models involves various kinds of elaborations of certain social-political units and processes. The student generates descriptions of future communities and seeks to discover whether or not they are superior to present patterns through the use of logical analysis and empirical research. *Superiority* is defined in terms of the *particular* values or preferences that inform the creation of the model, e.g., peace, justice, security. Three components are critical to any posited model: a detailed description of the new society, an examination of the assumptions that are explicitly stated or implied in the model, and a discussion of strategies designed to bring about the new social order.

SOURCES FOR IDEAS ABOUT ALTERNATIVE WORLD FUTURES

Perhaps the most difficult aspect of positing alternative world futures involves the preliminary process of describing the models. Since man is bounded by his experience, the most probable sources are the ideas and experiments of the past coupled with outcomes of current alternative living arrangements and laboratory experiments. The material below will briefly discuss some of the major sources for ideas about alternative futures. A central task of subsequent chapters will be to discuss the major historical proposals for alternative world futures.

First, students of alternative futures may draw upon those models proposed by social critics. These are writers and academicians who have maintained some distance from traditional academic boundaries and who have written broadly on social change and industrialized societies. Paul Goodman,[5] for example, has written widely on contemporary civilization and has proposed rather large-scale reorganization of society. In *Communitas*, he and his brother Percival posit three alternative social orders based upon markedly different value assumptions. They suggest that each model provides choices as to "technology, surplus, and the relations of means to ends,"[6] and each model implies certain things about economics, politics, education, culture, domestic life, and other community related functions. The three models are entitled "efficient consumption," the "elimination of the difference between production and consumption," and "planned security with minimum regulation."

One of the plans, "the elimination of the difference between production and consumption,"[7] emphasizes decentralized economic, political, and environmental systems. Here, workers participate in factory planning and decision-making. They do whatever is feasible in their homes, and they perform agricultural services during peak seasons. Farmers work in factories during the off seasons. Public services, city squares, shops, etc., are arranged so that all community activity is centrally located. Physically and socially the model resembles the Greek polis. It seeks to integrate industrial and agricultural life, and to stimulate productive and consumptive patterns that are in human scale. It seeks to create meaningful work and creative leisure, and most importantly to stimulate the growth of fruitful community relationships among people and between the community and natural environment.

Another critic and political theorist, Herbert Marcuse, has stimulated much controversy and political activism in recent years. His major early theoretical work, *Eros and Civilization*,[8] deals both with a critique of contemporary industrial civilization and with an alternative to such a civilization through "polymorphous perversity." This is the ability to gratify oneself in every sensual and sensory way. It can occur only when social organization has eliminated work as it is commonly defined. This condition can exist in an economy of abundance where technological sophistication has achieved its peak. Work based upon a repressive performance principle (the most oppressive form of Freud's reality principle) could be automated out of existence in an economy of abundance. Therefore, the "play impulse" is only achievable in a new non-work, non-repressive civilization. As Marcuse puts it, "The realm of freedom is envisioned as lying *beyond* the realm of necessity: freedom is not within but outside the 'struggle for existence.' Possession and procurement of the necessities of life are the prerequisite, rather than the content, of a free society. The realm of necessity, of labor, is one of unfreedom because the human existence in this realm is determined by objectives and functions that are not its own and that do not allow the free play of human faculties and desires . . . Play and display, as principles of civilization, imply not the transformation of labor but its complete subordination to the freely evolving potentialities of man and nature."[9]

Theodore Roszak[10] is a critic of technocracy. Technocracy is that set of social relationships in industrialized society that combines scientific and technological expertise and bureaucracy. The core of bureaucratic domination is the ideology that he terms "the myth of objective consciousness." This ideology involves science in the separation of researcher from researched, man from man, and ultimately the manipulators from the manipulated. The antidote, and in fact the only hope for a liberated alternative future, is the "counter-culture." The counter-culture seeks, through its thoroughgoing rejection of the myth of objective consciousness, to create a mystical communitarianism that goes beyond mere participatory democracy and creates human communities of experience. These communities presumably are decentralized, small, mystical, and sensual; in every way the obverse of the technocratic state.

A second significant source of ideas about alternative futures includes the utopian tradition (see chapter four) from Thomas More, Robert Owen, and Charles Fourier to Martin Buber, B. F. Skinner, and Aldous Huxley.[11] Students of alternative futures might compare, contrast, and synthesize the varied features of separate utopias to discover useful ideas for new forms of social organization. Utopian literature and experiments contain prescriptions relevant to work and play, sex roles, family structures, decision-making, conflict resolution, intracommunity and intercommunity interaction, technology, and deviance. Viable alternatives to social organization in post-industrial societies might be discovered from investigations of several utopias, past and present.

For example, Robert Owen,[12] the nineteenth-century utopian socialist, asserts that any human character can be formed by applying certain means of education and social organization. Hence, those men of affairs who are appropriately influential have the power to make societies harmonious or belligerent. In his proposals and experiments, Owen creates a system of cooperative community life based upon agricultural productivity, ancillary industrial production, and an equal distribution of wealth. A certain optimal population will live comfortably in a planned parallelogram of buildings with eating and play facilities, as well as schools and churches, in the center. Education will seek to socialize the young to accept the basic oneness of individual and community interests. Children living together and adults living and working together will provide the conditions that foster the growth of harmonious community life.

For Saint-Simon and Edward Bellamy,[13] nineteenth-century French and American utopians respectively, the harmonious society can be of the size of Europe or of the nation-state. Both theorists propose centralized and efficient control of the means of production and management of the economy to the mutual benefit of leaders and followers. The psychologist B. F. Skinner's *Walden Two* is a community controlled by skilled social engineers who are able to create the conditions for happiness of all community members by way of positive reinforcement. These rewards condition behavior to be cooperative and mutually beneficial. Utopian writer William Morris's[14] communities are anarchist and socialist, all self-regulating with few controls over the behavior of individuals and maximum opportunity for individual choice. The underlying assumptions and prescriptions are so varied in this tradition that it provides a rich arena from which to begin examining systematically the alternative structures and processes proposed.

A third speculative tradition involves classical and modern images of world order (see chapter six). The world order literature describes and hopes for the emergence of an integrative process that will ultimately lead to some form of global political, economic, and cultural organization. The student of alternative world futures should seriously consider this literature, comparing and contrasting those processes that theorists view as central to the creation of oneness among supranational movements of peoples.

W. Warren Wagar,[15] an historian, discusses the many themes in this tradition. He distinguishes among those theorists who speak of worldwide philosophical syntheses, cultural syntheses, or religious syntheses. An important source of debate concerns these theorists and others who presume the necessity for beginning the integrative process at the political or economic levels. The theologian Reinhold Niebuhr, for example, challenges the view that power politics can be tempered by strengthening an organization like the United Nations before the creation of more basic cultural and philosophical unity among world societies.[16] Quincy Wright, however, in his classical work of political science, *A Study of War*,[17] emphasizes those institutions and processes within the United Nations system that need to be expanded before cultural and philosophical unity can be created. Another political scientist, David Mitrany,[18] contends that the most basic integrative force is functional cooperation on nonpolitical and specific tasks that are central to all states. These tasks range from mail and health to extensive social welfare services.

Along with various differences about the critical processes needed for movement to an improved world order, there is also disagreement on the *kind of values* to be achieved. Different theorists emphasize the management of power, conflict resolution, or the fulfillment of self-preservation needs, community needs, or self-determination needs. Institutionally, different models emphasize a highly centralized world system, a loosely federative system, or an organic commonwealth of quasi-independent communities of relatively small populations. Other theorists[19] have studied the relationship between regional international organization and world order by looking at the European Economic Community. Since both world order and utopian theorists speak of organic community,[20] a significant question is raised about the feasibility of creating a world-in-community analogous to the close-knit small community of friends. Can a world be created that is analogous to supra-individual personality, organic growth, and union, or can the social solidarity presumed in organic analogies only be achieved in relatively small, self-contained communities?

Another source of ideas about alternative futures is less clearly related to any specific literary tradition, but emphasizes a conceptual process analogous to puzzle solving. What might be referred to as unit-process itemization consists of listing as many currently relevant political, social, and economic units and processes as exist in the world today and then speculating about the prospective desirability of a world if each unit or process increases or decreases in importance. The work of international relations scholar Morton Kaplan[21] is relevant here. Kaplan, in *System and Process in International Politics*, deductively elaborates assumptions about six models of world systems, only two of which have existed historically. The four systems that have no historical referents are developed from changes in institutions and processes of the two historical ones. Thus, students can evaluate a world without an international organization, nation-states, or international corporations. Moreover, they can conceptually magnify the importance of each. Political scientists have used this process in their analyses of domestic politics by evaluating the relative utility of increased community power or state governmental power, or enhanced national institutional power. Integration theorists have examined the adequacy for conflict resolution and need fulfillment of an international system comprised of strong regional actors. Varying the permutations of units and processes in the international system may lead to the "discovery" of some especially desirable combination.

17

A less orthodox source of ideas about alternative world futures entails a close scrutiny of children at play. Political science research about children's development of political beliefs tends to emphasize the understanding of how children become acculturated into the adult world. There is the implicit assumption that examination of childhood cognition, affectivity, and behavior is not interesting in and of itself. It is assumed that adults have nothing to learn from children.

One interesting exception to this is some of the work of Jean Piaget, the noted child development authority. In his *The Moral Judgment of the Child*,[22] Piaget analyzes the moral behavior of children at play. It may be helpful to see how untutored youthful members of society adjust their relationships with each other, create norms and rules of behavior, and deal with intense interpersonal conflict. From such findings, ideas about alternative futures might be suggested.

Piaget has described a capacity in children for what he calls "reciprocity,"[23] the ability to conceptualize other children as co-equal. Beginning at age ten or eleven, children have the capacity and the desire to perceive others and to evaluate them as equals. This kind of reciprocal awareness is stifled as the child grows older and is increasingly exposed to the political and social world of adult ethnocentrism. If reciprocity exists among the young, it may be useful to discover how to maintain and enhance it in adults. Also, since reciprocal awareness and respect often get sidetracked by external social forces, the problem is one of maintaining and expanding that reciprocity in the young that already exists at an early age.

A final unorthodox source of ideas about alternative futures can be real action experiments or laboratory simulations of new societies. Social scientists have already begun to study some of the many communes that have emerged in the United States. Others might become participant observers in such living experiments, evaluating the results in terms of need fulfillment, conflict resolution, and other concerns.

Peace researcher Paul Smoker[24] has argued that contrary to past simulation studies, the laboratory can be used to examine how experimental participants work out major problems. The researcher can then utilize the solutions from the simulation to deal with real world problems. Simulation has usually been used to study phenomena in the external world. The presumably better simulations are those that demonstrated a high measure of correspondence with that external world. Smoker has suggested that social scientists might reverse this interest and seek to make the external world more like the simulation world. As he suggests, "Such an approach is not only important in social creation of desired futures, it suggests an alternative perspective for social science that differs from the 'realistic' position of 'telling it the way it is.' "[25]

EXAMINING HYPOTHESES IN ALTERNATIVE WORLD FUTURES

Whatever the alternative future model examined, there are several hypotheses that serve to justify the creator's selection. To give serious consideration to any such model, these hypotheses have to be studied thoroughly. The multiplicity of hypotheses may necessitate the examination of works by political scientists, historians, economists, philosophers, and scientists. Although some of the tasks may be monumental, students must be made aware of the conditions critical to the creation of these alternatives and of the kinds of problems the different models raise.

Some examples of hypotheses are suggested in the utopian and social-critical literature. Several authors suggest relationships between the fulfillment of community and self-determination needs and changes in the selection and context of work. Some suggest the integration of many different kinds of work roles giving man the option or responsibility to work in industry, agriculture, and the arts. Others emphasize the relationship between psychic fulfillment and self-selection of work. Some concern equal payment for a day's labor or some gradation of credit based upon the amount of difficulty or lack of popularity of given work roles. Finally, Marcuse has contended that liberation can come only from the abolition of work as we define it today. These assertions can be "checked" against research done on work roles that utilizes responses to questionnaires, participant observation, and other techniques in different cultural and economic settings.

A second kind of hypothesis that pervades some of the utopian and anarchist literature posits a special relationship between small-scale autonomous communities of work and leisure and a mutual aid principle that will ensure cooperative interaction among community members. The statement links political and economic decentralization to cooperative intracommunity and intercommunity relationships. Since this idea is critical to any choice about change at the global level or moving toward community, it requires a many-sided examination. Of particular interest would be an analysis of historical and contemporary

19

examples of community. Such an examination could include a look at the Israeli kibbutz, decentralization in Yugoslavia and Cuba, and existing communes in the United States.

A very different kind of hypothesis derived from traditional world order and international organization perspectives assumes a specific relationship between the management of power or conflict and the degree of centralization of political institutions. Such an hypothesis has presumably guided many post-world war movements for world federal government. At the same time, the thesis has never been examined thoroughly. There may be historical analogues of the world government model that could provide some insight into the adequacy of the hypothesis. The pre-Westphalian system of Medieval Europe is a case in point.

CREATING ALTERNATIVE WORLD FUTURES

Much of the contemporary political debate in the United States in the last decade has involved questions of strategy. People in political movements and political parties have argued incessantly about *how* to bring about social change. In so doing, they have also neglected the *kinds of changes* that should be brought about. Because of the linkages between means and ends, present and future, the student cannot afford to ignore problems of implementation. Such concern must not, however, overshadow the prior matter of determining what the desired alternative should be.

Such concern *must* involve several kinds of issues. First, it must determine which *kind of social unit* is central to the desired change. Some emphasize the role of the individual, either in terms of a changed consciousness or a personal political commitment. Others view whole ethnic groups or social classes as the necessary agents of change. Still others speak of communities acting in concert. Various other kinds of social organizations with a marked cross-cultural membership are viewed as critical agents of change, particularly for movements toward world order. Second, activists and theorists have debated *methods of action*. These methods might pertain to electoral politics, various forms of civil disobedience and nonviolence, or to classical modes of revolutionary activity.

Strategies for social change require considerations of theories of change, an understanding of what various methods have been able to achieve, and what numbers, skills, amounts of time, etc., are needed for given strategies to be effective. Also, such considerations necessitate a thorough evaluation of the ethics of political action: Are means commensurate with the desired ends? Is violence justified to bring about social change? Should concern for the rapidity of change require a commitment to violence instead of slower but less destructive modes of action? A multiplicity of empirical and ethical questions must be pondered before the student begins to speak of creating an alternative world future. Such questions require historical and scientific analyses of social change, using appropriate historical analogues for the desired future and for the strategies that have seemingly produced the condition. Such questions also require the study of ethics and philosophy to highlight the perennial questions of personal and social commitment.

SUMMARY

Brief mention has been made of the kinds of strains, tensions, and violence-motivating activities that have characterized the post-World War II period in developed *and* third world societies. The argument was advanced that the student of international politics must, along with his study of present dynamics, give serious consideration to problems of the future and to the construction of futures that might alleviate potential disasters. It was then proposed that a checklist of values could be used to evaluate the prospective costs and benefits of certain kinds of alternative social orders. The kinds of social orders that maximize the productivity and distribution of basic survival needs may not be the kinds that maximize community or self-determination needs. Ideally, alternative futures should be constructed that offer the possibility of maximizing all or most of the values that their creators hold dear. In fact, of course, certain values may conflict and trade-offs may be called for.

From the articulation of values, the student can look to a variety of sources for guidance in the construction of alternative world futures. He can examine the works of social critics, utopians, anarchists, and world order theorists. He can map and remap the existing social and political units to fit new patterns. He can examine unconventional sources like the social organizations of children or the activities of persons participating in simulations or real-living experiments. From these many sources, students can then consider the underlying assumptions that emerge from the newly created societies.

After models are constructed and assumptions examined, the student of alternative futures can consider the question of moving from the present to the future. Strategies for social change must be considered in the light of units and processes of change, the time needed to bring about change, and the ethics of actions designed to bring about the changes. The strategy question must logically follow, not precede, the desirability question.

Lastly, it should be emphasized that the study of alternative world systems must not lead to the presumption that only those in academia have the expertise or the responsibility for creating more desirable world futures. While the thrust of this new area of concern within the study of international relations is oriented toward systematic scholarship, it does not presume the need or the desirability of a new scientific or technocratic elite. Academic studies should serve to stimulate the expansion and exploration of possibilities among *all those* who are interested in such issues. In the final analysis, the choice of alternative world futures rests not with select numbers of professors and students, but with publics throughout the world.

NOTES

1. A different version of this chapter can be found in Harry R. Targ, "Social Science and a New Social Order," *Journal of Peace Research*, 1971, 3-4, pp. 207-220.

2. Abraham Maslow, *Toward a Psychology of Being* (New York: Van Nostrand, 1962).

3. *The Port Huron Statement of the Students for a Democratic Society*, 1962, drew upon concepts similar to those of Maslow. Of particular importance to the New Left has been concern for self-actualization; in Port Huron terms "the object is not to have one's way so much as it is to have a way that is one's own."

4. Mulford Q. Sibley, "Apology for Utopia: I," *The Journal of Politics*, February 1940, pp. 57-74; "Apology for Utopia: II," *The Journal of Politics*, May 1940, pp. 165-188; Martin Buber, *Paths in Utopia* (Boston: Beacon, 1958).

5. Paul Goodman, *Utopian Essays and Practical Proposals* (New York: Random House, 1962); *People or Personnel* (New York: Vintage, 1968); and Paul and Percival Goodman, *Communitas* (New York: Vintage, 1960).

6. Goodman, *Communitas*, p. 121.

7. *Ibid.*, pp. 153-187.

8. Herbert Marcuse, *Eros and Civilization* (New York: Vintage, 1955).

9. *Ibid.*, p. 178.

10. Theodore Roszak, *The Making of a Counter Culture* (Garden City, N. Y.: Anchor, 1969).

11. Thomas More, *Utopia* (Baltimore: Penguin, 1965); Robert Owen, *Report to the County of Lanark, A New View of Society* (Baltimore: Penguin, 1969); Mark Poster, ed., *Harmonian Man: Selected Writings of Charles Fourier* (Garden City, N. Y.: Anchor, 1971); B. F. Skinner, *Walden Two* (New York: Macmillian, 1948); Aldous Huxley, *Island* (New York: Bantam, 1963).

12. Robert Owen, *Report to the County of Lanark, A New View of Society*.

13. Henri de Saint-Simon, *Social Organization, The Science of Man and Other Writings* (New York: Harper & Row, 1964); Edward Bellamy, *Looking Backward* (New York: Signet, 1960).

14. William Morris, *News from Nowhere* (London: Reeves and Turner, 1890).

15. W. Warren Wagar, *The City of Man* (Baltimore: Pelican, 1967).

16. *Ibid.,* p. 200

17. Quincy Wright, *A Study of War*, abridged by Louise L. Wright (Chicago: University of Chicago Press, 1964).

18. David Mitrany, *A Working Peace System* (Chicago: Quadrangle, 1966).

19. *International Political Communities, An Anthology* (Garden City, N. Y.: Anchor, 1966).

20. The *organic* analogy views persons as integrally related to some whole social system in the same manner as parts of the human body are related to the whole body. The organic view of social life is described further in chapter seven.

21. Morton Kaplan, *System and Process in International Politics* (New York: Wiley, 1957).

22. Jean Piaget, *The Moral Judgment of the Child* (London: Kegan, Paul, 1932).

23. Jean Piaget and A. Weil, "The Development in Children of the Idea of Homeland and of Relations with Other Countries," *International Social Science Bulletin*, autumn 1951, pp. 561-578.

24. Paul Smoker, "Social Research for Social Anticipation," *American Behavioral Scientist*, July-August 1969, pp. 7-13.

25. *Ibid.,* p. 11

Chapter 2
Social – Critical Theories
of the Modern State

Before critically examining the central forms of alternative world futures, this chapter and the next will briefly consider certain social-critical theories concerning current domestic and international political systems. Social-critical theory seeks to describe and explain particular relationships and often to predict future developments from current trends. Its findings are viewed as justification for criticisms of the present. As values inevitably tutor inquiry, the social critic's analysis recognizes the disparity between what he views as desirable and what actually exists. Through his analysis, the theorist tries to understand and signal the kinds of dangers to basic values that prevail within present forms of social organization.

The overarching emphasis of social-critical theory is on *change*. It recognizes that stability presumes the perpetuation of a social condition which the theorist finds wanting. Even though some theorists, particularly those studying international politics, may not presume the possibility or the desirability of change, their analyses serve to stimulate thought about a future that is different from the present. Traditional balance of power theory in the study of international relations fits in this category (see chapter three) as it describes a world without common authority, self-interested national actors, and periodic violence. However disconcerting to balance of power theorists, the implications of such descriptions will be considered as part of the social-critical tradition.

FIVE SOCIAL-CRITICAL VIEWS OF THE MODERN NATION-STATE

Five basic kinds of theories have characterized recent studies of national phenomena in the modern state. Each kind of theory emphasizes one set of factors as the central dynamic force for stability and change. While most of the theorists are writing about the United States in particular, the implications of their statements for similar developments in other parts of the world are alarming. If the United States is at the pinnacle of development and others are striving to achieve this position, the planet as a whole may soon experience the negative consequences for human need fulfillment that now appear uniquely American. Moreover, as the most powerful actor in the world system, the United States is significantly influencing others to develop in ways that conform to the American pattern.

Furthermore, the chapters that follow do not view alternative world futures solely from the standpoint of transforming national actors into larger, more homogeneous political and social structures. Those theorists like the utopians and anarchists who envision viable futures in terms of immediate and small-scale communities (see chapter four) will view any of the developments described below as a serious threat to human need fulfillment. For these several reasons, the social changes described should *not* be judged as America's distinctive problem, but should be viewed as an indicator of what *world society* will look like given current trends. The pictures painted by social-critical theorists dramatize the need for alternatives *within* states both for the sake of *intra*national improvement and *inter*national transformation.

THE ORGANIZATIONAL/TECHNOCRATIC CRITIQUE

This first critique makes of technology, science, and organization a vast, complex, quasi-mystical process that significantly controls or influences all human activity. It is a critique that takes account of the most contemporary characteristics of industrialized societies, making them into an "albatross." Theodore Roszak, for example, terms the complex of science, technology, and organization "a technocracy."[1] Technocracy goes beyond a conventional power structure with impressive mechanisms of control and repression. It is "a grand cultural imperative" which takes on the qualities of mysticism among the citizens of the state. The technocracy is also a "capacious sponge able to soak up prodigious quantities of discontent" and therefore able to nullify any resistance to it. For Jacques Ellul, a French theorist in this school, the problem is a method imbedded in the Western tradition. He calls the method a technique which "does not mean machines, technology, or this or that procedure for attaining an end. In our technological society, *technique is the totality of methods rationally arrived at and having absolute efficiency . . .* in *every* field of human activity."[2]

Roszak says that technocracy represents the highest form of organizational integration and social engineering based upon expertise, efficiency, social security, and coordination. The technocratic society is based upon three interlocking premises: (1) all vital needs require technical solutions; (2) any friction in society is primarily a breakdown of communications; and (3) experts exist within the hierarchy of the state or the corporate world. Elites justify their decisions through appeal to expertise and the experts justify themselves through the utilization of scientific research and knowledge. No knowledge or insight exists beyond that of scientifically accumulated knowledge.

The ramifications of technocratic norms for most social institutions are great. Education in actuality is training for functional roles within some bureaucracy. The economy is nothing more than the product of manipulation by oligopolistic forces. Democracy involves mechanistic polling of simplistic opinions of publics and of decisions by experts. All social processes are part of a grand machine, and people are replaceable parts of the machine.

Along with technology, technique, and the social organization of technique, there exists a scientific-ideological structure that provides the beliefs and values underlying the entire system. Roszak calls this structure "the myth of objective consciousness,"[3] an "arbitrary construct" chosen by people in a given historical period to provide meaning to life. There are three psychological constructs that characterize this objective consciousness: (1) the alienative dichotomy, (2) the invidious hierarchy, and (3) the mechanistic imperative.

The alienative dichotomy involves the separation between "in-here" and "out-there." The scientific epistemology separates the phenomena of the outside world, the phenomena beyond the scientist's person, from his own subjective experience. The self is expunged from the observation. This leads, particularly in social science research, to the growth of insensitivity or a "cool curiosity" rather than an engaged, sympathetic, and empathetic perspective. The dichotomy is skillfully created by abstract formulations, statistically based modes of analysis which extrapolate from individual experiences to broad generalizations, and questionnaire constructions that extract from the totality of an individual's personality very specific forced-choice responses. Essentially, the expert separates himself from the subject and maintains a dispassionate, unfeeling relationship with him.

Following the separation of "in-here" from "out-there" and

the denuding of "in-here" of any substantive, emotional content, "the invidious hierarchy" inevitably emerges. In-here (the expert) becomes superior to out-there (people or things being studied). The external world of necessity becomes subject to manipulation and control. " 'In-here' learns, plans, controls, watches out cunningly for threats and opportunities." Out-there is "drift, unpredictability, stupidity." Out-there is devoid of meaning and becomes prey to in-here, to the experts. Through research, in-here knows how out-there works and hence seeks total control.

Finally, the myth of objective consciousness leads to a mechanistic imperative, the motivation to make in-here, the expert himself, machine-like or to turn in-here over to machines. The clock, the computer, instruments of mass media, all routinize and transform our inner being: "The machine achieves the perfect state of objective consciousness and, hence, becomes the standard by which all things are gauged."[4] It is at this point that all culture is susceptible to mechanization.

Technology, organization, and science then proceed in an interlocking relationship to transform man from master to slave. This transformation takes place in most dimensions of being, usually with man having little or no cognizance of his oppression. For Roszak, two phenomena seem most characteristic of the manipulative aspect of the technocratic state: protest and sex.

In reference to the former, dissident groups organize and challenge the ongoing political system. The foci of protest attention yield resistance, struggle, and finally change. This might mean an alteration of policy, a renovated institution, or a budgetary reallocation. Each change is viewed by dissidents as a kind of victory, but in fact the technocratic "system" has skillfully manipulated and controlled the movement through its patterned resistance and conciliation. Roszak offers an analogy between political protest and persons pushing to open a closed door that does not budge. If the door is suddenly opened, those pushing against it come tumbling into the room. They have lost control of their minds and bodies; they are therefore subject to control. This is the political process, and dissent is always subject to systemic manipulation. Politics cannot bring social change in a technocratic state.

Finally, the discussion of sex suggests perhaps the most alarming possible tendencies of the technocratic state, the ability to mold and manipulate man's basic instinctual structure. Roszak's position is that sex, in what is perceived as a liberated society, is part and parcel of the technocratic state. The imagery of the liberated society is that of the Playboy Bunny, an image that suggests promiscuity as the reward for appropriate organizational behavior and appropriate conspicuous consumption. Sex is available for those who behave and consume "correctly." Since, for most people, the resources for appropriate behavior and consumption are drastically restricted, sexual liberation lives in the world of fantasy and myth. Furthermore, the objects of this fantasy are women who are perfect representations of "out-there." To the extent that men and women live by this mindless fantasy, they are subconsciously manipulated and oppressed. Herbert Marcuse calls this condition "repressive desublimation."

An organizational/technocratic theorist who more than any other thinker reflects the pessimism of the modern age is Roderick Seidenberg.[5] Seidenberg sees two organizational imperatives operant in all political and economic systems. First, organization seeks to create total cohesion and control of all those components, human and environmental, that exist within its bounds. Second, upon achievement of internal control, organization seeks to expand its parameters and scope of control beyond itself.

Organizational growth is a manifestation of the dynamic quality of human intelligence, the capacity to remember, to abstract, to generalize, and to routinize. Before the emergence of collective human intelligence, humans were motivated primarily by basic static instincts (food, sex, etc.). Therefore, the period of prehistory was dominated by instincts; the period of history is characterized by conflict between instinct and intelligence. Finally, posthistory will be dominated by intelligence and universal organization. The outcome of this final stage will be entropy, stagnation, and human destruction. Men will become robots.

Seidenberg says that organization implies machines and technology: "Organization, dissolving chaos and incoherence in ever wider arcs of life, moves toward universality; and nowhere has this inherent drift been more compelling in its sweep and more preemptory in its demands than in the expansive claims of the machine and its technology."[6] The machine accelerates the organization of life and demands human adaptation to its rhythm. Science has made manipulation of the physical world and man possible. As with other critics in this school, Seidenberg views machines, organization, and scientific technique as inseparable.

Generally the organizational/technocratic critique views with pessimism the application of science *through* organization to social, political, and economic life. The image of the gigantic machine vividly projects a future of billions of people around the world behaving like ants. The darkest side of this vision is that people will think that they are politically, socially, and even sexually "free" when in fact they are totally controlled. Indeed, for some, this totalitarian future already exists in the industrialized world and only awaits the infusion of technology in Asia, Africa, and Latin America to become global in scope.

THE STATIST CRITIQUE

The statist critique, derived from an earlier anarchist tradition, sees a connection between the development of the modern state and many social ills. The state replaced an earlier and presumably superior organic order manifested in primitive villages, Greek city-states, medieval guilds, and other small integrated and cooperative communities.

Accepting this analysis, Petr Kropotkin, the Russian anarchist, in the classic tract *Mutual Aid*,[7] sought to challenge an erroneous social application of Charles Darwin's evolutionary theory. Herbert Spencer, Thomas Huxley, and other nineteenth-century theorists argued that those organisms that were most successful in intra- and inter-species conflict were most likely to survive and stimulate evolutionary development. "Survival of the fittest" was viewed as central to human as well as to animal development. To the contrary, Kropotkin contends that such theorizing overemphasized conflict in human affairs, ignoring the propensity for "mutual aid." Natural selection meant that those species practicing mutual aid would survive and prosper.

In Kropotkin's judgment, the history of human life is a history of the emergence and re-emergence of natural communal life. Early man organized in ways that can be characterized as primitive communism. Tribes, villages, and cities owned property collectively, made decisions collectively, and grew in the context of a communal tradition. Those societies that practiced mutual aid were more likely to persist than those that became atomized and conflictful. The height of man's progress occurred in the early renaissance in city-states with men bound organically through geography, voluntary associations, and guild systems.

Because of ineffectual attempts at peasant assimilation, the medieval city-state fell prey to rural opposition. Acquisitive kings with peasant support destroyed the free cities and created precursors to the modern state. Organic unity was replaced by the distant state. The state gained control of social life through the development of law, the mechanisms of coercion, and education. It created a system of authority giving a minority power over the majority. Kropotkin contends that the creation of the state prevented "the direct association among men," shackled "the development of local and individual initiative," destroyed and prevented the reappearance of basic liberties, and subjected "the masses to the will of the minorities."

A similar argument has been made by the contemporary American sociologist Robert Nisbet.[8] His basic contention is that a normative order, a system of values guiding rules of behavior, depends on associative order, or community. The state, because of size, impersonality, and distance from people's lives, has destroyed those associative orders that transmit and create value systems. No large associations can meet the psychological needs of people because they are bureaucratized, complex, and "too aloof."[9] The state can create pseudo-community to maintain support for warfare and other causes, but it is unable to meet human needs for "recognition, fellowship, security, and membership."

The state developed at the same time that liberalism as a political theory was gaining dominance in the West. Autonomous man replaced community as the source of security, reason, passion, and values. As with Newtonian science and laissez-faire economics, society was redefined in terms of a complex of interacting "human atoms in motion," devoid of any significant group context. The end product was a highly centralized state comprised of atomized individuals associating only as an undifferentiated mass. Traditional forms of authority were replaced by state authority.

Finally, a formulation of the statist critique in terms of ethical theory has been articulated by a political philosopher, Robert Paul Wolff.[10] The problem raised by the state is the problem of authority. Authority involves "the right to command" as well as "the right to be obeyed." Drawing upon Kant, Wolff contends that the moral man must be autonomous, that he must act and be responsible for his own actions. There cannot be any such thing as a command for the moral autonomous man. The dilemma, therefore, is that the very nature of the state is obeisance to authority while the mark of man is his autonomy. All authority is illegitimate in that it interferes with autonomous man. The only possible form of political rule that would meet the ethical criterion would be unanimous direct democracy. Those political systems that practice representative democracy or majoritarian democracy fall prey to the will of authority. Wolff concludes that "the only logical political theory that one can defend is 'philosophical anarchism.' "[11]

Whereas the organizational/technocratic perspective emphasizes the interlocking effects of technology, organization, and science, the statist critique asserts a more basic concern. It contends that the Western state, by its very sovereignty, destroys community, erects a new political system, and makes of man an atomized individual facing an omnipotent ruler. Irrespective of its specific features, the state has created mass society and destroyed organic order.

THE ECONOMIC CRITIQUE

The economic critique involves an application and revision of earlier Marxist interpretations of the relationships between economic class, status, power, and policy. Capitalism is specifically characterized by a series of interlocking premises that affect the character of political systems and societies in general. Politics is governed overtly or covertly by an economic elite. Public policy is made to enhance control by the ruling class. Domestic and foreign policy are designed to serve several economic purposes: to increase foreign markets for domestically produced goods, to create a cheap labor supply, to have sources for raw materials, and finally to induce compulsive consumption.

Carl Oglesby[12] adds that since capitalist economic systems must continuously grow and expand productivity while increasing foreign markets and domestic consumption, military spending is an attractive ideal. Military hardware is either used up or becomes obsolete as soon as it is produced, thus ensuring endless production. Oglesby goes on to describe the nexus between economics, policy, and international relations in the United States. He contends that peace is defined by American elites in terms of the easy, tension-free access of American business to the rest of the world and by the capacity of ruling elites in the United States to control counterparts in third world countries. If foreign elites do not cooperate, the last resort is always the American marines. The domestic ramifications of such an analysis are reflected in historian Gabriel Kolko's assertion that "the United States is a class society fostering great differences in wealth and power between upper and lower classes. This rigid class structure has not changed in the twentieth century."[13]

Sociologist Norman Birnbaum, in *The Crisis of Industrial Society*, applies the terms of the critique to Britain, France, and West Germany, integrating Marxist sociology with contemporary bureaucratic and technological phenomena. He begins with a definition of class revised from traditional Marxist formulations: A class is "any grouping in a similar relationship to the means of production, regardless of the degree of social consciousness or political cohesion it had attained."[14] Relationship to the means of production encompasses ownership, control, proximity, or profit. The means of production include distribution, administration, and, with increasing governmental and economic interaction, political institutions.

A new class situation exists in the industrialized societies. The elites are no longer just the owners of the means of production, but reflect a symbiosis of ownership and management. Indeed, the new elites are truly the managers of industry. They may not even own property, but they are surely in a position to manipulate it. Power for the new managerial elite is not necessarily inherited, but family background, level of education, and a particular kind of life-style and culture still distinguish potential managerial elites from others. The new managers are complemented by a middle class of technicians, administrators, and a semi-skilled expendible working class that has developed life-styles and consumption patterns of the middle class. Lastly, there exists a substratum, a new proletariat, made up of underemployed or unemployable men and women.

The class system prevalent in Western industrialized societies has changed since Marx wrote, Birnbaum says, but it still manifests itself in politics and culture and is still the source of potential oppression and class conflict. The new class system and elite organization is less conspicuous than the old. General definitions of roles and functions of managers and executives conceal large amounts of power and influence. Birnbaum suggests that the integration of "property managers" and "political managers" is most effective because it is informal, a "happy coincidence," and reflects shared perceptions of common interests.[15]

The economic system projects the image of a division of labor and integration. It leads capitalist ideologues to argue that the inherent antagonisms of the old class system no longer exist. For example, a broad sector of the middle class does contain a measure of autonomy in decision-making and does have considerable prospects of upward mobility. Furthermore, with the new working class living by middle class life-styles and the new proletariat excluded from the economic system, the worst stereotypes of a capitalist class system are not visible.

The invisible quality of the class system is reproduced in the political system. Here the exercise of power by economic elites is "veiled." Those who exercise power typically deny that they do so. In many cases such denials are based on sincere beliefs held by economic elites that their input does not carry more weight than other citizens. For Birnbaum, politics at the level of parliamentary interaction is mere surface play and policy is usually made by those far away from the centers of democratic institutions. The state is interlocked with economic institutions.

The industrial state, the integration of the control of the means of production and the political apparatus, ensures order through violent repression or manipulation. It adjudicates and coordinates the workings of society, allocates production and distribution, and provides some services to the population. Property in alliance with the state can be found at the legislative level, in regulatory agencies, and through mass manipulation of the electorate. The welfare state dominates the working class which pays its own benefits. It assumes the role of maintaining a disciplined and productive labor force.

In sum, domestic and foreign policy is a direct reflection of the new opaque economic elite; those who are not visible but who control the means of production. These men are not viewed as vulgar conspirators but members of a class with common interests. These features are characteristic of all capitalist societies. Many third world elites are clients of Western nations. For some economic theorists, the Soviet and Eastern European regimes are in reality "state capitalist" and hence not too dissimilar from Western capitalist nations. These theorists therefore view the technocracy and state as instruments of capitalism.

THE POLITICAL ELITIST CRITIQUE

The political elitist critique, though often sharing some assumptions with the economic critique, assigns more emphasis to political institutions and to the corruption of traditional definitions of legitimate power and influence. In the United States, concern is often manifested over the breakdown of traditional distributions of power. Some emphasize the emerging disequilibrium of influence among national institutions over policy-making. Writers during various historical periods have worried about the excessive power of the Supreme Court, or of Congress, or of the presidency. Since the New Deal, political theorists have been increasingly concerned with the dramatically expanding powers of the presidency, particularly in the realm of foreign policy.

Those who speak of a military-industrial complex emphasize the creation of a mixed decisional system based upon highly organized private sectors of business and labor. Business and labor leaders are seen in loose cooperation with certain critical sections of the executive branch, including the president, the Department of Defense, and members of the National Security Council.

Some political elitist critics speak of other corrupting tendencies such as those that increase national power at the expense of state and local control of public policy. A final critical problem involves the emergence of a mass society. This results in reduced public input through representatives on decisions of major policy import. Elites rule and masses follow. All of these formulations suggest that public policy is always a function of the magnitude of organizational power and the ideological orientations of those elites who dominate the critical organizations in society.

In his controversial study, *The Power Elite*, sociologist C. Wright Mills asserts that a relatively small number of individuals who command the major hierarchies in American society comprise an elite that has the power to make the most critical political decisions. Even if they choose not to decide or are not precisely aware of the power they hold, these men have the capacity to rule. "They rule the big corporations. They run the machinery of the state and claim its prerogatives. They direct the military establishment. They occupy the strategic command posts of the social structure, in which are now centered the effective means of the power and the wealth and celebrity which they enjoy."[16] Essentially they rule the economic, military, and political domains of modern America.

The existence of a power elite relates to modes and styles of access to organizational dominance, the kinds of values that these men acquire as a prerequisite to rule, and finally, the immensely expanded size and power of elite-run organizations. Mills tells us that each of the big three institutions involving economy, military, and politics has dramatically increased in size, resources, and scope of operations. Each major institutional force has acquired the benefits of modern technology which is used to full advantage. The economy has become controlled by some three hundred major corporations that are increasingly interrelated. The military has moved from a small force tempered by the existence of the much preferred state militia to the largest and wealthiest manned institution in society. The political system has moved from a relatively impotent national structure paying homage to state and local authority to a highly centralized, aggrandizing organization.

As time passes, the elites of each institution become more interlocking. Conflict may still exist between elites and between institutions, but the power elite all hold to a common system of values and global perceptions. Marc Pilisuk, psychologist, and

Thomas Hayden, political activist,[17] for example, offer a distinction between competition over the allocations of budgetary and other resources from one branch of the elite to another and cooperation and consensus on fundamental values. They contend that a quasi-pluralism of power exists in resource allocation, but that elite consensus reigns in basic values. Elites compete with each other for scarce resources but agree on basic policy premises. These include: (1) the acceptance of efficacy over principle in decision-making, i.e., the acceptance of violence as an instrument of policy; (2) the acceptance of private property over collectivization in domestic and international policy; and (3) the acceptance of limited representative democracy over other political forms, both domestically and internationally. It could be argued that another premise overwhelmingly accepted by elites in these institutions involves the total support of technological invention and application. Such reasoning derives from power's relationship to technical control.

Stressing the concept of mass society and implying a preference for social and political pluralism, William Kornhauser[18] has posited a set of conditions that may lead to the centralization of political power. Kornhauser postulates a need for elites to maintain some insulation from pressures by unorganized masses, what he calls the "exclusiveness of elites." Similarly, he seeks protection for non-elites from manipulation by elites, what he calls the avoidance of "high availability of a population for mobilization by elites." Those societies that are characterized by low access to elites and low access to citizens he calls "communal societies." These societies are circumscribed by traditions and customs that set limits on elite manipulation and mass popular pressures on elites.

Those societies where access to elites is high and the capacity to manipulate masses is low he calls "pluralist societies." In this case, citizens are members of numerous salient political and social groups that protect them from direct manipulation by any potential power elite. Those societies where access to elites and masses is high are referred to as "mass society." This condition is characterized by a mutually reinforcing relationship between a mass of people, not hundreds of groups, and aspiring elites. Finally, a society where there exists high access to masses and no access to elites is labeled "totalitarian." Usually the mass society two-way relationship between elites and masses is broken down by a successful ascension to power by the charismatic elite figure. His new power provides him with the resources to lessen reliance upon mass direct support.

The Kornhauser formulation emphasizes some four major

socio-political layers in pluralist society. Between the powerful state apparatus and the individual there exist meaningful groups, communities, and the nuclear family. In mass society, all the intervening layers between the individual and the state decrease in importance, leaving masses of atomized individuals susceptible to manipulation. The classic illustration of this, according to many mass society theorists, is Nazi Germany. With the loss of pride after World War I, the decline of traditional religious and aristocratic beliefs, and the chaos of the German economy, traditional groups lost their relevance. This left millions of German citizens seeking new leadership and guidance. In the setting of the 1920s, the social disarray provided Hitler with circumstances from which to mobilize and lead the atomized who, in Erich Fromm's terms,[19] sought to "escape from freedom."

Although many theorists would question Kornhauser's faith in pluralism as an antidote to potential mass societies and totalitarianism, the theory does point to the corruption of power whereby publics are transformed into masses and political representatives are transformed into uncontrollable elites. The Nazi example further suggests possible ramifications of mass society for domestic and foreign policy.

Other theorists have criticized pluralism as a viable alternative to elitism. Some like Theodore Lowi,[20] have argued that even though there is no small, potentially conspiratorial elite, input into governmental decision-making is tempered by one's group affiliations. Political decision-making is a function of conflict and consensus among relatively small numbers of highly organized groups. Executive or legislative institutions serve as brokers or mediators between big group contentions. The "new public philosophy" assumes that decision-making is fundamentally the mediation between disputing groups. The allocation of resources is based on the strength of groups in the system. As Wolff[21] suggests, all decisions in a pluralist system are subject to equitable compromise. Hence, neither nondistributive questions nor moral imperatives can be heard in governmental institutions (opposition to the war in Vietnam must yield a "compromise" whereby troops are withdrawn and bombing is intensified). Finally, power is a function of membership in large, legitimate groups. Individual citizens have no meaningful say in or access to decision-making. It may be hypothesized that the outcomes of Mill's elitism or Lowi's "interest group liberalism" amount to much the same thing.

The political elitist critiques all share a perception of the narrowing range of power sources in modern societies. Access to decision-making centers is limited and the definition and administration of policy is increasingly a reflection of a military-industrial complex, or an elite freed from public pressures, or a variety of highly organized interest groups. However one defines these elites, they seem to be more varied than a homogeneous economic class but less than representative of broad publics. The heart of the problem is *decaying political structures*. Similar arguments in non-Western societies stress the breakdown of traditional authorities and the rise to power of military or civilian dictators. The cultural contexts are different from the West, but the same lack of public representation prevails.

THE CULTURAL CRITIQUE

This final kind of criticism is reflected in many popular and scholarly writings since the onset of the Eisenhower years. The central assumption here is that culture (broadly defined to encompass life-styles, value systems, art forms, modes of interaction, ways of perceiving reality, and even the quality and intensity of religiosity) is a critical determinant of political, economic, and social systems. Whereas other theorists begin with organization and technology, or the capitalist system, or political elites, the cultural critique explains the malaise of modernized societies in terms of one or several cultural variables.

Although more of a political activist than a cultural critic or academic theorist, Eldridge Cleaver vividly expresses the kinds of cultural concerns so characteristic of this literature as it is applied to the United States:

> The boxing ring is the ultimate focus of masculinity in America, the two-fisted testing ground of manhood, and the heavyweight champion, as a symbol, is the real Mr. America. In a culture that secretly subscribes to the piratical ethic of "every man for himself"—the social Darwinism of "survival of the fittest" being far from dead, manifesting itself in our ratrace political system of competing parties, in our dog-eat-dog economic system of profit and loss, and in our adversary system of justice wherein truth is secondary to the skill and connections of the advocate—the logical culmination of this ethic, on a person-to-person level, is that the weak are seen as the natural and just prey of the strong. But since this dark principle violates our democratic ideals and professions, we force it underground out of a perverse national modesty that reveals us as a nation of peep freaks who prefer the bikini to the naked body, the white lie to the black truth, Hollywood smiles and canned laughter to a soulful Bronx cheer.[22]

In this quotation Cleaver makes several assumptions about American culture that reflect the concerns of other theorists:

1. The model for man in the United States is the brutal activity of the fighter. It incorporates the interaction of the boxing ring into the social, economic, and political life of society. It measures success in terms of the imagery of dominance.

2. The dominant political and economic ideology remains the crassest form of Social Darwinism, tying change and success to "survival of the fittest." The most durable people and institutions within domestic and international systems will succeed while the docile, cooperative, humane people and institutions will become extinct. The measure of man in the United States is his ability to compete, not to cooperate.

3. Aggressive competition is the dominant motif in all American institutions. The party structure, the court system, the economy, the educational system all reward the cut-throat competitive behavior of man in the state of nature.

4. Such competition makes religious values of the Judeo-Christian and Eastern traditions "irrelevant." That is, they become inadequate to the "facts of life" in a dynamic and powerful state. However, since the Western tradition is presumed to be governed by a cooperative ethic, competition must be couched in the context of a symbolic, humane, mythical structure. This myth system fools people into thinking that American institutions are not actually motivated by the ethos of Social Darwinism.

Other cultural theorists view the modern state in terms of value systems that are based upon possession of goods. The acquisition of goods becomes a major indicator of success and social status. The object orientation or materialism of modern society gets reflected in life-styles that devalue cooperative human interaction and interaction between men and nature. Life becomes "privatized" as each citizen uses others as objects for personal advancement. At the same time, man seeks conformity with others, rejecting spontaneity and uniqueness in himself and others as a threat to personal security. C. B. MacPherson terms the liberal tradition from which this world view springs "possessive individualism."[23]

Paul and Percival Goodman[24] discuss the interactive effect of city plans and architectural forms on possessive individualism. In an attempt to maximize healthful suburban living, the greenbelt communities built in the post-World War II period created localities of isolated families far from work and connected by miles of freeways. Man lives distant from both his workplace and the centers of political and cultural life. He seeks pleasure in his home or backyard. People get separated; families get isolated; work, play, politics, and culture get separated. The net result is atomization.

The models discussed give preeminent consideration to those emerging values and life-styles that temper and structure political and economic life. Although most of the cultural theorists would not necessarily accept a rigid causal chain from culture to politics to economics, they would emphasize the critical role that emerging cultures have played in all nations. Political and economic forms reinforce and escalate those values derived from the culture. To the extent that modernity in Western terms is spilling over into the third world, increasing materialism, possessive individualism, and atomization may dominate a new world culture in the future.

SHORTCOMINGS OF SOCIAL-CRITICAL THEORIES

Social-critical theorists see the modern state as inhibiting human need fulfillment. Capitalism maximizes exploitation, maintains classes of rich and poor, and makes third world peoples prey to corporate profit. Materialist cultures justified by a Social Darwinian ethos stimulate the objectification of self and others, redefine persons in terms of possessions, and encourage perpetual competition among peoples. Political elitism places control over peoples lives in the hands of a select few. The technocracy victimizes people through subliminal controls over minds and bodies. Lastly, the impersonal state minimizes human control, interpersonal interaction, and mutual aid. The end product of all this is that preservation, community, and self-determination needs remain unfulfilled.

These claims are usually challenged in two ways. First, some argue that the critics are wrong, that the modern state and its emerging offshoots in the third world are increasingly meeting more needs of more people. Second, others argue that all social systems in the past, present, and, of necessity, the future require elites, technocrats, bureaucracies, sources of sovereign authority, and certain specific kinds of cultural patterns. These features are necessary for the maintenance of stability within society and between societies. Some "realists" might accept the critics' points of view but contend that "given the nature of man" these conditions are inevitable in any social system.

From the perspective of alternative world futures *any* limitations on human need fulfillment must be challenged. Further, *no* state of affairs is inevitable. If the apologists are wrong and social-critical theories have at least a kernel of worth then dialogues on alternatives are justified. It is important, however, to look critically at the five kinds of theories presented above to see if singly or in combination the dangers are sources of societal and global problems.

The organizational/technocratic theory presumes the malevolence of bureaucracy, science, and technology. Roszak seems to be a modern Luddite who wishes to strike the machine dead, replacing it and its inventors with a kind of primitive mysticism and communitarianism. He and Seidenberg assume the inevitability of destruction or human stagnation from continued commitment to technology and science. This argument ignores the human input. Technocracy is a by-product of people. Hence it is people that may be able to "humanize" its application to social problems. Some argue that technology can be used for good or ill and other variables may determine to which use it is put. Perhaps the problem of the technocracy is really a problem of self-interested economic or political elites, misguided or psychologically depraved decision-makers, or a culture that is motivated by acquisitiveness and disregard for the natural environment.

Descriptions of the dehumanizing tasks to which science is put, the totalitarian character of large-scale bureaucracy and technological manipulation, reflect one trend or process among many in industrializing or industrialized societies. Yet, other descriptions are possible. If society is analogous to a well-oiled machine beyond human control, one wonders how Roszak's hope for the future, the counter-culture, can in fact develop the will and the power to bring the machine to a halt. Either the social machine is capable of being stopped or it is not. If it is, then man must do it.

A different kind of determinism characterizes economic critical theory. This paradigm emphasizes the dynamics of capitalism as it relates to imperialism, conspicuous consumption, political elitism, and alienation. Two questionable suppositions are found in this analysis. First, the kinds of outcomes attributed to capitalist societies are found in noncapitalist societies as well. Imperialism, for example, seems to have been stimulated by several nations with different kinds of economic structures. The propensity for encroachment among nations can be explained better by examining great powers during different historical periods. The experience of the Soviet Union in Eastern Europe or the Peoples Republic of China in Tibet suggest that imperialism is not necessarily peculiar to Western capitalism.

Second, the economic paradigm emphasizes a rigorous class structure in explaining systems of power and the character of cultures within societies. Such an analysis ignores the input to decision-making that results from large institutional and non-institutional pressure groups. For example, in the United States the labor hierarchy has been ready and willing to support the Cold War. Power groups like the American Medical Association, the National Rifle Association, and sub-bureaucratic groups from the Department of Defense have consistently influenced public policy. Such pressure does not reflect any visible class system as much as the interests of a small number of highly placed groups. There may be greater explanatory power from a model that integrates class with organizational elitism, technocratic expertise, and political elitism. In sum, the economic paradigm points accurately to a "tendency," but neglects a variety of equally important factors.

The political elitist critique adds more dimensions of power and can better explain policy-making in different societies. This explanation, however, necessitates more specific research in given nations to discover the character, organization, and kinds of access that elites have in these particular environments. The elitist arguments are less precise and hence less generalizable across societies than the technocratic arguments. Although Latin American dictators may be generically similar to elites in the United States, their means of acquiring and maintaining power differ greatly. Further, elitist charges often neglect class interests and the use of technocratic expertise. Finally, there has been lengthy debate among social scientists about the Mills' position. It is often charged that power elite theories are conspiratorial and do not offer proof of common interests and actions of elites from different institutional spheres. However, even though conflict between elites is visible to observers in most societies, this does not negate the assumption that elites do share major values that maintain the system of power as it is constituted.

The cultural critics have emphasized values, life-styles, and world views to the neglect of institutional forces. Politics and economics are assumed to emerge from cultural imperatives that dominate a given society. However, such cultural imperatives seem to be a product of the manipulation of symbols by elites. Or at most, perhaps, the culture serves to reinforce or support elitist structures and self-serving policies that characterize given societies. Further, questions concerning the "quality of life" that have been examined in recent years are not assessed by cultural critics in terms of the kinds of political and economic choices made by elites. Cultural variables are relevant, but not all-important. Possessive individualism is critical in a society that reinforces it through political decisions.

Finally, the central assumptions expressed by the statist critics seem to accurately reflect the breakdown of community and the creation of impersonal hierarchical systems. However, one might still suggest that the existence of states only provides the precondition for atomization. Within state systems, communities still survive, perhaps with great difficulty, but they survive nonetheless. This suggests that the state reduces the capacity for human need fulfillment but that such reduction is hastened by a complex of other factors.

Generally, the relative accuracy of the five theories varies from country to country. Perhaps a synthesis of *all* the theories points to dangers *inherent* in every society. The state is the context in which social behavior occurs. It atomizes peoples and demands obeisance to authority. Within each state, parallel systems serve to reinforce each other. These include *culture*, *political structure*, *economy*, and *technocracy*. The political institutions and economy generate policies that reinforce the state and feedback into the culture. Without significant resistance, the state and its components sustain themselves or increase their power over their citizens.

Specifically, the extent of applicability of the theories beyond the Western industrialized states involves an extensive analysis of each country. Five questions can be asked in *each* national context: (1) Does the state have a capitalist economy and has this economy created a rigid class system that relates to power and culture *or* is the economy socialized with no noticeable relationship between economic class and power? (2) Does the culture, through myths, symbols, heroes, and a generalized ethos, maximize competition and struggle between isolated individuals and nuclear families *or* do the dominant values and beliefs stress cooperation and affiliation? (3) Do numbers of elites in critical institutions, particularly in the government, make decisions without regard for communities, groups, or publics *or* is the political system broadly representative? (4) Is the society increasingly dominated by scientific expertise through public institutions *or* are technocrats in roles subordinate to public choices on general values and specific decisions? (5) Finally, is the role of the state expanding at the expense of communities of people *or* is it subordinate to local affiliations? If all or most of the central forces described by these theorists exist, the student must ask if the predicted poverty, powerlessness, competition, and alienation are genuinely emerging. This book assumes that the social-critical theorists are, at a minimum, accurately portraying strong *tendencies* within the United States and industrialized societies, and visible *potentialities* in nonindustrialized and industrializing societies.

IMPLICATIONS OF DOMESTIC SOCIAL-CRITICAL THEORY FOR ALTERNATIVE WORLD FUTURES

From a global point of view, there are at least four reasons for discussing social-critical theories that emphasize domestic social change. First, the notion of alternative world futures assumes the possibility, and for some the desirability, of emphasizing smaller political units than states. As much of the utopian and anarchist traditions below suggest, the maximization of human need fulfillment may in part be a function of smallness of units. If this is true, then national processes and institutions may be the major inhibitors of human needs. Historically, utopians have been concerned about decentralizing economies, polities, cultures, and technologies. For W. Warren Wagar, the two most significant alternative futures have been "utopia" and "cosmopolis," roughly community and world order. Therefore, community is fundamentally a domestic problem. At a minimum, it may be expected that community and self-determination needs necessitate some intranational adaptations.

A second reason for considering domestic social-critical theory involves the cross-national linkages that some of the theories imply. Many theorists of conflict and war from Thucydides to modern-day social scientists assume a direct relationship between domestic instability and international conflict. If the social critics accurately document domestic trends toward increasing social malaise, one might expect such a condition to lead to external conflict. The mass society theorists, for example, have shown how the emergence of an elitist system in Germany coupled with widespread alienation and sense of powerlessness provided the preconditions for an expansionist foreign policy.

A third reason for considering domestic phenomena in a global context is that the implications of trends within the theories are external. The economic critique assumes strong connections between the central capitalist states and third world nations. The very basis of the class system at home is the level of interpenetration of foreign markets. The organizational/technocratic argument also presumes an ever-expanding network of organized relationships between people under its control, first domestically, then internationally. One can expect such expansiveness from political elites, but of a less intensive sort. Finally, there have been historic examples of states being motivated by cultural imperatives that necessitate foreign expansion. From the era of missionary zeal to one of possessive individualism, institutionalized values have encouraged foreign war and political interpenetration of other states. The logic of each critique thus has worldwide implications.

Finally, an integrated analysis of the five kinds of theories suggests trends inherent in the most industrialized states. If these states become the ideal which all others strive to imitate, the future might witness the spillover of what are now national phenomena into a general global pattern. Global society may become the contemporary industrialized state writ large.

However one feels about the validity of specific theoretical positions, it seems clear that in a world of increasing interrelatedness the warnings made must be given serious thought. No viable alternative world future can be expected that does not reduce the urgency of the factors discussed.

NOTES

1. Theodore Roszak, *The Making of a Counter Culture* (Garden City, N. Y.: Anchor, 1969).

2. Jacques Ellul, *The Technological Society* (New York: Vintage, 1964), p. xxv.

3. Roszak, *The Making of a Counter Culture*, pp. 205-239.

4. *Ibid.*, p. 230.

5. Roderick Seidenberg, *Post-Historic Man* (Boston: Beacon, 1950).

6. *Ibid.*, p. 27-28.

7. Petr Kropotkin, *Mutual Aid* (Boston: Extending Horizon Books, 1902).

8. Robert A. Nisbet, *Tradition and Revolt* (New York: Vintage, 1970).

9. *Ibid.*, p. 136-137.

10. Robert Paul Wolff, *In Defense of Anarchism* (New York: Harper & Row, 1970).

11. *Ibid.*, p. 19.

12. Carl Oglesby and Richard Schaull, *Containment and Change* (New York: Macmillan, 1967).

13. Gabriel Kolko, *The Roots of American Foreign Policy* (Boston: Beacon, 1969), p. 9.

14. Norman Birnbaum, *The Crisis of Industrial Society* (London: Oxford, 1969), p. 6.

15. *Ibid.*, p. 13-14.

16. C. Wright Mills, *The Power Elite* (New York: Oxford, 1959), p. 4.

17. Marc Pilisuk and Thomas Hayden, "Is There a Military Industrial Complex Which Prevents Peace?: Consensus and Countervailing Power in Pluralistic Systems," in Robert Perrucci and Marc Pilisuk, eds., *The Triple Revolution, Social Problems in Depth* (Boston: Little, Brown, 1968), pp. 77-111.

18. William Kornhauser, *The Politics of Mass Society* (New York: Free Press, 1959).

19. Erich Fromm, *Escape from Freedom* (New York: Holt, Rinehart & Winston, 1941).

20. Theodore Lowi, *The End of Liberalism* (New York: Norton, 1969).

21. Robert Paul Wolff, *The Poverty of Liberalism* (Boston: Beacon, 1968), p. 137.

22. Eldridge Cleaver, *Soul on Ice* (New York: Delta, 1968), p. 84.

23. C. B. MacPherson, *The Political Theory of Possessive Individualism* (London: Oxford, 1962).

24. Paul and Percival Goodman, *Communitas* (New York: Vintage, 1960).

Chapter 3
Social-Critical Implications of Selected International Relations Theories

The material in the last chapter emphasized characteristic problems *within* states. International relations theories examine interactions and problems *between* states. Several international relations theorists have addressed themselves implicitly or directly to the problem of human needs. The classic formulations of balance of power theory describe a condition of perpetual conflict and violence in international relations and a frame of reference for statesmen that serves to justify such conflict. Stratification and rank disequilibrium theories point to the great disparities in wealth and power between states in the international system and the implications this has for continued violence. Theses about the endangered planet and uncontrollable worldwide change speak most directly in a problem-oriented way to the urgency of creating alternative world futures. Each theory suggests a dimension of crisis in *international* relations that must be added to those of *intranational* relations.

BALANCE OF POWER AND POLITICAL REALISM

The history of international relations thought is largely the history of the theory of balance of power. Balance of power thinking also dominates the writings of those political philosophers who dealt only peripherally with the international system before the twentieth century. Today, some form of such thinking is popular among statesmen and scholars alike.

Aside from Thucydides' history of the Peloponnesian War (431-404 B.C.), balance of power thinking drew its initial impetus from Machiavelli and Hobbes.[1] Men are described as seekers of security. Since the primary motivation for man is self-preservation, it must be the case for city-states or nation-states as well. Consequently the central guide to national policy must be protection. To that end, the accumulation and wise use of power is critical.

Political theorists such as Locke, Montesquieu, and Madison emphasize the need for domestic structures and processes that limit the acquisition of power by the few or by the masses.[2] Each theorist says that a viable society necessitates a balancing of forces to create equilibrium. This is the case so that no single faction can become dominant in the political process. The notions of self-preservation, power acquisition, and balancing of power paralleled the acceptance by most European nations of similar precepts in the international realm. For example, beginning with the Renaissance, the idea of a balance of power incorporates three basic assumptions: (1) the security and independence of any single state depends upon power, (2) power is relative and the power of any single state can be measured only in terms of the capacities of surrounding states, and (3) any increase in the power of one state means a decrease in the power of its neighbors and a threat to their security and independence.[3] Whether among groups within states or states within the international system, a balance of power ensures stability and precludes any gross disproportionalities of capability.

Several theorists stipulate the assumptions which guided the behavior among statesmen during the centuries of the balance of power's most persistent use. First, a viable balance of power international system must have at least five independent national actors. The greater the number of states in the system, the less the likelihood of dominance by any one of them. If the system is composed of three major nations, two will almost automatically band together to counter the third. Second, for the theory to be applicable, an equilibrium of military power is necessary. It is a system based upon a stand-off in terms of power determinants. Third, to reinforce the need for power equilibrium, there are norms supposedly governing the accumulation of power by one or a handful of nations. These norms set limits on how much each state can take from other states in situations of conflict. Statesmen from victorious states would not try to annex land from defeated states.

Corollary to the third, a fourth assumption is that there are accepted limits to the extent of international conflict. Because war was the sport of kings and soldiers were mercenaries, it was considered relatively easy to limit the scope of violence. Conflict and war may have occurred even more frequently but the intensity and scope of conflict were more limited. These assumptions also relate to a fifth: that each national actor in the system is interested in the preservation of all other actors in the system.[4] A healthy, limited conflict system necessitated the continued participation of the several states that were members. No state was to be subjected to such an overwhelming defeat that it was for all practical purposes no longer a member of the system.

Sixth, the continued equilibrium that is prerequisite to stability precludes the imposition of any international organizations or permanent alliances. Any new non-national institutions (like a United Nations) add a new and potentially disequilibrating dimension to the international system. Finally, the rules assume the desirability of a state that can play the role of balancer, maintaining its distance from immediate struggles of the day and imposing itself in quarrels when there is some danger that one power or group of powers will gain too much and destroy systemic equilibrium. Great Britain was considered the balancer in the eighteenth and nineteenth centuries, keeping her distance from the continent's strife until such time as the system required her participation.

Morton Kaplan[5] has recently extrapolated several rules of behavior from European history that presumably governed the conduct of each state during the major balance of power epoch. Aside from the assumptions already cited, Kaplan adds that each actor seeks to increase its capabilities but negotiates rather than fights for them. However, it fights rather than fails to increase its capabilities. Each state depends solely upon itself or its allies for self-preservation and advancement. As sovereign entities, states are the ultimate source for the monopolization and utilization of legitimate violence. Supranational institutions are a direct threat to the balance of power system.

Kaplan further posits a model that seems to reflect the Cold War system of power. His "loose bipolar system" differs from the balance of power system in that new actors and processes have emerged. Along with states, the postwar system also consists of supranational actors that significantly include two blocs (reflected in the North Atlantic Treaty Organization [NATO] and the Warsaw Pact) and an international organization (the United Nations). Most nations belong to the international organization and several are also bloc members. Finally, there remains a significant number of non-bloc or neutral nations. Consequently, the new inter-

national system consists of two blocs, an international organization, and nonaligned nations, each governed by its own rules of
behavior. Blocs can either be organized in a hierarchical (one
nation with the most influence) or nonhierarchical (all nations
have equal influence) way, depending on the obligation of bloc
members to pay homage to great power authority.

Several of Kaplan's rules of behavior illustrate the conflictful
and perhaps inadequate nature of the loose bipolar system from
the perspective of human need fulfillment and alternative world
futures. For example, central to this system is the assumption on
the part of both blocs (East versus West) that their fundamental
reason for existing involves the elimination of the other bloc. For
the hierarchical bloc, rules suggest (1) negotiating rather than
fighting, (2) fighting minor wars rather than major wars, and finally, (3) fighting major wars rather than failing to eliminate the rival
bloc. For the nonhierarchical bloc, the rules include (1) negotiating rather than fighting, (2) continually increasing military and
economic capabilities, (3) fighting minor wars rather than failing
to increase capabilities, and (4) refraining from initiating major
wars.

The balancing function in the loose bipolar system is to be
attempted by the non-bloc nations (neutrals) and the international
organization (United Nations). Non-bloc nations must subordinate
the goals of the blocs to those of the international organization.
Both nonaligned nations and the United Nations are to seek the
limitation of inter-bloc conflict. Bloc actors, however, may subordinate the objectives of nonaligned nations and the international
organization to their own objectives but must give the nonaligned
and international organizational objectives precedence over the
objectives of the opposing blocs. The United States and the Soviet
Union will emphasize their own goals first, then those of the
United Nations, and last the goals of the other great power.

Together with the four systems he presumes could emerge in
the future, Kaplan's balance of power and loose bipolar systems
are based upon national sovereignty, international conflict, and
national self-interest. Each of his six systems presumes the state as
the smallest salient political unit.

The most popular formulation of *realpolitik* in the tradition
of balance of power theory is articulated by Hans Morgenthau. [6]
For Morgenthau, primary concern for human need fulfillment or a
peaceful world order is misguided. His theory of political realism
presumes only limited prospects for change in the international
environment. The theory of political realism has four basic principles: (1) National interest is defined in terms of power.

(2) Those factors that determine power change throughout history; consequently, so does the national interest. (3) Because of the fundamental truths about power and national interest, morality should not stand in the way of a state's "practical" political action. (4) Political realism denies that national moral aspirations are universal moral laws. In sum, Morgenthau suggests that "International politics, like all politics, is a struggle for power. Whatever the ultimate aims of international politics, power is always the immediate aim." Power encompasses the "control over the minds and actions of other men." Political power is psychological control and military power is physical control.[7]

Theories of balance of power and political realism present a picture of a world in struggle with the most salient political units governed by an overarching quest for security. Security might entail maintaining military power, control over land, people, and resources, or it may mean increasing the accumulation of all of these. The only genuine constraints in the balance of power system are "the rules of the game." It is a violent world. Even if the theory does not adequately explain international relations, it is of critical importance because statesmen and politicians over the centuries have believed it to be true. As is well known, beliefs and expectations about the social world will sometimes have a self-fulfilling effect.

STRATIFICATION AND RANK DISEQUILIBRIUM MODELS

Whereas balance of power and realist thinking emphasizes national sovereignty, self-interest, and systemic conflict, other theorists of international politics employ stratification analogues to domestic class systems in their descriptions of the international order. A. F. K. Organski[8] incorporates stratification notions in what he calls a theory of power transition.

Organski's formulation involves a challenge to traditional balance of power thought. In the period of the modern state system, it is argued, international politics have not been characterized by actual balances of power, but by the *predominance* of power by certain states. The system, then, has always been one of dominance and submission rather than equilibrium.

Organski elaborates on the determinants of international power which include (1) wealth and industrial strength, (2) population, and (3) efficiency of governmental organization. He suggests "an industrializing nation typically gains simultaneously in wealth and industrial strength, in population, and in efficiency of governmental organization. Since these are the three major determinants of national power, an increase in them inevitably results in a great increase of power for the nation that is going through the process of industrialization."[9]

Given the determinants of power, nations progress through three stages of power transition. First, they may be in the stage of power potential which is characterized by a total lack of industrialization, agricultural and rural dominance, and extensive illiteracy. Those nations in stage one that have large populations have potential for movement to stages two and three. Stage two nations are in the process of transitional growth in power: industrial growth begins, urban centers emerge, the national income begins to rise, the scope of national government increases, and literacy increases. Nations in stage two are significantly more powerful than nations in stage one. A few nations have reached the stage of final power maturity. Nations in this stage have experienced continuous and broad-based economic growth, extensive economic and political bureaucratization, thorough urbanization, and spreading literacy. Great bursts of economic growth cease as newer industrializing nations develop at a more rapid pace than older industrialized states.

Since power is defined as a relation, the power of nations in stage three may decline as newer nations move from stages one and two: "Its *relative* power declines because other nations are entering the second stage of transitional growth, and as they do so they begin to close the gap between themselves and the nations that industrialized before them."[10] Therefore, changes in the international system involve the differential spread of industrialization and consequently transitional power distributions rather than "some automatic balancing process."

Given the theory of power transition, three international systems are conceptualized. The first such system probably existed from the beginnings of the state system until the onset of the industrial revolution. During this time no states were industrializing; hence, all were in the stage of power potential. Differential power was based on other variables than those discussed above. For example, military tactical skills or leadership capabilities probably affected a nation's power position. Since the onset of the industrial revolution, states have been moving from stage one to stages two and three, creating the stratified international system that still exists today. Finally, a third international period might be expected in which all states have reached the stage of power maturity. Differences in power in this international system will be based upon factors that are not yet known.

If balance of power theory was relevant at all, it was during the first international epoch, i.e., before industrialization. The best theoretical explanation of the contemporary international system now is the theory of power transition. The achievement of world-wide industrialization will necessitate the creation of new theories.

Organski introduces another variable to understand the dynamics of his stratified international system. He suggests that nations may either be satisfied or dissatisfied with the distribution of power and its consequences. Thus, the international system consists of four possible kinds of nations: the powerful and satisfied, the powerful and dissatisfied, the weak and satisfied, and the weak and dissatisfied. War is judged most likely to occur when there emerges a significant challenge to the powerful and satisfied nations from some powerful and dissatisfied nations in conjunction with several weak and dissatisfied nations. In terms of the power dimension, Organski portrays the international system as a triangular structure with one dominant power at the apex followed by several great powers, then a layer of middle powers and small powers, and finally colonies. If extensive dissatisfaction is introduced into the system, instability results.

There are several implications of this argument. Organski implies that a small number of states dominate the international system in every epoch. This means that they regulate and control international economic transactions, verify norms of diplomacy, generate international law, structure international organizations in their own images, and actually define the very character of the international system. If other states object to the ongoing definition and have the attributes of power to challenge the dominant coalition, then extensive international conflict seems inevitable. The German and Japanese challenge to Western dominance prior to World War II is an illustration of powerful and dissatisfied nations responding to an international decision-making structure from which they were excluded: "Indeed, the major wars of recent history have all been wars involving the biggest power in the world and its allies against a challenger (or group of challengers) who had recently risen in power thanks to industrialization. One could almost say that the rise of such a challenger guarantees a major war."[11]

Given the theory of power transition, there are two possible routes to peace and stability in a changing world system. On the one hand, peace can be maintained via a power distribution that favors the few at the expense of the many. The greater the asymmetry of power, the greater the likelihood of peace. Second, relative peace can be maintained during a transitional distribution of power if the new rising power accepts the central values, norms, and beliefs of the ongoing system as defined by prior dominant and great powers. The transition of power from British to American dominance is an example of a relatively peaceful transfer in that the United States accepted the basic "rules" of the ongoing international system. America's rise to power was unobtrusive; consequently, it did not stimulate British reaction. Further, the United States accepted the main features of the Anglo-French international order that preceded it. Working rules, ideologies, and domestic political structures did not change. American power dominance in the twentieth century has been a perpetuation of the European system of the nineteenth century which was created by the French and British.

Johan Galtung, a Norwegian sociologist, has developed a theory of aggression[12] and more recently a theory of imperialism[13] that draw primarily upon the structural properties of political and social institutions. He suggests that two commonly held theories of aggression, which he defines as the "drives towards change, even against the will of others," ignore the importance of social structure in stimulating aggressive behavior. The statement that war begins "in the minds of men" does not tell us anything about the social conditions that create the critical attitudes. Explanations of aggression that emphasize hunger or poverty do not account for the settings of poverty that create the opposite of aggression, i.e., passive acceptance. Attitudes and poverty may both explain aggression, but only in the context of social structures.

Galtung talks about systems of goal-oriented actors, be they individuals in groups, groups in nations, or nations in the international system. Each system is characterized by a kind of division of labor whereby actors perform different tasks. Actors in each system are ranked on several dimensions including those that concern the division of labor. A certain stability of rank and labor task characterizes each system. In essence, "*stratification* seems to be a universal phenomenon." Within any social system there exists a multidimensional system of stratification.[14]

If ranks between persons, groups, or nations are broadly defined as high and low, topdog (T) or underdog (U), three kinds of relationships between actors can be conceptualized. An actor can be topdog on all relevant dimensions (TTTT, for example). An actor can be underdog on all relevant dimensions (UUUU). Finally, an actor can have mixed rankings on these dimensions (TUTU). The first two possibilities are equilibrated positions; the latter, one of rank disequilibrium. From the three possible positions, Galtung hypothesizes that:

*Aggression is most likely to arise in social positions in rank disequi-
librium. In a system of individuals it may take the form of crime, in a
system of groups the form of revolutions, and in a system of nations
the form of war. But these extreme forms of aggression are unlikely to
occur unless (1) other means of equilibrium towards a complete topdog
configuration have been tried and (2) the culture has some practice in
violent aggression.*[15]

This hypothesis about rank disequilibrium assumes that
actors in the disequilibrated position develop self-concepts by
reference to those actors that are totally in the topdog position.
The TUTU position will stimulate actors to try to rectify the
unbalanced ranking in favor of the TTTT position. If there are no
avenues for the actors to move up nonviolently, they will consider
aggressive means to do so. The actors in total topdog positions
(TTTT) will have no need to aggress. The topdogs may be ex-
ploiters, but they will not be aggressors. The total underdog
(UUUU) does not possess the mental set, the requisite skills, the
desire, or the tools to seek to change its status.

In a later article, Galtung elaborates upon an imperial relationship between two or more nations. Instead of topdog and
underdog, Galtung uses the terms *center* and *periphery*. Nations or
groups in the center of a sociopolitical system are the holders of
power. They are the ones who rank first across a multiplicity of
dimensions (the United States is an example). The periphery
groups and nations are polar opposites in terms of any number of
status and power dimensions (African, Asian, Latin American
nations). Imperialism is that relationship between two or more
nations whereby the center nation has power over the periphery
nation in such a way as to increase or bring about a "disharmony
of interest" between the two. A disharmony of interest occurs
when there is an inverse relationship between the living condition
of one nation and another and there exists some causal connection
between the two nations. Simply put, the power, prestige, material
and psychic well-being of one nation, the center nation, increases
at the expense of the other nation, the periphery nation. Galtung
thus defines the structural relationships between the two nations
in an imperialist situation in terms of three conditions:

(1) There is *harmony of interest* between the *center in the Center
nation* and the *center in the Periphery nation*, (2) there is more *disharmony of interest* within the Periphery nation than within the Center
nations, (3) there is *disharmony of interest* between the *periphery in
the Center* nation and the *periphery in the Periphery* nation.[16]

The imperialist nation establishes mutually beneficial relationships with elites in periphery nations so that the gain of the center nation is also the gain of the elite of the peripheral nation. Since the interests of elites in the periphery nation are in accord with the interests of the center nation, the elites are acting in ways that are antithetical to the living conditions of the periphery in the periphery nation. Finally, the third condition suggests that all citizens in the center nation as well as elites in the periphery nation are in a position of disharmony of interests with those peoples in the periphery of the periphery nation.

The imperialist relationship is based upon two overlapping mechanisms. The first is "vertical" interaction, whereby asymmetrical distributions of value prevail which have differential effects domestically in center and periphery nations. The second is feudal social structures, whereby periphery nations are suppliers of wants to center nations. These periphery nations and peoples are kept separate from other peripheries. The periphery of the periphery nation is at the service of the center nation and its allies in the periphery nation. The important point is that imperialism has a dramatic effect on the two interacting nations, both in terms of interstate relations and intrastate relations. For example, a gap in processing raw materials into finished products affects the trade relationship between the center and periphery nations as well as the political, cultural, economic, and ecological systems of each nation. The periphery nation sells the raw materials for a small price and the center nation uses them for industrial, defense, and consumer purposes.

Although the validity of the imperialist relationships between center and periphery nations in two-nation or multiple-nation combinations is difficult to substantiate, the substance of the theory seems to describe many current interaction patterns and their domestic consequences. The implications of the Organski and Galtung models suggest a world of unequal distribution of values that creates a number of adverse international and domestic effects. Internationally, dissatisfaction and rank disequilibrium are stimuli for aggression and violence. Domestically, dissatisfaction and rank disequilibrium stimulate poverty, powerlessness, and political instability. Both theorists emphasize the critical linkage between international and intranational politics in a much more substantial way than the balance of power theorists. Peace becomes a function of the extent of control from the powerful and hence depends upon a thoroughgoing exploitation. As the exploited develop, violence increases internationally and domestically.

ENDANGERED PLANET AND FUTURE SHOCK MODELS

Very recently, a few international relations and world order theorists have begun to look at the international system from the perspective of current and expected problems of a global nature. Moving beyond the individual problems of perpetual conflict and stratification, two such theorists, Richard A. Falk[17] and W. Warren Wagar,[18] attempt to draw a portrait of the international system that highlights the interconnectedness of global problems. These problems can no longer be separated from a traditional concern for military and political power or from the domestic context in which they have most often been discussed. While these analysts have not constructed theory in the strict scientific sense, they offer a holistic portrayal of international relations that encompasses major actors, processes, and dilemmas.

In his development of the endangered planet thesis, Falk argues that for the first time in history man and his natural setting are being threatened by terrible destruction. The physical, natural, and social realities of the planet are in obvious unity, says Falk. Yet, the world of authority and power is fragmented. If the world system does not become unified to resolve the four basic planetary dangers—nuclear war, population pressure, pollution, and resource depletion—the future of the planet and its inhabitants appears dim; in essence, "the present framework for problem-solving in international society imperils human survival."[19]

The history of liberal and socialist thought in the West presumed inevitable progress, first conceived of, perhaps, as the kingdom of God in the Old and New Testaments. With rising population, increasing technological sophistication, the rationalistic spirit of the Enlightenment, and the tangible improvements in the human condition over the last two hundred years in Europe and North America, Western man lost his sense of the finite. With a sustained and sophisticated struggle against nature, man became god. The medieval unity between man and nature was replaced by the new Darwinian struggle of man *against* nature. Such a struggle for the survival of the fittest between men and men and men and nature may have been productive. It may not have been much of a threat to human survival in an historical epoch when population was small and population groups were relatively isolated from each other. In the twentieth century, the accent on struggle accepted by both Western and non-Western man, coupled with burgeoning populations, scarcity of space and resources, and communications and technological networks that blanket the entire globe, yields unenviable preconditions of disaster.

The endangered planet problem is accentuated by the stated goals of third world peoples to adopt development models of either corporate capitalism or state socialism. Both models accept ecological disruption as a price to be paid for rapid development. Both models further assume that development can and must proceed in the context of a competitive state system. The perplexing irony is that to the extent that such third world goals are not realized, domestic violence and revolution will probably increase. To the extent that third world peoples are "successful," the dangers of ecosuicide will almost certainly increase. In Falk's words, "We are confronted, then, with a fundamental dilemma: *success* in industrializing the poor countries is likely to result in less poverty and turmoil, but in a rapidly and possibly decisive worsening of the ecological situation, whereas the *failure* to industrialize these countries is likely to generate political behavior that would be likely to increase risks of general war."[20] The task Falk poses for world citizens is the discovery of ways to end misery without threatening ecological suicide.

At a minimum, several kinds of structure, policy, and consciousness changes are required. First and foremost, an equilibrium between man and nature is needed. Only as much technology and industrialization as can satisfy real, tangible human needs should be utilized. Such utilization must proceed from an ecological ethic that recognizes man as a part of nature; he is inextricably bound up with it. This requires planetary planning that can reduce and recycle waste, maintain the earth's resource base, and limit superfluous consumption patterns. Second, the world system must be redefined so that national security is no longer the preeminent consideration. Third, fundamental policy changes must be carried out to dramatically alter patterns of resource and product redistribution. Finally, institutions and attitudes must be changed so that the inviolability and legitimacy of the state is reduced. As long as the state is the central political unit in the world, interaction will be based on a security conscious and competitive model of existence.

Falk then discusses six underlying reasons for the endangered planet thesis. First, as implied above, the state system itself has maximized competitive international interactions and has minimized cooperative interactions. The three overarching goals of any state are economic growth, political stability, and international security and prestige. These goals tend to be incompatible with world cooperation. To the extent that there is cooperation between states, it is only a by-product of temporary mutual interests. Superimposed on the competitive state system is the mix of a few large bureaucratized nations and far greater numbers of small and underdeveloped ones. The symbiotic relationship between the two kinds of nations is characterized by dominance and submission. Of related concern is the extraction and utilization of excessive percentages of world resources by the few.

Second, Falk discusses what he calls the "paradox of aggregation," whereby the collectivity of individual interests is presumed to equal the interests of the collectivity. Both domestic and international systems presuppose the existence of some kind of invisible hand that will adjust and equalize individual and national pursuits to maximize stability in the larger whole. The reality of the four dimensions of planetary danger is that there are no mechanisms to perceive or act upon world interests.

A third critical stimulus to planetary danger involves the pervasive belief in, and institutionalization of, the efficacy of violence. Social change is often a function of violent action by revolutionary or counterrevolutionary groups and stability is maintained by threat, fear, or physical repression. In a world of scarce resources and extensive maldistribution, violence is ultimately the major mechanism of all political groupings. Fourth, a cycle of destruction motivated by fear and greed seems to characterize all politics. Attitudinally, world and domestic actors have casually accepted the destruction of human life and ecology as inevitable by-products of human existence.

The final two causative factors are particularly interrelated in that they pertain to the "hazards of velocity" of change and increasing alienation, manipulation of peoples, and the creation of false consciousness. Technological advances exceed social adaptation to these changes. The spirit of change is maximized in the most developed nations through conscious policies of planned obsolescence. This in turn stimulates the pervasive feeling of powerlessness and purposelessness in mass man that makes him susceptible to manipulation. His thought and action become contrary to self-interest and collectivity interests.

Each of these phenomena serves to create and reinforce the war system, patterns of human relationships that are based upon structural violence (dominance, fear) and direct violence (revolution, repression), escalating population pressures (space and food shortages), increasing insufficiency of resources (air, water, food, fuels, minerals, etc.), and environmental overload (pollution, destruction of limited planetary resources). Complementary and interconnected processes are creating the four planetary dangers. Any viable alternative future, Falk is suggesting, must grapple with these problems in a holistic or planetary way.

In discussing many of the same problems and processes, W. Warren Wagar looks at explanations of root causes of planetary danger. He argues that all the traditional enemies which men have conjured up to explain social malfunctions are inadequate to the twentieth-century crisis. Capitalism, technocracy, totalitarianism, mass society, pathological leaders, etc., are all old and discredited ideologies. The real crisis-inducing phenomenon is the rapidity of change itself. As suggested by Michael Harrington,[21] we are living in an accidental century characterized by value systems derived from the nineteenth-century industrial revolution and a twentieth-century cybernetic revolution. Or the malaise is derived from what Toffler[22] calls future shock, rapid sociotechnological developments that do not provide adequate time for human adaptation.

Wagar's terms are *fission* and *fusion*. Old orders are breaking down; "we are living in an age of simultaneous fission and fusion, of violent forces that promise to tear us apart and of violent forces that promise to whirl us together into a solid mass."[23] Old organic relationships are destroyed and people find themselves in a society that has properties of individualism and collectivism. Every previous value system, every current form of social organization has lost its credibility as men are hurled together by communications, transportation, and a common economic system. Again in Wagar's words:

> What a confusion! Irresistible pressures crush rapidly decaying local centers of civilization into a precarious new geophysical unity in a world where space and time have been virtually annihilated. Centrifugal force threatens the organicity of every historic structure of life and thought; centripetal force squeezes the broken fragments of these structures into a single, hard, compact sphere of aggregated humanity. Here, for a short while, the one kind of force prevails. There, for a little time, the second. Now one, now the other; or both bashing away together.[24]

The forces of change lead to five kinds of interlocking calamities: war, poverty, ecocide, dehumanization, and nihilism. The basic calamity is the continued threat of nuclear war. For Wagar, the underlying quarrels that stimulated the Cold War have not yet been eased. Hostilities are exacerbated by the dynamics of a competitive nation-state system supplied with the tools for nuclear annihilation. Increased defense spending affects the distribution of resources for basic needs, the quality of the environment, and the mechanisms of control and manipulation within societies that magnify alienation and anomie. For Wagar, as for Falk, the only resolution is a unified world order.

59

What the theorists of the endangered planet bring to the study of international relations, therefore, is a sorely needed problem focus. Beginning with the kinds of worldwide dangers they see as characteristic of the contemporary epoch, they seek to relate these dangers to their sources. Their conceptualizations are worldwide and organic in character; that is, they view the morass of domestic and international problems as integrally related. From this perspective, solutions must be holistic; they must provide institutions and/or processes that can deal with all of the dangers together.

NATIONAL AND INTERNATIONAL DIMENSIONS OF SOCIAL-CRITICAL THEORY

Chapters two and three have illustrated many of the current and future problems that face national societies and the entire planet. Each perspective emphasizes one kind of force that can inhibit the fulfillment of human needs. Some may view one argument or another as singularly decisive to an explanation of the present and the future. Others may see several interlocking forces as the most accurate means of explaining major trends. Still others may view the positions of several theorists as contradictory and therefore of limited use to an understanding of the condition of man in his national and world system milieu. This volume assumes that in varying degrees, *all* of the forces described are characteristic of *intranational* and *international* relations.

Starvation, poverty, and lack of personal security are tied to elitism, capitalism, and cultures of competition domestically and nation-state competition, stratification, population explosion, and resource depletion cross-nationally. Loss of community, loneliness, and alienation relate to expanding technocracies, elites, and classes nationally and to the balance of power, stratification, and uncontrolled change internationally.

The maze of interrelated causes and effects between what happens in states and what happens between them is extraordinarily complex. National properties affect individuals and the larger global system. Global properties affect the nation and its people. Properties act on each other. A more satisfying alternative future must replace certain by-products of the state and its central components *and* certain components of the international system. Only through a holistic view of "what is" can the student of alternative futures decide "what ought to be." Only through a holistic view of "what ought to be" can the student of alternative futures think of ways to change "what is."

NOTES

1. Thucydides, *The Peloponnesian War* (Baltimore: Penguin, 1954); Machiavelli, *The Prince* (New York: New American Library, 1952); Hobbes, *Leviathan* (Baltimore: Penguin, 1968).

2. See Mulford Q. Sibley, *Political Ideas and Ideologies* (New York: Harper & Row, 1970), pp. 384-387.

3. See Per Maurseth, "Balance-of-Power Thinking from the Renaissance to the French Revolution," *Journal of Peace Research*, 2, 1964, pp. 120-137.

4. Morton Kaplan and others write of the balance of power rules that supposedly governed eighteenth- and nineteenth-century international politics. They often ignore contradictions in their elucidation of the several rules. For example, there is a discrepancy between states being motivated by self-interest and their seeking the preservation of other states. Kaplan does not address himself to this apparent contradiction.

5. Morton Kaplan, *System and Process in International Politics* (New York: Wiley, 1957).

6. Hans Morgenthau, *Politics Among Nations* (New York: Alfred A. Knopf, 1960).

7. *Ibid.*, pp. 27-29.

8. A. F. K. Organski, "The Power Transition," in James N. Rosenau, ed., *International Politics and Foreign Policy* (Glencoe, Ill.: Free Press, 1961), pp. 367-376.

9. *Ibid.*, p. 367.

10. *Ibid.*, p. 369.

11. *Ibid.*, p. 370.

12. Johan Galtung, "A Structural Theory of Aggression," *Journal of Peace Research*, 2, 1964, pp. 95-120.

13. Johan Galtung, "A Structural Theory of Imperialism," *Journal of Peace Research*, 2, 1971, pp. 81-119.

14. Galtung, "A Structural Theory of Aggression," p. 96.

15. *Ibid.*, p. 98-99.

16. Galtung, "A Structural Theory of Imperialism," p. 83.

17. Richard A. Falk, *This Endangered Planet* (New York: Random House, 1971).

18. W. Warren Wagar, *Building the City of Man* (New York: Grossman, 1971).

19. Falk, *This Endangered Planet*, p. 8.

20. *Ibid.*, p. 33-34.

21. Michael Harrington, *The Accidental Century* (Baltimore: Pelican, 1965).
22. Alvin Toffler, *Future Shock* (New York: Bantam, 1970).
23. Wagar, *Building the City of Man*, p. 5.
24. *Ibid.*, p. 7.

Chapter 4

The Utopian and Anarchist Traditions as Alternative World Futures

INTRODUCTION

The concept of utopia has many meanings. It is most often used by "realist" thinkers to pejoratively label an idea as fanciful. Some theorists, however, like Lewis Mumford and Martin Buber,[1] regard utopias as visions of desirable social orders. To them, these visions are motivating forces for needed social change. Utopian speculation, expressed as concern for alternative futures, is a prerequisite for social change. The idea precedes the act.

A similar position emphasizes the notion that utopia implies a method of political action. Mulford Sibley, In "Apology for Utopia,"[2] challenges the view that the only reality is the reality of the empirical world, that men are solely products of biology, their social heritage, and their social and material environments. Even though all thought is derived from facts, says Sibley, the selection of appropriate facts for political action is a value choice. Every action implies the pursuit of utopia. All action is pursued in the name of some changed state of affairs. Utopia is a method of reflection, value-ordering, and action, whatever the nature of the thought that precedes the action.

Others have viewed utopia more narrowly as a specific body of thought and writing. Its task here is the description of a society that does not exist, or one that is being experimentally constructed. This perspective leads one to point to a literary tradition and several key figures, beginning with Plato or Thomas More and proceeding through the nineteenth century to contemporary figures like B. F. Skinner and Paul and Percival Goodman.

63

Finally, some authors identify the utopian tradition in terms of those social orders that are usually small-scale societies of several hundred or several thousand people. W. Warren Wagar, for example, talks about "Utopia" and "Cosmopolis." Utopia is "the perfect town, a community of friends and neighbors, an uncomplicated warm nest from which all the noise of the real world is excluded." Cosmopolis is the center of a viable world order, a world-city, "the inevitably large spiritual and intellectual and administrative capital of a civilization, of the whole known civilized world."[3]

In terms of the two polar traditions concerning alternative futures, Wagar's conceptions are particularly useful. Each of the models discussed in chapters four through seven of Part I is an approximation of either the utopian or cosmopolitan forms or a synthesis of them both. Most of the utopians discussed below emphasize small-scale social organization or community. Within these parameters, however, two tendencies will be noted separately. Utopians who talk almost exclusively about community per se are referred to as the "microcosmic" utopians. Utopians who seek to incorporate community forms into some larger networks of economic, political, and social relationships are the "macrocosmic" utopians. From the standpoint of thinking about alternative *world* futures, the latter variety of utopian speculation is of direct interest while microcosmic theories are of more *indirect* interest. This means that microcosmic schemes may contribute creatively to our concern where their recommendations are extended beyond their intended bounds (individual communities) to create a world of communities *or* a world society that resembles one community.

The anarchist tradition has also provided a rich collection of proposals for alternative world futures. Often such proposals have been derived from or stimulated the utopians. Since the central thrust of anarchism has involved the abolition and replacement of the state with some kind of community and/or federation, selected anarchists are included in the discussion of micro- and macrocosmic utopians. For some theorists of alternative futures, therefore, peace, justice, and welfare seemingly require extensive centralization of certain institutions and obeisance to a world sovereign (see chapter six). For most utopians and anarchists, however, the gravest human plights can only be alleviated by dramatic decentralization of all institutional forms and the creation of some kind of community.

It should be emphasized further that the utopian tradition has stimulated interest in a variety of problems relating to human need fulfillment. The utopians and anarchists have examined the single most basic issue: *the nature of man.* These writers have speculated about man's capacity for passion, reason, goodness, or evil. Man is usually defined as capable of cooperation, industriousness, and creativity. Some theorists view man as potentially good only in the appropriate utopian setting. Utopians and anarchists have examined in depth the question of the *most desirable form of social organization.* This usually comes from their criticisms of the negative by-products of the industrialized state, i.e., its bureaucracy, impersonalism, and elitism. These writers have considered the *interaction between proposed social organizations* the critical concern, for cooperation and conflict between two or more communities emerges as central to anarchists' speculation in particular. Also central to discussions of man, community, and community interaction is the *style of community decision-making.* Modes of decision-making in utopian and anarchist thought range from certain forms of benevolent elitism to participatory democracy.

Other questions are also given serious consideration. Theorists differ on how they treat the *processes of work and productivity.* Some presume that alienation results from continuous, dull, and repetitive work and thus propose schemes for work rotation. Others, emphasizing agricultural and craft jobs, propose to abolish the factory. Still others seek to limit work time to those activities which provide for community members' basic needs. Along with work, *property* is usually subjected to serious consideration. Many writers in the utopian and anarchist tradition contend that private property is the source of greed and avarice. Others contend that certain forms of private property are supportive of individual liberty, while other kinds are sources of oppression.

Most utopians and some anarchists offer extended discussions of the processes and substance of *education.* Maintenance of community support and productivity is usually tied to an efficiently operating educational system within the community. For some, education becomes both the mechanism for bringing about social change and the means by which the new order will be maintained. Integrally related to work and education is the *structure of sex role distinctions.* A few anarchists and utopians have pointed to the relationship between rigid sex role distinctions and oppression in industrialized societies. They have called for redefinitions of the family, "male" and "female" work, and the access of women to political participation in the affairs of the community. Significant discussions of community and the *response to deviance and crime* are also found in the anarchist literature. Some of the writers consider the problem of community responses to dissent; others simply assume that such dissent will not occur.

A final significant issue developed in the utopian literature involves the appropriate *reaction to technological developments*. Some utopians have prescribed model forms that totally reject the technological by-products of the industrial revolution. Others seek a partial acceptance of such advances, and some unconditionally accept the latest developments in science, engineering, and behavioral science.

In the pages that follow, we will seek to analyze the alternative futures proposed by utopians and anarchists. The fundamental thrust of the models relates to the creation of *community*. Along with this, selected thinkers examine the nature of man, alternative forms of decision-making, community interactions, work roles, sex roles, educational processes, and technological adaptation. Even if the utopian position must be tempered in a complex and interconnected world, the kinds of issues raised by utopians and anarchists are an important part of any alternative world future.

MICROCOSMIC FORMS OF UTOPIAN SOCIAL ORDERS

Although not actually the first utopian proposal, Thomas More's *Utopia*[4] seems to have set the precedent for the use of the utopian form to condemn ongoing societies and to postulate new ones. Many features of *Utopia*, which was written in 1516, still have a remarkably contemporary ring to them. Raphael is More's traveler who spends five years in Utopia and returns to Europe to relate his experiences. In "Book One" of *Utopia*, Raphael and More argue about the efficacy of reformers serving as counselors to monarchs. More's expressed view is that people with the innovative ideas of Raphael (derived in good part from his visit to Utopia) should share them with the king in the hope that the evils of European society might gradually be changed. Raphael contends that monarchs would only ignore what they were told about Utopia. Kings and nobles are presumably interested only in war-making and personal flattery. Furthermore, the reformer himself would be corrupted by the necessity of modifying his views to please his superiors.

As a result of what he learned in Utopia, Raphael believes that no significant social change can be expected until private property is eliminated. Without an equal distribution of goods, poverty will still remain, the rich will be idle, the poor will act in criminal ways, and elites will continue to punish crimes of thievery with death. Only the creation of the unique characteristics of Utopia can lead to the maximization of pleasure and to social behavior that is moderate and virtuous.

Although Utopia represents a network of rather large towns (up to 50,000 people) on one island, the major emphasis of Raphael's portrayal is upon a single town. All towns in Utopia are almost exactly alike in geography, tradition, law, and social norms. The underlying philosophy of Utopia centers about the maximization of pleasure. There are two kinds of pleasures: the mental or contemplative pleasures and the physical or sensory ones. Only those activities that are "naturally" enjoyable are really pleasurable. Men naturally derive joy from mental activities like contemplation and thinking about the past and future. The physical pleasures encompass basic bodily activities that create excitation in the whole organism as well as other kinds that seemingly satisfy no organic need. These latter ones act in a "mysterious" way upon our senses and give us joy. The enjoyment of music is a good example. The most favored physical pleasure is simply good health. Being in good health gives one a good feeling.

While Utopia is based upon the motive to maximize real or natural pleasures, other societies are said to be based upon illusory and false pleasures. These false pleasures include addiction to the acquisition of excessive amounts of clothing, a passion for jewels, the accumulation of superfluous wealth, gambling, and hunting.

Although Raphael feels that the Utopians are too hedonistic, he describes the argument Utopians make for the pursuit of pleasure. Man is created by God to be happy and is rewarded by behavior in the next world. If man follows his "natural" impulses or pursues real pleasures he not only creates the greatest happiness for himself, but because of future reward behaves in a virtuous way that does not impinge upon the pleasures of others. Contrary to ascetics who purge themselves of pleasure so as to create it for others, the Utopians believe that if the virtuous life means seeking pleasure for others, it must mean seeking pleasure for oneself as well. Consequently,

> The Utopians therefore regard the enjoyment of life—that is, pleasure—as the natural object of all human efforts, and natural, as they define it, is synonymous with virtuous. However, Nature also wants us to help one another to enjoy life, for the very good reason that no human being has a monopoly of her affections. She's equally anxious for the welfare of every member of the species. So of course she tells us to make quite sure that we don't pursue our own interests at the expense of other people's.[5]

From this ethic, the Utopians come to the conclusion that men must keep their promises in private life while supporting public laws that are made wisely and properly. Man has an obligation to pursue private pleasures and the pleasure of the community. To the extent that men must make personal sacrifices for the public good they are rewarded by a sense of spirituality and "perfect joy."

"Book Two" of More's *Utopia* then discusses those structures and processes that the Utopians have created to achieve and maximize pleasure. All members of each town perform agricultural activities for two-year periods in rural areas. They develop some expertise in a given trade when they are not serving the community in a farming capacity. Persons work six hours a day, three in the morning and three in the afternoon. They spend the remainder of time in modest entertainment and self-education, including study and attending lectures. The light work schedule can be sustained because the economy of Utopia produces only the necessities that aid in the attainment of natural pleasures. Everyone wears the same clothes and public housing is built solely for permanence (with repairs as soon as needed). Hence, excessive consumption for dress and shelter is precluded. Work involves only what is necessary, but necessary work is emphasized and idleness is scorned. Work is for the community and each individual or head of household has free access to goods and services upon demand. In substance, unnecessary production is obviated, industriousness is encouraged, leisure is narrowly defined in terms of the life of the mind and certain limited gaming activities, and goods are distributed "to each according to his need."

Politically, Utopia is characterized by a settled hierarchy of decision-making authority, beginning with the election of representatives to the town council by a specified number of households, the selection of higher authorities from among these representatives, and finally the selection of a mayor from the higher authorities. Citizens exercise indirect input in the decision-making process through discussion with their own representatives. An island-wide parliament also exists.

The hierarchical structure of the political process corresponds to some of the other inflexible features built into Utopia's social system. Citizens need passports to travel between towns, they are enslaved for nonparticipation in the work process, and they are ordered to take part in agriculture seasonally and for two-year periods of service. Although Utopians tolerate religious differences, the founder Utopos made it law for citizens to believe in some divine being, viewing atheism as destructive of the spirit of the island. Some work is carried out by slaves who are either deviants and criminals from Utopia or convicts from foreign lands who are purchased by the Utopians. Finally, the Utopian household is rigidly patriarchal, with the wife periodically required to ask her husband for forgiveness for various sins.

In terms of participation in war, the Utopians will engage in such activities only for self-defense, to protect allies from invasion, to liberate others from dictatorship, or to punish aggressors. Every attempt is made to minimize violence. A major strategy of the Utopians is to encourage and support domestic conflicts among her enemies. If that does not work, they seek to purchase the services of mercenaries. In either case, they utilize gold received from foreign trade. The only use Utopians have for gold is to entice foreigners to act in ways the Utopians desire. Although Utopians have no use for gold domestically, it is acquired for purposes of buying the services of peoples who do value it highly.

More was a significant precursor to modern utopians and visionary social thinkers. He sought to ground his utopia in a philosophic position that viewed the good life in terms of particular physical and mental pleasures. After defining human potential, he created a ficticious community to maximize it. To a large extent, however, he may have failed. Utopia represents a land of harsh rules and sanctions; agricultural and other work is compulsory, direct political participation by citizens is minimized, leisure activities are narrowly circumscribed, and women remain as servile as those in the Europe of his day. Lastly, Utopia is a static society that seeks to isolate itself from both external and internal sources of social change.

Despite these flaws, Thomas More was successful in popularizing the utopian genre. The model treats general philosophical issues and is at the same time structurally specific. It successfully criticizes and ridicules certain shortcomings of sixteenth-century Europe. Finally, More introduced communism to modern Western thought. Some of his contemporaries also posited utopias, but More's communism and utopianism seem a remarkably direct influence on nineteenth- and twentieth-century utopian schemes. More recently, utopianism was influential at the outset of the industrial revolution, partly because of the works, experiments, and movements of three figures labeled by Marx and Engels as "utopian socialists": Robert Owen, Charles Fourier, and Henri de Saint Simon. Both Owen and Fourier were microcosmic utopians. Saint Simon offered proposals that were designed to encompass all of Europe. These will be examined later.

Robert Owen (1771-1858), a successful factory manager,

began to develop some of the schemes that led him first to write about labor reform, then to pressure for parliamentary action, and later to create certain cooperative communities in Britain and the United States. Throughout his writings, one fundamental assumption presages all of his schemes: "Any general character, from the best to the worst, from the most ignorant to the most enlightened, may be given to any community, even to the world at large, by the application of proper means; which means are to a great extent at the command and under the control of those who have influence in the affairs of men."[6]

Five kinds of forces, Owen states, created the multiple malaise of industrializing England (poverty, unemployment, crime, and alienation). First, and encompassing all of the others, is the quality of the environment. Environmental variables entail a complex of the characteristics of the political and social systems, the factory, the gulf between man and nature in his physical setting, and the distance between man and his food supply. The qualities of moral man and pleasure-maximizing man are judged a function of all those physical and social forces that surround him. If the environment is radically changed, then one might expect men to change radically.

Second, and more specifically, Owen attacks the institution of religion as a stimulus for the creation of false consciousness. This is so because man is a product of his environment and can rationally discover how to properly change it and himself, while religion preaches that man cannot control his environment. Governments should extricate educational processes from the Church so that proper attitudes can be taught instead of the faulty religious ones.

Third, the educational process serves to instill erroneous ideas in each individual. It teaches that man is responsible for his own actions. The environment supposedly has no necessary relationship to human character. Further, children are not educated to view the interests of individuals and the community as one. Instead, each is defined as being in continuing competition with all others.

Fourth, the economy has created the structural conditions by which each person is pitted in a competitive relationship with all others. The industrial revolution created a society of atomized individuals; in the process, it destroyed pre-industrial organic communities. Manufacturing leads new capitalist elites to strive for more acquisition of riches. Masses of people are thus subjected to ebbs and flows of demands for employment. The lower classes are victims of structural unemployment and poverty. The rich become debased and the poor become impoverished. Political economy has created the distinction between private and public welfare.

Finally, Owen views the unreasoned assimilation of machine technology as a further source of atomization and unemployment. It is the machine that provides the tools for increasing competition among the rich for wealth and serves to degrade the laboring poor. The factory system divides man from man, making rich and poor alike selfish.

Since human society is a function of environment, education, economy, the application of technology, and the impact of religion, redirection of these features in a new systematic whole could create a social system that lacks all of the pathologies of nineteenth-century England. In *Report to the County of Lanark*, Owen describes his plan by answering six questions concerning: the size of the community; the extent of land to be cultivated; arrangements for feeding, lodging, clothing, and education; governance of the community; distribution of goods in the community; and the relationship between the community and the larger society and political system.

Owen's communities are to consist of from 300 to 2,000 people, with the ideal number for the predominantly agricultural villages ranging from 800 to 1,200 persons. This figure is presumably derived from the principle that *"there should be the largest amount of intrinsically valuable produce created, at the least expense of labour, and in a way the most advantageous to the producers and society,"* and the communities would reflect *"the principle of united labour, expenditure, and property, and equal privileges."*[7]

Since the communities are defined primarily in terms of agriculture, with manufacturing as an appendage, the amount of land to be utilized is to be based upon what is actually needed to sustain the community. Agriculture would also provide some surplus crops for the possible use of other communities and for those not employed in farming. If greater emphasis is placed on manufacturing, the acreage for agricultural surpluses would be reduced. What seems critical for Owen is the closeness of man to his food. The quality of life generally and physical sustenance has been impaired by the separation of agriculture from manufacturing in industrializing society. Man is to be at one with the products of his labor and his needs for survival.

Owen's discussion of living arrangements leads to his most specific proposals. The buildings of the village are to be built in the form of a parallelogram situated as close to the cultivated land as possible. Dwellings will encircle the central open space used for children's play. In the central portion of the parallelogram will stand the church, school, and meeting halls. Members of the community dine together. Men and women are each to share a common dress. Children will be trained in common "as though they were literally all of one family." One school will train children from ages two to six and the other school will train children six to twelve. Children will receive a general education which places them in the context of their past, their present place in the community, and their prospects for the future. They will be taught the integral relationship between each individual and the community, the harmony between private and public interest. As the children grow older they will be increasingly exposed to the physical labors that are needed to sustain their community.

Owen contends that the communities could be created by large capitalists, landed proprietors, large companies, parishes and counties, working and agricultural associations, or middle- and working-class farmers or laborers.

> As land, capital, and labour may be applied *to far greater pecuniary advantage* under the proposed arrangements than under any other at present known to the public, all parties will readily unite in carrying them into execution as soon as they shall be so plainly developed in principle as to be generally understood, and as parties who possess sufficient knowledge of the practical details to direct them advantageously can be found or trained to superintend them.[8]

Governance will depend upon who establishes the community. In cases where capitalists have created the communities, superintendents will be chosen to manage the affairs of the community. In communities established by members of the middle and working classes, community members within certain ages (35 to 45) will make group decisions. Here, particular value will be placed upon advice of those who are older and have more experience.

In terms of the acquisition and distribution of goods, the community will ascertain a labor standard of value (the expenditure of time and effort) as the criterion for exchange. As the community prospers, surplus goods will be distributed on the basis of request. Given the proper education, members will not seek to acquire and hoard goods but will take only what can be personally used. As individual communities grow and prosper, others will form as a result of the example. This will lead to intercommunity exchanges of surplus goods, thus adding variety to those commodities available to all members.

Finally, the success of the community will reduce government services such as law enforcement and prison maintenance. The new human character will reduce the incidence of criminality and hence a major reason for government. Similarly, war will become less likely as associations of men spread and change human character. Advances in the science of what influences man will lead peoples to realize the "folly" and "evils" of war.[9]

The substance of the Owen scheme entails the creation of a physical, social, and economic plan that will create a common bond among community members. The interests of individuals and the community are defined as one. Through education and the creation of proper community institutions, cooperation and affiliation will replace conflict and personal isolation. The holistic framework in which both the proposed alternative and the criticism of nineteenth-century Europe is cast sets the standard for future utopian schemes and experiments.

Owen's insights do have some flaws. His central conception of man is shared by contemporary behaviorists (see B. F. Skinner below). In this view, man is totally a by-product of his environment; hence, he is limited in his capacity for freedom, spontaneity, and choice by existing institutions. This leaves him two chief options: to be conditioned by bad institutions and education or by good institutions and education. The latter will result from humane social "engineers" like Owen himself. Further, the community Owen proposes is potentially static and austere; life revolves around agriculture, work is emphasized, pleasures are limited, and intellectual and cultural deviance is discouraged.

Charles Fourier was Owen's French contemporary and the second utopian socialist. Contrary to Owen's *tabula rasa* conception of man (human character a function of only environmental forces), Fourier contends that man is motivated by a multiplicity of passions that can be fully satisfied in a nonrepressive setting. God has divined a plan for the universe in which planetary bodies, human beings, and other living things may maximize their potential in unity and contrast. More specifically, Fourier contends that humans are subjects of twelve basic passions: five sensory passions—taste, touch, smell, sight, and sound; four affective passions—friendship, honor, love, and family or kinship; and three distributive passions—the desire for intrigue, variety or change, and the unity of man with nature. According to Fourier:

> The passions—variously called sentiments, affections, instincts, etc., are the motor forces, the springs of action in man; they are the parts of a unity or a whole, which is the soul or the spirit. God, in implanting in man these impelling forces, must have calculated mathematically their mode of action, their tendencies, and their functions. Passional attraction implies all these; it is equivalent to the mode of action and tendencies of the passions. As the passions come from God, this attraction expresses or reveals to us the will of God; it is his voice speaking

through the soul; it is the power which he employs to impel us to fulfill
the destiny he has assigned us.[10]

The twelve basic passions are manifested in different nuances.
Their possible combinations, together with some subtypes, yield
some 810 human types. Although Fourier manifests a compulsion
to quantify and mystify his analysis, the basic contention that he
raises is unambiguous: human potential must be realized through
the gratification of passions. The ideal society is one that can best
serve to maximize human potential.

There were, claims Fourier, several fundamental forces in
industrializing France that blocked the achievement of human
potential and stimulated evils through the repression of passions.
Most basic was the emerging bourgeois morality that distinguished
between reason and passion. By implication, this distinction suggests that passion is a source of evil that must be moderated or
repressed through reason. Parents teach their children deferred
gratification, a rigid rationalism, and emphasize an ethic of calculating self-interest. Contrary to this, the theory of "passional
attraction" assumes that creativity and the purging of evil are tied
inextricably to the fulfillment of all the passions. Most critically, it
assumes a universal unity of man with man, man with the universe,
and man with God. This is opposed to the repressed and isolated
individualism of the bourgeois ethic.

A second negative force, the economic system, was built
upon the assumption that progress is tied to the inevitable conflict
between man and man, that individual and collective interests are
always in conflict. Further, the duality between an ethic of
Christian virtue and commercial practice is a continual source of
hypocrisy. Commerce creates a whole nonproductive class of
middlemen who gain unfairly from buyers and sellers. The ultimate result of the rise of commerce is that it overpowers the state
of which it is a part.

The isolated and competitive social structure is most significantly manifested in the nuclear family because each family is in
competition with all others. The male is subject to unhappiness,
great expense, and the obligation to watch over family members.
The female in the household is made a house slave, her intelligence
is belied, and she is socialized into incompetence. Family life,
therefore, entails passional repression, not gratification.

Fourier contends that there is only one answer to the competitive, hypocritical, and isolating political-economic system in
existence. That answer presumes the maximization of "passional
fulfillment," which is possible only within the structural context

of universal association. Association to him means the creation of "Phalansteries" consisting of 1,600 people living in one large building with several wings to account for dwelling, recreation, and sexual interaction.

The Phalanstery would be primarily agricultural. Members would regularly rotate their work roles. Groups of people could maximize job satisfaction by performing no one task for more than two hours. Along with the diversification of work roles, Fourier proposes the abolition of the nuclear family. It should be replaced with free-flowing heterosexual interaction. Mates are to be temporarily selected for a number of purposes (companionship, common intellectual interests, friendship, or sexuality). Individuals would receive a share of the community's productive output based upon their capital holdings, labor, and talent. All communal members would receive a certain minimum subsistence allowance irrespective of these three criteria. Although the Phalanstery would seek to provide basic sustenance for its members, it would not abolish private property or capital accumulation.

Women, although perceived as having certain specific kinds of skills, were to be equal. They would have access to a number of roles beyond those in bourgeois society. Essentially women in the community are to form work groups not subservient to men. Education would maximize those passions and talents that the young of either sex evidenced. It would be pursued through familiarization with both material and spiritual education, encompassing the body and the mind.

Finally, the ultimate harmonization was to occur when the entire population of the world became organized in Phalansteries. The world would organize after the first several experiments were deemed successful and after others chose to experiment themselves. Initial efforts were expected to be supported by the rich and later the general populace.

Fourier, therefore, introduces a myriad of provocative proposals about alternative communities. Contrary to Owen's static model, and More's lifeless definition of pleasure, the Phalanstery would be a place where happiness would be achieved by the full satisfaction of the passions. The growth of community would be a function of the contrasting passions; thus, heterogeneity rather than homogeneity is preferred. The satisfaction of the passions, for Fourier, is possible only in some kind of association where conflict and cooperation lead to a unity of being. However, Fourier was still willing to maintain relative privilege within the community based upon differential property holdings, skill, and effort.

Two twentieth-century theorists, B. F. Skinner, a psychologist, and Aldous Huxley, a novelist, have posited microcosmic utopias that are remarkably similar to those of Owen and Fourier respectively. Skinner's Walden Two[11] is a fictitious community in New York state that is organized around the principles of behavioral technology and "positive reinforcement." Human behavior is judged a function of antecedent conditions of two kinds: genetic endowment and environmental circumstance. Inner states, attitudes, beliefs, and emotions do not seem to determine human behavior; hence, they are irrelevant to a science of behavior. The only question, Walden Two's director Frazier contends, is what kinds of antecedent conditions are most likely to create desirable behavior patterns from the standpoint of the community.

Frazier tells the visitors to Walden Two that three kinds of human reactions to external stimuli can be found. Some stimuli bring no reaction, others bring a negative reaction, and lastly, some bring positive reactions. According to Frazier:

> . . . if it's in our power to create any of the situations which a person likes or to remove any situation he doesn't like, we can control his behavior. When he behaves as we want him to behave, we simply create a situation he likes, or remove one he doesn't like. As a result, the probability that he will behave that way again goes up, which is what we want.[12]

This is positive reinforcement. Psychology has shown that it yields desired behavior patterns much more successfully than punishment. At best, negative reinforcement (punishment) creates the desired behavior for short periods of time. The kind of lifelong conditioning to which citizens of Walden Two are subjected is designed to create the environmental conditions which lead to positively reinforced behaviors. Experiments in education, work roles, leisure, marriage, and basic sustenance are all directed to this end.

All goods and services are available without charge to members of the community. Each member has a reciprocal obligation to earn a certain amount of work credits per year. This usually amounts to four hours of work per day. People may choose the kind of work they desire to do. Onerous work brings more credit than desirable tasks. All members of the community, including managers and scientists, perform a certain amount of work credits in manual labor. Frazier tells his guests that the community can sustain itself with participants working only four hours a day for several reasons. In Walden Two, four hours of work is more productive than eight hours in the larger society because jobs are

self-selected and hence satisfying. Both men and women participate in the work process. The traditional family household and
isolated cleaning and cooking activities are eliminated by communal kitchens and communal raising of children. Useless jobs,
such as those in banking and insurance, are eliminated. Finally, the
community is willing to assimilate the most advanced labor-saving
devices available.

Central to Skinner's theories of behavioral technology are
certain processes of educating the young. In Walden Two, children
grow up in various environmentally controlled living arrangements
that are designed to minimize nonproductive emotions like anger
and jealousy. They move from incubators to small living and play
rooms, to dormitory living for children up to the age of thirteen.
At this time, they can choose to build and occupy large and
private rooms for themselves.

Early ethical training involves children in the gradual toler-
ation of minor frustrations comparable to those experienced in
adult life. Children are exposed to situations where, when hungry,
they must wait for their food while others eat. They are given
lollipops and are trained to avoid devouring them until an appropriate time. The ethical training at Walden Two teaches the child
to endure naturally uncomfortable situations without reacting
negatively to peers. Those raised exclusively in the community do
not develop egoistic and antagonistic attitudes toward others.
Competition with others, as opposed to competition with self and
nature, is avoided. Finally, as children mature they are increasingly
socialized by their peers and older children.

As they mature children are also taught the "techniques of
learning and thinking." They proceed at their own pace. Guidance
is available in any of several subjects. Children are exposed to the
experiences of the community. Hence they develop the skills
needed to perform useful community services. In terms of educational policy, as with all other policy in Walden Two, experimentation is central. Policies that do not produce the desired
experimental results are dropped. New ideas are tested as they
emerge.

Men and women do marry in Walden Two. They may do so
when they reach the adolescent years. As privacy presumably
increases happiness, married persons live in individual rooms.
Children are raised collectively. Parents, as well as all community
members, visit and enjoy the children, providing the love that
children require. Most basically, Frazier tells his guests, "The
family is an ancient form of community, and the customs and
habits which have been set up to perpetuate it are out of place in a

society which isn't based on blood ties. Walden Two replaces the family, not only as an economic unit, but to some extent as a social and psychological unit as well. What survives is an experimental question." The raising of children via scientifically tested planning, Frazier asserts, is far superior to the haphazard socialization that children are exposed to in the extant nuclear family, in which children are poorly socialized because parents are dissatisfied with their marriage relationship.

Roles in Walden Two are not determined by traditional definitions of what each sex can best perform. Community child raising is a job for both men and women. Traditionally defined female roles are judged to approximate slavery. Frazier is adamant on this point: "What does the ordinary middle-class marriage amount to? Well, it's agreed that the husband will provide shelter, clothing, food, and perhaps some amusement, while the wife will work as a cook and cleaning woman and bear and raise children. The man is reasonably free to select or change his work; the woman has no choice, except between accepting and neglecting her lot. She has a legal claim for support, he has a claim for a certain type of labor."[13]

Frazier states that the historic enslavement of women has been coupled in recent times with the mythology of equality. While she is restricted to the home, the woman is told that she is of equal importance to men. Walden Two redistributes household chores from the private household to the community and actualizes sexual equality. Each individual, man or woman, is judged of equal worth to the community. A woman's sense of self-worth is no longer linked to child raising and being a homemaker, but to her performance of important tasks for the community. Essentially, Walden Two has become a more radical departure for women than men. The transition, Frazier tells us, has been somewhat difficult for those members who were socialized in the larger society. However, after appropriate adjustments were made, women have found themselves much happier in the new situation.

The maintenance and development of Walden Two is directed by a board of planners which makes general policy and oversees the work of various sector managers. Along with planners and managers, the community supports a coterie of scientists who provide the insights for community policy through experimental research. Frazier repeatedly emphasizes the premium placed upon experimentation with new policies of behavioral engineering. For him, since man is a product of his environment, the choice for any government is rational control or haphazard policy. Either man utilizes the best means at his disposal to build rational institutions or he loses control of his destiny to contradictory and misguided forces. If man is not free, which Frazier says science assumes, control must be taken out of the hands of the acquisitive, the competitive, and the aggressive and placed in the hands of scientifically trained planners. Further, such planning necessitates large-scale structural change, not just piecemeal change in the schools, the family, or the economic system. The science of behavior technology must inevitably lead to a systemic, holistic world view and the complementary solutions to all significant problems.

As with Robert Owen, B. F. Skinner offers an image of man that is totally a reflection of his environment. Attitudes, values, and passions are extraneous to the significant causal link between stimulus and response. Nevertheless, Frazier, the narrator, describes the work satisfaction and the forms of creativity and artistic achievements experienced by citizens of Walden Two. What remains puzzling is where the stimulus for creativity, spontaneity, and individuality comes from. Although critics of Skinner may overemphasize the manipulative and social control dimensions of his thought (because community policies *are* a reflection of citizen behaviors), it seems more appropriate to construct an alternative future that allows man the freedom to transcend environmental constraints. Of course, for Skinner this is not possible because man is *not* free to self-actualize.

Aldous Huxley's positive utopia, Island,[14] is a small integrated island republic. It is based upon a unique kind of spirit blending Western rationalism with Eastern notions of the primacy of immediate experience and the relationship between man and nature. The psychic state of Island's members is based upon total self-awareness, of being what one is rather than what one might become. Happiness is a function of various institutional, psychic, and biochemical means. These are all designed to maximize a kind of total sensuality, one that encompasses the entire being as opposed to more conventional notions of sexual gratification. Children are taught to understand themselves, to be extremely aware of their environment, to avoid dogmas of any kind, and to pursue the natural pleasures of life. Island's book of philosophy says, for example, that "Good Being is in the knowledge of who in fact one is in relation to *all* experiences. So be aware—aware in every context, at all times and whatever, creditable or discreditable, pleasant or unpleasant, you may be doing or suffering. This is the only genuine yoga, the only spiritual exercise worth practicing."[15]

The maximization of experience and pleasure means that social institutions must be supportive of experience. Each political ideology, each crusade, falsifies experience and creates the dualism whereby people seek to become what they are not. Local democratic participation exists on the island, and except for the existence of a hereditary monarch with limited power, the society is self-regulating with a minimum of political institutions. Nuclear families remain, but groups of people throughout the island form Mutual Adoption Clubs whereby children within families may temporarily or permanently adopt new parents when household strains make such an adoption advantageous.

Nothing is sacrosanct except the pursuit of pleasure and the maximization of experience. As with skepticism concerning institutions (political, family, organized religion), the application of Western technology on the island is measured. Only those means that can expand human experience and pleasure are assimilated into the society. The bulk of technological developments are rejected since they might expand populations, encourage power seeking, foster the dualist pathology, and stimulate unnecessary consumption. In essence, the utopian community begins from *within the individual*. From there, it spills over to create the small-scale community that is a social manifestation of psychic utopia.

As Skinner emphasizes environmental factors at the expense of the states of conscious awareness, Huxley highlights psychosexual liberation at the expense of structural reform. It is not that Huxley ignores political and economic institutions, but that at the core of his views of utopia are certain kinds of psychic states of awareness. More than any other utopian, he sees human liberation almost totally in psychological terms.

MACROCOSMIC FORMS OF UTOPIAN AND ANARCHIST SOCIAL ORDERS

The emphasis of the utopians considered thus far has been upon small community for its own sake. Little concern has been evidenced for the world beyond the borders of this community. The *macrocosmic* utopians and anarchists continue to emphasize the life of the community as central to productive human experience, but they also begin, if rather haltingly, to propose some mechanisms for *intercommunity interaction*. The usual institutional pattern for such relationships takes the form of some kind of overarching federal structure. While the microcosmic utopian visions might be regarded as models for extension to the entire planet, macrocosmic ones are *originally* conceived from the world system perspective. The interactive dimension is an *intrinsic* feature of their recommendations.

P. J. Proudhon,[16] a nineteenth-century French anarchist illustrates this interactive component. He was especially concerned with the system of capitalist exploitation that was emerging in industrializing Europe. The worth of man's labor, he contends, should be the standard of value. Instead, factory production has created a system whereby the collective value of the labor of the work force is controlled by the employer. Workers live under conditions of bare subsistence while the owners of labor live in wealth. Proudhon argues that social science involves the study of the relationship between justice and economics. Rational analyses can discover the way to maximize justice in an evolving economic system. Justice is possible, therefore, only if the economic system and all institutions that support inequitable economics, particularly the state and religion, are radically changed.

Proudhon then reasons that political economy, or that theme in political economy that emphasizes the necessity of each against all in a continuous self-interested struggle, is the source of the exploitation of labor. He further contends, however, that socialism, the antithesis of political economy, denies that historic experience of man. Socialism especially ignores the fact that man has struggled with man to reach personal gain and also seeks to maintain his liberty in the process. According to Proudhon, the answer to the conflict between political economy, which emphasizes struggle, and socialism, which ignores individual liberty, is *mutualism*, a socialism of credit and exchange.

Mutualism represents a balance between socialism and capitalism. Its central premise is that justice is best served in an economic system where exchange in kind of products and services between independent individuals is the primary mode: "Its law, they say, is service for service, product for product, loan for loan, insurance for insurance, credit for credit, security for security, guarantee for guarantee. It is the ancient law of retaliation, *an eye for an eye, a tooth for a tooth, a life for a life*, as it were turned upside down and transferred from criminal law and the vile practices of the vendetta to economic law, to the tasks of labor and to the good offices of free fraternity."[17] All relationships should be based on the freely chosen contract between people. With the establishment of the freely chosen contract, sovereign state authority would be minimized. What would develop over time in its place would be a series of interacting relationships, first between people who have products and services to exchange, then between communities. Finally, there would be relations between states in larger and larger networks of economically based inter-actions.

In Proudhon's words, contracts between people and communities should be "synallagmatic" and "commutative." Synallagmatic contracts are those that bind two parties together by way of mutual obligations. Commutative contracts are those in which each party binds himself to do something which is equivalent to what is done for him. The mutual binding and equivalence criteria are critical to the existence of democracy. A federation is a binding contract for mutual benefit between two or more parties. The federal contract between peoples ensures the liberty and autonomous actions of all participants. As more contracts are made between people, groups, regions, and states, the diversity of products and services available to all will increase. The federal structure will facilitate specialization and a freely chosen division of labor. To the extent that the state still exists, it could serve to initiate public services. As these are established, the state could withdraw its power and control over the institution. The essence of the Proudhon proposal, therefore, is a freely chosen contract between individuals and the replacement of the political state with a network of individual and group contracts.

Mutualism proposes networks of relationships between individuals and collectivities. Unfortunately, a social order based solely on contractual relationships does not yield the kind of organic community posited by other utopians and anarchists. Mutualism may be a useful basis for intercommunity interaction where interpersonal affiliations are less feasible. However, the mutualism of the community must be supplemented by common institutions and a spirit of communalism for it to replace the world of capitalism and competition that Proudhon was criticizing.

Petr Kropotkin,[18] the Russian anarchist discussed earlier, based his proposals for a more desirable future upon lessons learned about animal and past human organization. Those species that have survived and prospered in given periods of history, we are told, did so because they practiced mutual aid, an instinctive feeling of solidarity that promoted cooperation for the collective good of all species members. In animals, Kropotkin found several common characteristics: the existence of complex forms of social organization, division of functions, hunting and feeding in common, common migration, sociability, and group punishment of rule violators.

Among humans, bands, tribes, or societies were presumably

the first organizational forms. Discrete families of people emerged rather late in evolution. The earliest humans were characterized in their social organization by peacefulness, sharing, kindness, primitive communism, common work, periodic redistribution of wealth, and common rule. After the demise of the Roman Empire, barbarian organizations of villages led to the emergence of confederations of tribes. These tribes held property in common and provided collective defense and support for all members. In each case, while conflict did exist with external groups, Kropotkin suggests that mutual aid under a structure of primitive communism prevailed within communities. The height of man's social achievement was accomplished in the medieval city-state. These city-states had cross-cutting forms of voluntaristic association based upon territoriality and occupation.

Persons who were members of small associations in parts of cities were also members of occupationally defined guilds that provided guaranteed sustenance. Beyond neighborhood and guild associations, the city itself provided basic services such as the acquisition and distribution of goods and services from other cities. The city organized itself as a federation of guilds and village communities. Kropotkin describes the medieval city as a "double federation" made of "small territorial unions" and "individuals united by oath into guilds." The first was an offshoot of earlier villages, the second a result of new occupational patterns.[19]

In terms of the future, if the state is destroyed or loses its legitimacy people will be sufficiently free to form in local associations, to share land and produce in common, and to develop a "free federation." Kropotkin contends that groups of freely forming communes and towns have emerged in France, Spain, England, and the United States. "In actual life this tendency manifests itself in thousands of attempts at organization outside the State, fully independent of it; as well as in attempts to take hold of various functions which had been previously usurped by the State and which, of course, it has never properly performed."[20] Although questionably relying upon the spontaneous construction of communities and federations of communities, Kropotkin portrays a future of both salient immediate groups *and* loose organizations among groups. Essentially, he integrates the mutualism of Proudhon with the community life of the microcosmic utopians, both at the expense of the state.

Three twentieth-century theorists, Paul and Percival Goodman and Martin Buber, have drawn heavily upon Proudhon, Kropotkin, and the utopian tradition to posit similar communities within larger federated structures. The Goodmans wrote *Commun-*

itas[21] shortly after World War II to challenge the prevailing drift of American social, economic, and environmental policy. In this work, they seek to stimulate a reconsideration of man's relationship to his natural and man-made environment, and to relate the means of his livelihood to particular ways of life. They question whether available means best fit the desired ends, if the ends themselves are desirable, and how the idea of means and desirable ends might be integrated. Their utopian plans are based upon an interrelationship of technology, standards of living, political and economic decisions, and the geography and history of a setting. They seek holistic communities that are based upon articulated central values. From these values, physical, social, political, and economic plans are to be derived.

After discussing three contemporary town plans (green belt, industrial, integrated), they propose three alternatives based upon fundamentally different values. The first plan, "a city of efficient consumption," seeks to maximize efficient distribution of goods and services to an urban populace. The second plan, "the elimination of the difference between production and consumption," seeks a totally integrated life, and develops themes expressed in the writings of Owen, Fourier, Proudhon, and Kropotkin. The third plan, "planned security with minimum regulation," emphasizes minimum subsistence guarantees to an entire national population with limited government.

The second plan, "the elimination of the difference between production and consumption,"[22] is an elaboration of four basic principles. First, the Goodmans call for an increased interrelationship between personal and productive environments. Second, workers are to be involved in all phases of the work process and to be experts in some of them. Third, work is to be scheduled with psychological and moral considerations in mind as well as efficiency and technological needs. And fourth, the socioeconomic features of the community are to yield a considerable amount of self-sufficiency and independence in its interaction with the larger society.

In elaborating these four principles, the authors offer several proposals to enhance the feasibility of the self-maintaining organic community. To reduce the separation between work and home life, more work tasks must be returned to the home. Certain home tasks, cooking and other housework, must be considered as part of the productive economy. Both in terms of communities and households, they contend that the advent and ready distribution of electrical power reduce the necessity of large concentrations of people and work forces in massive factories.

As to necessary factory work, the worker is to be schooled in the entire productive process so that he may understand his particular role in the production of goods. Not only does this have the effect of reducing alienation, but the workers might then begin to participate in the making of factory decisions. The Goodmans envision a factory system based upon participatory democracy whereby the factory becomes a source of power from which interactions with the external world can be pursued. The end product, they say, will be syndicalism or "simply an industrial town meeting." Along with industrial democracy, the community must provide comfortable, diverse kinds of work. This includes the possibility of men and women performing different tasks at different times, even to the point of farmers working in factories and factory laborers working on farms during appropriate seasons.

Painting the portrait of the region encompassing the community, the Goodmans call for diversified farming. This is designed to enhance regional autonomy, mutually dependent industrial centers, and industrial development in conformity with regional resources and capabilities. The town-country and farm-factory linkages with ready movement of adults and children can create an "industrial region" with "independent bargaining power in the national whole."[23]

The Goodmans then write of various architectural blueprints for the community, drawing upon plans and norms derived from the Greek polis and European piazzas within cities. Their plans emphasize central space for social intercourse, nearness of home and workplace, and the increasing integration of work, social activity, and public service buildings like libraries and shops. They also talk of schooling the young on farms as well as in the central urban area. The economy and the polity are designed to increase regional self-sufficiency as much as possible (local consumption of produce, local control of factories and public services), but these communities must still exist within a network of national and international economic and political systems. The desire is to create tangible community so that interactions with the external world are based upon mutual interchange rather than submissiveness in the face of distant and faceless authority. They contend that the decentralized societies they propose will create a new kind of integrated and efficient life-style. "But we are aiming at a different standard of efficiency, one in which inventions will flourish and the job will be its own incentive; and most important, at the highest and nearest ideals of external life: liberty, responsibility, self-esteem as a workman, and initiative. Compared with these aims the present system has nothing to offer us."[24]

The final utopian discussed here, Martin Buber (*Paths in Utopia*), examines the visions or "wish-pictures" of selected nineteenth- and twentieth-century utopians, anarchists, and Marxists. The totality of this literature leads Buber to postulate new social and spiritual forms that maximize organic community and a commonwealth of organic communities. Community can only be built upon the foundations of socialism and spiritualism. Socialism without religion is like a body without a spirit. Religion without socialism is the spirit without the body. Rather than structuring a blueprint, Buber contends that political and social institutions should be decentralized (what he calls the decentralized social principle) as much as possible. This he juxtaposes with the centralist political principle characteristic of Marxist-Leninist thought.

Like Kropotkin, Buber argues that the history of man is a history of collectivities that have sought to maximize functional autonomy, mutual recognition, and mutual responsibility. The "life between man and man" or Buber's "I-Thou" relationship was destroyed as the state took more and more power and responsibility from individuals and communities. Instead of being a critical member of the community, man became a functional object in the large social machine known as The State: "Just as his degenerate technology is causing man to lose the feel of good work and proportion, so the degrading social life he leads is causing him to lose the feel of community. . . ."[25] Buber poignantly describes what he means by community:

> Community is never a mere attitude of mind, and if it is *feeling* it is an inner disposition that is felt. Community is the inner disposition or constitution of a life in common, which knows and embraces in itself hard "calculation," adverse "chance," the sudden access of "anxiety." It is community of tribulation and only because of that community of spirit; community of toil and only because of that community of salvation. Even those communities which call the spirit their master and salvation their Promised Land, the "religious" communities, are community only if they serve their lord and master in the midst of simple, unexalted unselected reality, a reality not so much chosen by them as sent to them just as it is; they are community only if they prepare the way to the Promised Land through the thickets of this pathless hour . . . . A community of faith truly exists only when it is a community of work.[26]

The task before man, therefore, is to act to achieve the "wish-picture" or utopias he desires. This action must progress in the context of tangible social relationships that lead to community. Community means sharing work and responsibility, mutual respect, and individual autonomy. The religiosity of the community is the meaningful relationship between man and man. From the formation of communities, which represent the skeletal structures of the universal alternative future, will come the overarching community of communities. This will maximize cooperative interaction between communities.

The architectural forms and social structures of the Goodmans can profitably be blended with the spiritualism and socialism of Buber to construct a synthesis of all that the utopians and anarchists set out to achieve. The Goodmans show how community can be created in the industrial age and Buber illustrates how the best features of the entire community tradition fit together.

THE RELEVANCE OF THE UTOPIAN AND ANARCHIST TRADITIONS FOR ALTERNATIVE WORLD FUTURES

The above discussion of selected utopians and anarchists is designed to highlight both a method of positing alternative world futures and historically significant responses to varying societal pathologies. These traditions raise questions about structures, processes, and values that require radical changes. Moreover, they raise the kinds of questions that receive little attention in other perspectives on alternative world futures (many of the world order theorists, for example).

Perhaps most important to all of the theorists, and particularly Buber, is the basic problem of meaningful human relationships. With the possible exception of More, all of the theorists see the escalating destruction of face-to-face relationships among people in all but market interactions. These theorists seek to revitalize the commitment of men to live, work, and seek pleasure together. Buber is most directly influenced by the important conceptual distinction drawn by German social theorists, that of *Gemeinschaft* and *Gesellschaft*.

Gemeinschaft is the immediate community with common life-styles, values, and work patterns. Its essence is the primacy of the village, the town, the small city in the life of man. The organic nature of these communities is analogous to the inextricable union of the organs of the human body. Just as all organs are critical to a healthy body, individuals are all central to the healthy life of the community. And they are central as total persons, not just as specialized economic functions. *Gesellschaft*, on the other hand, is the emerging mechanistic large-scale society that destroys community and replaces it with certain values of individualism. These values are coordinated through the mediation of the centralized state. It is the state that destroys the mutual aid principle, mutual respect, responsibility, and psychic support for individual action. It is to individual "aloneness" in mass society that this tradition speaks most clearly.

All of the theorists discussed also give considerable attention to the problem of work. Since work is the most commonly shared human activity, several kinds of issues require analysis. Most basic, the utopians and anarchists see the need for rendering the relationship between human effort and human sustenance more satisfying. Each theorist sees the necessity of providing the worker with sufficient basic and material goods to justify his labor and to provide him with a comfortable existence. Whether the prescription is for sharing community produce on an egalitarian basis or simply reducing the disparity between rich and poor, poverty is to be eliminated or minimized. Some theorists go even further, raising the question of the relationship between work and psychic, passional, or spiritual gratification. In the industrialized state, the concept of meaningful labor has become a source of tension second only to the question of sustenance.

An issue related to the hours of labor is the time spent at leisure. This includes eating, resting, sensual pleasures, and cultural and artistic activities. The literature points to various different conceptions of pleasure, some reflecting certain staid notions of the ongoing society, others reflecting extreme deviations from these societies. For modern theorists of human needs, like Abraham Maslow, the potential for self-actualization is critical. Some of the theorists seek to provide the structural and environmental parameters in which actualization is possible.

For some of the theorists, conventional sex role distinctions are thinly veiled forms of oppression. Owen, Fourier, and Skinner are especially sensitive to the oppression of women. They want to change the nuclear family, the marriage bond, or the generalized conception of woman's place in the community. Any mix of goals encompassing egalitarianism and self-actualization must look carefully at proposals about the reformation of traditionally held sex role distinctions.

Each theorist addresses himself in some way to communal decision-making and cooperative interaction. Some see the special utility of boards of managers, elders, or philanthropists benevolently governing the life of the community. Others see the sharing of decision-making in government and business as critical to communal life. The utopian and anarchist traditions raise the issue of the relationship between policy-making and expertise, authority, and participatory democracy. Proponents of the traditions would agree, however, that the vast impersonal state cannot make decisions for the benefit of communal members. There is a common assumption that the successful construction of community, meaningful work, and provision for basic sustenance would all reduce the propensity toward intracommunity conflict and hostility.

Finally, and here the theorists take varying positions, the application of technology to communal life is examined. Utopians and anarchists range from a total rejection of technology to a partial assimilation of its useful features, to an almost total acceptance of machines and scientific expertise. If the option of total rejection for the developed world is not a real one, there still remain the questions of how much to accept, in what social and economic spheres, and for what purposes. For example: to what extent can technology be utilized in the context of a commonwealth of communities? The theorist of alternative world futures, if he seeks to improve the life of the community, must discover to what extent technology can be adapted to the community. He must discover whether the prerequisites of technology are in fact antithetical to community.

THE SHORTCOMINGS OF THE UTOPIAN AND ANARCHIST TRADITIONS

The argument made in this chapter is that the traditions of utopian and anarchist thought raise issues of critical importance to any student of alternative world futures. Despite the importance of the literature sampled here, however, it is clear that several kinds of shortcomings can be found in the visions discussed. It is only through the mix of perspectives from utopian, regionalist, and cosmopolitan positions that a thorough set of prescriptions can be derived.

The most central problem with the utopian perspective, even among the macrocosmic utopians, involves the problem of intercommunity interaction. The history of political thought has emphasized the necessity of authority and legitimate political institutions to bind different peoples together. Even if one could expect life within the community to be cooperative, the problem of binding communities together in larger wholes remains pressing. One might expect intense personal contacts and relationships to lead to a spirit of community among peoples, but one ought not to expect such community between peoples that do not directly relate to each other in continuous, tangible ways. Proudhon, Kropotkin, Buber, and others presume the emergence of a "commonwealth of communities" or a federation of communities after the basic communal structures are formed. Yet none of the theorists adequately describes the process of growth nor do they deal with the possibility of asymmetrical growth of communities and states at the same time. In essence, the community theorist must be able to respond to Professor W. Warren Wagar's charge that such proposals are no more than isolated pockets of good living with little or no prospect for meaningful interaction.

A nagging doubt also remains about the self-sustaining prospects of small-scale communities in the twentieth century. Some contend that technology can be decentralized. Others speak of the tremendous potential for distribution of peoples across the entire globe. Most utopian theorists have not yet systematically explored the constraints on the creation of human community.

The utopians and anarchists have also relied on one or another special strategy of social change to achieve their desired future. Either educational reform, or a multiplicity of community successes, or the stimulus of philanthropists, or the actions of revolutionaries have been seen as sources of change. The experiences of those utopians and anarchists who sought to actualize their visions over the last two hundred years have led only to marginal successes. (Of course this charge can be leveled at regionalist and world order theorists as well.) Viable social change probably necessitates several kinds of strategies which give special consideration to the particular historical setting, the varying levels of commitment and consciousness of potential members, and the personalities and dispositions of those seeking change. The problem of creating communities and "communities of communities" is extraordinarily complex. It requires thorough reflection.

Finally, the utopian and anarchist traditions stem from a period when Richard Falk's four planetary dangers were barely recognized or even nonexistent. Community visions speak most profoundly to alienation, feelings of powerlessness, and the need for self-realization or self-actualization at the expense of concern for nuclear war, population explosion, environmental pollution, and resource depletion. No matter how desirable communal life may be from the former set of standpoints, it may still warrant rejection if it cannot respond to the threatened destruction of life and life-support systems. If the *quality of life* and *the maintenance of life* can be distinguished, then the former is probably best achieved through *community* and the latter through *world order* of some kind. If this is true, then the basic problem for the student of alternative world futures is to posit a world system model that reconciles these two traditions.

NOTES

1. Lewis Mumford, *The Story of Utopias* (New York: Viking, 1922); Martin Buber, *Paths in Utopia* (Boston: Beacon, 1949).

2. Mulford Q. Sibley, "Apology for Utopia: I," *The Journal of Politics*, February 1940, pp. 57-74; "Apology for Utopia: II," *The Journal of Politics*, May 1940, pp. 165-188.

3. W. Warren Wagar, *The City of Man* (Baltimore: Pelican, 1963), pp. 14-15.

4. Thomas More, *Utopia* (Baltimore: Penguin, 1965).

5. *Ibid.*, p. 92.

6. Robert Owen, *Report to the County of Lanark, A New View of Society* (Baltimore: Pelican, 1969), p. 99.

7. *Ibid.*, p. 226, p. 227.

8. *Ibid.*, p. 252-253.

9. *Ibid.*, p. 262.

10. Mark Poster, ed., *Harmonian Man: Selected Writings of Charles Fourier* (Garden City, N.Y.: Anchor, 1971), p. 37.

11. B. F. Skinner, *Walden Two* (New York: Macmillan, 1948).

12. *Ibid.*, p. 259-260.

13. *Ibid.*, p. 146.

14. Aldous Huxley, *Island* (New York: Bantam, 1962).

15. *Ibid.*, p. 36.

16. Stewart Edwards, ed., *Selected Writings of P. J. Proudhon* (Garden City, N.Y.: Anchor, 1969).

17. *Ibid.*, p. 60.

18. Petr Kropotkin, *Mutual Aid* (Boston: Extending Horizon Books, 1902); Roger N. Baldwin, ed., *Kropotkin's Revolutionary Pamphlets* (New York: Dover, 1927).

19. Kropotkin, *Mutual Aid*, p. 181.

20. Baldwin, ed., *Kropotkin's Revolutionary Pamphlets*, p. 185-186.

21. Paul and Percival Goodman, *Communitas* (New York: Vintage, 1960).

22. *Ibid.*, pp. 153-187.

23. *Ibid.*, p. 160.

24. *Ibid.*, p. 160.

25. Buber, *Paths in Utopia*, p. 132.

26. *Ibid.*, p. 134-135.

Chapter 5
Regionalist Thought and Alternative World Futures

PRECURSOR TO CURRENT REGIONALIST THOUGHT

Regionalist thought describes a commitment to certain patterns of social, political, and/or economic organization at a level more comprehensive than the state, but less than the entire world. Typically, the regionalist position is unconcerned with immediate, tangible community per se. It is interested in managing economic competition or political conflict among states via supranational institutions in a given geographic area. As defined by Ernst Haas and Bruce Russett,[1] two prominent theorists of regionalism, such institutions exist "above and beyond" the state, exercising sovereign authority over state actors on certain matters. Essentially, these institutions can make decisions that participants are obliged to accept. The material below will examine some of the theories that seek to describe, explain, and predict the activity of integration (particularly in Europe). Most importantly, it will describe the implied alternative world future that certain theorists seem to favor. Regionalist or integration theory provides a commonly preferred condition lying somewhere between utopia and cosmopolis.

Aside from early planners for world government who assumed European dominance of the international system, the first regionalist (and technocratic) theorist since the onset of the industrial revolution was Henri de Saint-Simon (1760-1825).[2] Labeled by Marx and Engels as a "utopian socialist," Saint-Simon sees an historical progression of cultures, moving from polytheism to monotheism, to metaphysics, and to positive science. Dominated by the Church and a theological-intellectual elite, the medieval world was challenged by the onset of metaphysical commitments to natural law, equality, and liberty. Saint-Simon contends that nineteenth-century developments in science and industry presaged a new age where universal science would become the new religion and scientists the new theological elite.

Saint-Simon describes the emergence of three classes of peoples: scientists, nonproductive property owners, and the masses of workers. A new social order must evolve that reduces the likelihood of mass insurrection. Such an order would represent the product of an administrative and economic system whereby public policy is made by scientists. His plan, first for European nations, and then for the continent of Europe itself, involves the creation of institutions that would allow for central economic planning. These would provide sustenance for the masses and systematic organization of useful work.

In his essay on *The Reorganization of the European Community*, Saint-Simon discusses his technocratic-regional plan. Since the most effective and stable form of domestic government is presumed to be parliamentary constitutionalism, this is to be the new form of organization for Europe. Three different levels of authority are seen to exist in parliamentary systems: the authority representing the common interest, the authority representing particular or local interests, and the authority which arbitrates between the first two. In England, the king represents the common interest, the House of Commons represents the particularistic interests, and the House of Lords serves as the mediating agency. In a viable system, every resolution emanating from one body must receive the support of the other two bodies. Therefore, *"Europe would have the best possible organization if all the nations composing it were to be governed by parliaments, recognizing the supremacy of a common parliament set above all the national governments and invested with the power of judging their disputes."*[3]

The European House of Commons should consist of men of business, scientists, magistrates, and administrators. Professional bodies should select one of their distinguished members to represent each million European people. The House of Lords should be chosen by the king from among men who have served the European community in the sciences, law, or industry. These men should be given a certain amount of property to parallel the condition of peers within national societies. Saint-Simon does not indicate how the king of the European community should be chosen, but he does indicate that the monarchy is to be hereditary. The king is to organize and convene the European parliament.

93

The parliament is to handle each issue that is of common interest to the entire community and to adjudicate disputes between conflicting parties. In further conformance with the strictures of creating a European community, Saint-Simon suggests that state education in the entire European continent be administered by the parliament. A similar recommendation extends to the drawing up of "a code of general as well as national and individual ethics." As a result of these measures, European peoples would be bound by "uniformity of institutions, union of interests, conformity of principles, a common ethic and a common education."[4]

The vision of Saint-Simon was prophetic in two ways. First it predicted the rise of the modern state. Saint-Simon knew the impact science, technology, and organization would have in industrializing societies. What he did not understand was the potential negative consequences of the technocratic state. Second, he posited a model of regional organization that was to capture the imagination of politicians and social scientists 125 years after his death. Regionalists today have largely accepted his image of social organization and human need fulfillment and its relation to science and centralized planning.

THE CONTEMPORARY REGIONALIST VISION

Contemporary integration theorists have been concerned with the forces and processes by which states form cooperative relationships with each other. Many different "preferred worlds" or desired futures can be found in this large body of international relations literature. Some theorists like Ernst Haas and Leon Lindberg define integration as a *process* of achieving certain goals. Others like Karl Deutsch and Amitai Etzioni define it as the actual *outcome* itself. Further, J. S. Nye indicates many of the ways in which regional organizations have been distinguished by major function, by number of functions per organization, by political versus technical functions, by the equality or inequality of members in terms of power, and by the degree of geographic proximity of members. Lindberg views political integration as a critical subset of larger social, economic, and cultural transformations of a region.[5] Without getting embroiled in the debate over "what integration really means" and how one defines regional organization, it is possible to talk about several desired *end states* that regionalists would like to achieve. It is these *end states* that circumscribe the regionalist vision.

If the varying dimensions of this vision can be viewed as a continuum, one can find several levels of cooperative interaction between states. A "minimalist" regionalist vision seeks the end to physical violence between two or more states. Deutsch, for example, in his early study entitled *Political Community and the North Atlantic Area*, states that integration entails "the attainment, within a territory, of a 'sense of community' and of institutions and practices strong enough and widespread enough to assure, for a 'long' time, dependable expectations of 'peaceful change' among its population."[6] A community exists when members assume that social problems will be solved by peaceful means. "Security-communities" preclude physical violence between members. There exist two kinds of communities for which there are historical referents: *amalgamated security-communities* and *pluralistic security-communities*. The former are characterized by the merging of sovereign entities into a new form of political union (from thirteen colonies to the United States, for example). The latter communities are comprised of fully sovereign actors that have attained the condition of peaceful relations (e.g., United States-Canadian relations).

Other orientations emphasize increasing collective action by two or more states to achieve outcomes of mutual benefit. State actors that begin to act in concert are moving beyond the minimal step of avoiding violence. They are beginning to move toward greater total cooperation. Similar in kind to common collective action is the agreed upon pursuit of common domestic policies by foreign policy elites of several nations. Cooperation and domestic policy in support of United States-Canadian interaction concerning the St. Lawrence Seaway is illustrative of this kind of integration. Not only do nationals of both countries expect a future of nonviolent relations; they may also work periodically for the achievement of common policies in areas of mutual concern.

From nonviolent interaction, collective action, and the formation of supportive policies within polities, one can look to the building of institutions that may regularize interactions between states. These institutions may be functional in character. That is, they may be created to systematize relationships in specific issue areas, whether the common problem is mail flow, health, labor standards, or drug abuse. They may be loose, nonbinding, general-purpose organizations like continental parliamentary bodies. The creation of certain institutions, parliaments, bureaucracies, and commissions may illustrate the willingness of states to relinquish some of their sovereignty for prospectively beneficial results.

A more significant outcome of integrative processes is the creation of a condition of shared consciousness among members of two or more states. The sought-after state of consciousness might encompass both elites and mass publics. Philip Jacob and James Toscano, two theorists of integration, write of the vision of a new consciousness: "Political integration generally implies a relationship of *community* among people within the same political entity. That is, they are held together by mutual ties of one kind or another which give the group a feeling of identity and self-awareness. Integration, therefore, is based on strong cohesiveness within a social group; and *political* integration is present when a *political*-governmental unit of some sort is cohesive."[7] This perspective emphasizes the existence of common values, beliefs, and life-styles rather than just periodic common policies or the existence of common institutions. As will be seen in the next chapter, some theorists of both regional and world persuasions emphasize changed consciousness as even more fundamental to the control of physical or structural violence (social injustice) than the creation of new regional or world institutions. In fact, central to any alternative future is the question of whether changed consciousness must precede institutional change *or* whether institutional change must occur before a new consciousness is created.

Finally, some theorists look to the creation of political/economic institutions that make decisions which are legitimate and binding on all participating actors. Institutions that have the authority and/or force to make binding decisions for all member states are often referred to as "supranational." Amitai Etzioni portrays the outcomes of "unification" efforts as those in which three conditions exist: the new central institutions effectively control the means of violence; these institutions influence the distribution of rewards and resources to member units; and the new institutions become the key focus of political identification for most peoples and groups.[8] Ernst Haas describes political community as the desired *end state*, and integration as the *process* of achieving it. The "end state" encompasses "loyalties, expectations, and political activities toward a new and larger center, whose institutions possess or demand jurisdiction over the pre-existing national states."[9]

Haas, who has written extensively about this vision, concerns himself with discovering those processes that stimulate and support the achievement of supranational institutions that generally resemble the industrialized and constitutional state. Drawing upon his research on the European Economic Community, Haas writes that supranationalism is the "counterpart" of the industrial state in the "post-capitalist age" because welfare needs require interdependence.[10]

Those who share the supranational vision, like Saint-Simon, recognize the utility of increasing bureaucratization of the decision-making process and the increasing use of technical expertise for the solution of continent-wide problems. For Haas, supranationality implies a style of decision-making that is unique to international relations. This is because of the nature of the participants, the context in which decisions are made, and the quality of decisions produced. Within the EEC, participants are bureaucrats who represent the individual states or EEC itself. Also, there are spokesmen for all major national and European-wide interest groups. The context of decision-making involves those social, economic, and technical problems shared by the member European states.

Haas suggests that there are three qualitatively different ways to solve common problems: accommodation on the basis of a minimum "common denominator," accommodation on the basis of "splitting the difference," and accommodation by "upgrading common interests." The first kind of policy is the result of the minimum thread of agreement among sovereign units. Policy is a function of the position which the least cooperative national participant is willing to accept. The second kind of policy involves the making of concessions of relatively equal value to all participants. Finally, accommodation on the basis of upgrading common interests involves supranational institutions in a mediatory role that leads to extensive national cooperation and policy. These are guided by the judgments of experts and pressure groups. In Europe, Haas finds the achievement of policies through upgrading common interests in several major areas. This is so because the European supranational structure is:

... able to construct patterns of mutual concessions from various policy contexts and in so doing usually manages to upgrade its own powers at the expense of the member governments. Yet these governments do not feel as if they had been bullied: common interests are upgraded also in the sense that each feels that by conceding something it gained something else. The final compromise, far from somehow debasing the bargaining process, induces a feeling of commitment, of creativity, and of gain in the participants.[11]

Haas predicts that extant supranational institutions, the

quality of decision-making (upgrading the common interest), the kinds of problems that need solution (social, economic, technical), and the major political actors (administrators, interest group elites, experts) all lead to continuing integration and the further solidification of supranational institutions. The "New Europe" is a Europe of "adaptive interest groups, bureaucracies, technocrats and other units with modest but pragmatic interests."[12]

According to Haas, this New Europe should be based on mass production and mass consumption achieved by a pragmatic synthesis of capitalism and socialism. In this system of democratic planning, industry, based on either private or public ownership, "easily produces enough to make everybody comfortable. Minimum standards of consumption are assumed for the entire citizenry." The future Europe

> features the continuous participation of all major voluntary groups in European society through elaborate systems of committees and councils. The technical bureaucracies of trade unions, industrial associations, bankers and farmers sit down with the technocrats for the ministries of finance, labor and economics—or with central government planning offices—to shape the future. Statistics tend to replace ideology and dogma. Permanent negotiation and occasional conciliation tend to replace active confrontation, doctrinaire discussion and class warfare. The symbol is of compulsory arbitration rather than the general strike.[13]

In substance, therefore, the regionalist vision that is most at variance with the classical international relations image of competitive actors vying for power describes a new set of supranational institutions. These institutions incorporate major processes and policies from existing states. A "successful" regional organization is one that is characterized by bureaucratic and policy input by leading interest group elites from across the region. As suggested by Saint-Simon during the onset of the industrial revolution and by contemporary integration theorists like Ernst Haas in a period when the industrial epoch in Europe seems to be "complete," the region will replace community and state in a new era of mass consumption and technocratic leadership. For Haas and others, bureaucracy and oligarchy in voluntary associations represent central features of the regionalist alternative future. Highly organized associations will be adaptive in the sense that they will be making new demands and seeking changes cooperatively within the new regional supranational institutions that conform to economic and political necessities.[14]

THE PROCESS OF INTEGRATION

After defining integration and the kind of outcomes that have most often been sought by state actors, several researchers examine successful and unsuccessful integrative efforts. This is done in order to discover necessary and sufficient conditions for implementing the regional vision. Research on past and present integrative efforts has been carried out by Karl Deutsch, Ernst Haas, Amitai Etzioni, Leon Lindberg, Joseph Nye, and others.

In a volume edited by Philip Jacob and James Toscano, *The Integration of Political Communities*, several theorists speculate about community-building within urban, national, and international contexts. The introductory essay by Jacob and Toscano summarizes ten factors that researchers have most often deemed relevant to the process of integration. These variables can be characterized according to whether they are *static, dynamic,* or *immediate* factors in the integrative process. The static factors are those that change very slowly, if at all. The dynamic factors are in a state of flux. The direction these variables take can be reversed or enhanced. The immediate factors are of such import as to be necessary and sufficient conditions for the promotion of integration in the cause of peaceful change, common action, and/or building common institutions.

The least changeable static factor that may relate to the integrative process involves the relative *proximity* of actors. For example, it is hypothesized that the closer peoples or states are to each other, the greater the likelihood of successful integrative efforts. Jacob and Toscano indicate that "preoccupation with international regionalism, especially since the Second World War, has led to a kind of rough geopolitical calculation that international integration among nations is facilitated by their regional contiguity."[15] But as some slow change has been evidenced in the postwar period through dramatic improvements in transportation and communication, the historic importance of contiguity may be replaced by *travel time* and *information transmission time.* The most extensive integrative success is still the geopolitically contiguous European Economic Community. Jacob and Toscano point out, however, that such proximity in itself is insufficient for creating a regionalist future.

A second important variable concerning integration is *homogeneity*. The "closer" two states are to each other along a number of social and economic indicators, the greater the presumed likelihood that these people will integrate. Jacob and Toscano offer several indicators of homogeneity that have been widely used by researchers: wealth or income, education, status or class, religion, race, language, ethnic identification, attitudes, and values.[16]

Next, we may consider the notion of *communal character*, a concept similar to older ideas of "national character." Jacob and Toscano discuss the hypothesis that different national value orientations may increase or decrease the propensity of the state to participate in integrative processes. Those societies that place a premium upon competition or theories of struggle are judged less likely to partake of integrative efforts with other states than those that value cooperative interaction very highly. In David McClelland's *The Achieving Society*,[17] three communal motivations are isolated: the affiliation motive, the achievement motive, and the power motive.

The variable *structural frame* has intranational and international implications. It has been hypothesized by Haas and others that pluralist societies and democratic polities are more supportive of integrative processes than authoritarian ones. Citizens of authoritarian regimes may resent and resist governmental policy. If further research corroborates this relationship, one might prescribe that regional political structures be organized around mass participation and large amounts of pressure group inputs into decision-making centers. Further, hypotheses have been drawn from the relationships between domestic political structures and their propensity to support integrative efforts between states. Here again, Haas says that pluralistic societies are most willing and best able to interact in greater and greater regionalist forms. Cross-national ties are more likely to form among societies with many influential political and economic groupings.

Jacob and Toscano suggest that the quality and character of *previous integrative experience* may be a determinant of an actor's desire to participate in new cooperative interactions. This variable relates to the much discussed question of "spillover" which is raised in the writings of David Mitrany,[18] the functionalist theorist (see chapter six for an extended discussion of Mitrany and functionalist thought). Mitrany argues that successful prior cooperation between peoples on specific welfare problems will lead to expanding cooperation on more and more nonpolitical tasks. Cooperation "spills over" from one task to another until regions and ultimately the globe itself will be organized around institutions that fulfill a multiplicity of welfare tasks.

In a more recent formulation of the spillover concept, Haas argues that prior integrative experience in economic realms must be related to political elites and powerful groups within states to stimulate further integration.[19] Classical functionalists assumed that prior positive integrative efforts in nonpolitical issues would almost automatically yield new and expanding efforts. Neo-functionalists like Haas believe that for such prior experiences to have lasting effects, they must mobilize political forces within cooperating states.

The perceived extent of actor *independence* has also been related to the propensity to integrate. Theorists have argued that the more a state judges itself autonomous in politics, economics, and culture, the less likely that integrative progress will result. This suggests that the regionalist vision must have less appeal among great powers than among lesser powers. States with a similar sense of interdependence and power might most optimally pursue integration. As national power may be declining in the contemporary world because of increasing technological and ecological interdependence, resistance to integrative moves may be reduced in the future.

Jacob and Toscano also speak of three variables that are subject to relatively rapid change. This means that they may be critical to the integrative process. *Mutual knowledge* of potential integrative partners, their cultures, political systems, and economic systems provides the basis of trust and understanding that could be a prerequisite to extensive cooperation. Mutual knowledge can serve to break down stereotypes that have impeded interaction in the past. Integration requires not only knowledge per se, but a special kind of knowledge that either challenges negative stereotypes or provides uncompromisingly positive images of other states.

Governmental effectiveness refers to the perceived level of success that existing international integrative efforts are currently achieving. If, for example, several states find that their cooperation in some specific functional organization is succeeding, the likelihood of the continuation and escalation of cooperation is increased. "The hypothesis is that governmental effectiveness is necessary to retain the loyalty of the members of the community, and such loyalty is necessary to maintain internal integration in the community."[20]

Transactions between nations have been widely studied by integration theorists. Deutsch, Russett, and others say that the frequency and quality of transactions, defined in terms of trade, communications, and mobility, are useful indicators of intensity of integration and stimuli for integration. The more two states interact with each other, the greater the probability of increasing cooperation. Further, Deutsch conceptualizes political communities in terms of the magnitude of communications links between peoples. A necessary condition for any social organization is the existence of communications between parts.

Finally, the immediate stimulus for integration involves the convergence of *functional interests*. Elites from political parties, labor unions, industrial associations, or professional associations may recognize tangible and specific benefits to be derived from international cooperation. They may seek to create broad support for integrative policies in their own polities and to build coalitions with parallel interest affiliations in other nations.

Proximity, communal character, previous experience, structural similarities, homogeneity, and common levels of autonomy provide the preconditions for integration. Changing knowledge, increasing integrative effectiveness, and intensifying transactions provide the dynamic conditions for changed policy and increased cooperation. Converging functional interests among elites and the willingness of those elites to maximize their benefits in terms of cooperation is the immediate precondition for integrative activity.

Other regional theorists have conceptualized the crucial determinants of integration in different ways. Haas distinguishes between social-frame factors, economic and industrial development factors, and ideological pattern variables. His study of European processes leads him to believe that integration efforts would be most successful among politically pluralist societies characterized by high levels of economic and industrial development and common ideological patterns between cultures and between political parties and interest groups. The regional vision would be least attainable among authoritarian, underdeveloped, and ideologically heterogeneous actors.

More recently, Joseph Nye has drawn extensively from earlier research to posit a model of integrative processes that follows upon initial creation of a regional economic organization.[21] His approach also highlights those institutions and forces that may lead to the initial formation of a regional organization. Nye speaks of the *integrative potential* of states involving both *structural* and *perceptual conditions* that may lead to a regional organization. From the formation of some common economic policies among states, expansion or contraction of integration depends upon certain *process mechanisms* that yield *dynamic outcomes*. Positive integrative outcomes then affect the structural and perceptual conditions which stimulate further regional cooperation.

Among the structural conditions of importance to integration, Nye suggests that *symmetrical* patterns of economic growth and achievement among integrating nations may increase the likelihood of cooperation among them. Since elites control economic policy, the greater the likelihood of *elite value complementarity*, the greater the stimulus for integration. The existence of *pluralism* in member states facilitates intersocietal interaction. Also, the more *stable* the societies that are considering integrative policies, the more successful those policies will be.

The perceptual conditions are less constant and may be dramatically affected by the integrative process itself. For example, continued integrative activity depends upon the *perceived equity of distribution of benefits* among key elites in participating states. Integration is also served by a *common perception of forces external to the region*. Finally, *the less visible the cost* of integration, the more amenable will elites be to participation.

Seven *process mechanisms* determine the direction integration takes after initiation of common policies. *Functional linkages of tasks* may cause common policies in one economic area to spill over, of necessity, to the development of common policies in other economic areas. Less automatic forms of spillover may result from *deliberate linkages and coalition formation* among groups that consciously seek to gain from more cooperation. The linkages of tasks are stimulated by generally *rising transactions*. Such group interaction might lead to *elite socialization* or to the development of cross-national affiliations and a sense of community loyalty. *Regional group formation* among economic elites from several states might increase transactions and by implication the legitimacy of the regional organization they wish to influence. At some point, elites and masses are attracted to *identification* with the new regional organization. Finally, *external actors*, like non-regional states giving foreign aid, can enhance the movement to integration.

Given the processes and conditions described, Nye assumes four outcomes of evolving integration that feedback to the conditions, the existent organization, and future processes. First, the interactions among member states and groups will become more *politicized* over time. Issues move from the technical and non-controversial to the emotionally charged and conflictful ones. Second, integration brings continued redistribution of "welfare, status, and power." Third, as groups interact and pressures on elites increase, policy *alternatives are reduced*. Finally, the region will *externalize* its interests and beliefs, developing common policies concerning nonregional members.

Although the Nye model specifically seeks to understand economic integration after initial institution building, the interaction of the complex of variables vividly illustrates what many theorists view as the process of integration. The potential for political, social, and economic integration can be seen as linked to similar integrative preconditions, processes, and outcomes of partial cooperation.

John W. Sloan and Harry R. Targ provide[22] a summary list of variables deemed critical to the integration process and of the kinds of outcomes or regional visions that have been achieved.

Table I: *Sloan and Targ List of Integration Variables Commonly Studied*

Preconditional Factors	Institutional Factors	Process Factors	Outside Factors	Outcomes (Level of Integration Achieved)
GNP	Bureaucracy	Communications	Neo-Colonial	End of Violence
Literacy	Industry	Trade	Relationships	Common Political Decisions
Culture	Parties			
		Inter-Elite	Alliances	Trade, Aid, and
Geography	Military	Relationships	External Enemies	Disarmament Cooperation
	Church			
			UN	Common Institution Building
				Supranationalism

Certain *preconditional* variables inhibit or enhance the growth of regionalism across political systems. Similarities in economic conditions (usually high levels of GNP), levels of literacy and culture (life-styles, art forms, hierarchies of values) create the common ground on which regional political institutions may be built. These preconditions are enhanced by geographic proximity. *Institutional* factors include a similarity of bureaucratic organization, political parties, industrial development, military power, and church organization. The *process* factors emphasize the most salient interactions states have with each other. The more that selected states interact with each other in these ways, the greater the probability of movements toward some kind of regionalism. *Outside* factors have been examined by some theorists who have related integrational processes to extraregional forces. Neocolonial relationships, the threat of outside force, alliances, or the imposition of international organizations may have dramatic effects on the dynamics of integrative growth. Finally, the *outcomes* involve several conceptualizations of what regionalism "ought to be."

AN ASSESSMENT OF THE REGIONAL VISION

The regional visions discussed above have been motivated by a great many international and domestic concerns. Of the three kinds of alternative world futures discussed in Part I of this book—community, regionalism, world order—the second perspective has undergone the most visible kinds of experimentation. An intensive assessment of regionalism must entail analyses of the visions and of how they seem to be faring in the contemporary world. Since the evidence on regional successes is still being gathered, our discussion will deal primarily with the visions themselves. Only occasionally will reference be made to the European Common Market or other such experiments.

Most regional theorists have sought to minimize international conflict by positing regional schemes to increase cooperative interaction. It seems reasonable to assume that if states begin to make policies in common, if their populations begin to share some common values, loyalties, and affiliations, and if some authoritative institutions are ultimately created that bind states to their decisions, international violence would decrease at least within regions. The critical sensitivity of people to national sovereignty, a source of resistance to international cooperation since the "construction" of the state system, may gradually be reduced as actors begin to surrender some of their independence to achieve economic, political, or security benefits. One long-term possibility may involve the progressive surrender of sovereignty, first to regional agencies, then to universal international ones.

A second kind of concern to which the regional vision is addressed is *economic development*. As Haas suggests, the European region should function to maximize both production and consumption in the most efficient way for European peoples. It may be that regional planning can reduce waste, decrease unnecessary regional competition, and develop a sophisticated division of labor based on the special skills and environment of each participating actor. For third world states in particular, academic theorists and political activists alike have suggested a direct relationship between economic development, the end to neo-colonial exploitation, and regional organization.

Regionalists have also taken typically "global" problems and issues and sought to develop solutions to them at a "local" (and presumably more manageable) level. The psychic dimensions of political, military, and economic conflict—stereotyping, displacement, mirror images, etc.—have often been viewed with alarm by international relations students. If, as the UNESCO charter contends, "War begins in the minds of men," then the processes of interaction and the institutionalization of interaction through regional political and economic units may break down dangerous misperceptions and mistrust. Increased trade, travel, communication, and cross-national work may have the desired effect of changing peoples' perceptions of the world and its citizens.

Finally, Joseph Nye[23] writes of five kinds of possible "linkages" between regional organizations and peace. First, some have looked with alarm at the postwar condition of bipolarity. Consequently, the emergence of one, two, or several regional organizations might constitute a new form of multipolarity in the international system. Such a system would increase the flexibility of alliances, thereby reducing the potential for nuclear confrontation between superpowers.

Second, the growth of regional organizations might provide small states with the opportunity to unite in viable economic, political, and military units. This would provide such actors with the opportunity to combat exploitation from big powers and enhance the possibilities for economic development. If exploitation is reduced and security is expanded, the propensity for small-state conflict to "spill over" into big-power confrontation may be reduced.

Third, it is contended that microeconomic institutions might spill over into political cooperation. The long-term effect of integration in one or another problem area is to stimulate states to move to the optimal level of organization. Some problems may involve disparate local solutions; others may necessitate region-wide solutions.

Fourth, regionalism may create a web of functional relationships between states that increases cooperation and reduces the propensity for conflict. This argument emphasizes the creation of a sense of community among peoples. Functional interdependence plus a common "we" feeling may make conflicts between sovereign actors less volatile and less likely to lead to violence.

Finally, it is argued that by enhancing regional cooperation, institution building, and the functional network, political problems that arise between states in one region will be solved within the region. Political problems that begin within a region will remain there; they will not become part of a larger global confrontation.

Although Nye's examination of some regional organizations reveals that success at conflict resolution is mixed, his five hypotheses are not unimportant. Historically, the processes of community building, growing functional interdependence, and the construction of "legitimate" institutions has led to a reduction of violence within societies. Ongoing analyses of regional organizational behavior may at some point yield insights as to the kinds of conflicts that are most susceptible to solution, the kinds of institutions that are most likely to solve them, the kind of community that is needed to institutionalize nonviolent conflict resolution, and the kinds of institutions that can maximize economic development.

What remains most troublesome about the regional vision, however, is that ultimately it cannot satisfy the kinds of needs the world order vision or community vision is intended to satisfy. Regionalism suffers from the fact that it represents neither utopia nor cosmopolis. In terms of violence reduction, the regional logic reconstructs the international system into a small number of relatively autonomous regions. These would presumably "behave" like the states of the contemporary international system. At best, the end product would be a reconstruction of the nineteenth-century European state system. Balance of power politics would be revitalized with individual units able to amass more human and natural resources to carry on the competitive struggle between regions. In essence, intraregional conflict may be reduced, but at the possible expense of heightened tensions in the global system.

So far, the research on processes of integration seems to suggest that regionalism is especially likely to occur among peoples who share common values and beliefs and who have achieved relatively high levels of economic development. Although generalizing from the EEC experience may be risky, such generalization leads to the very tentative hypothesis that integration will increase the economic, military, and hence political capabilities of the developed world at the expense of the third world. Haas may be right when he says: "The established nation-state is in full retreat in Europe while it is advancing voraciously in Africa and Asia. Integration among discrete political units is a historical fact in Europe, but disintegration seems to be the dominant motif elsewhere."[24] The consequences of this include more concentrated wealth amidst more intense poverty, and potentially greater violence in the third world spreading to the developed world.

The regional solution, therefore, may be no solution at all to the problem of violence and war. It may also provide no solution to the problems of community satisfaction and self-determination discussed earlier. What the Haas vision entails is the creation of large, viable, bureaucratized welfare states to manage each geographic area of the globe. The problems raised by theorists of technocracy, elitism, statism, and economic determinism are likely to be magnified in the worlds of Saint-Simon or Haas. Even if the Europe of the EEC successfully increases production, consumption, and the power to consume, the needs for love, a sense of belonging, self-esteem, and self-actualization may be thwarted. Sloan and Targ went so far as to contend that "there may be an inverse relationship between the fulfillment of preservation needs and the fulfillment of community and self-determination needs."[25] They further conclude:

> The frame of reference for our criticism has been the burgeoning literature describing the problems of the nation-state. In examining this literature, we have concluded that the modern nation-state, by means of its advanced technology and efficient bureaucracies, has been able to provide satisfaction for man's preservation needs but appears to be thwarting man's community and self-determination needs. Despite increased standards of living for the bulk of the population in post-capitalist states, there seems to be a decreased standard of what is generally called the quality of life caused by the dehumanizing aspects of technology, the growth of bureaucracy and the lack of meaningful political participation.[26]

NOTES

1. Bruce M. Russett, *Trends in World Politics* (New York: Macmillan, 1965); Ernst B. Haas, "International Integration, The European and the Universal Process," in *International Political Communities* (Garden City, N.Y.: Anchor, 1966), pp. 93-131.

2. Henri de Saint-Simon, *Social Organization, The Science of Man and Other Writings* (New York: Harper & Row, 1964).

3. *Ibid.*, p. 46.

4. *Ibid.*, p. 49.

5. Ernst B. Haas, *The Uniting of Europe* (Stanford, Calif.: Stanford University Press, 1965); Leon N. Lindberg, *The Political Dynamics of European Economic Integration* (Stanford, Calif.: Stanford University Press, 1963); Karl Deutsch et al., "Political Community and the North Atlantic Area," in *International Political Communities* (Garden City, N.Y.: Anchor, 1966); Amitai Etzioni, *Political Unification* (New York: Holt, Rinehart & Winston, 1965); Joseph S. Nye, Jr., *Peace in Parts* (Boston: Little, Brown, 1971); and Leon N. Lindberg, "Political Integration as a Multidimensional Phenomenon Requiring Multivariate Measurement," *International Organization*, autumn 1970, pp. 649-732.

6. Deutsch et al., "Political Community and the North Atlantic Area," p. 2.

7. Philip E. Jacob and James V. Toscano, eds., *The Integration of Political Communities* (Philadelphia: Lippincott, 1964), p. 4.

8. Etzioni, *Political Unification*, p. 4.

9. Haas, "International Integration, The European and the Universal Process," p. 94.

10. Ernst B. Haas, "Technocracy, Pluralism and the New Europe," in *International Regionalism*, Joseph S. Nye, Jr., ed. (Boston: Little, Brown, 1968), p. 159.

11. *Ibid.*, p. 153.

12. *Ibid.*, p. 155.

13. *Ibid.*, p. 156.

14. Ernst B. Haas, *Beyond the Nation State: Functionalism and International Organization* (Stanford, Calif.: Stanford University Press, 1964), p. 117.

15. Jacob and Toscano, eds., *The Integration of Political Communities*, p. 17.

16. *Ibid.*, p. 18.

17. David C. McClelland, *The Achieving Society* (Princeton: Van Nostrand, 1961).

18. David Mitrany, *A Working Peace System* (Chicago: Quadrangle, 1966).

19. Haas, *The Uniting of Europe.*

20. Jacob and Toscano, eds., *The Integration of Political Communities*, p. 43.

21. Nye, *Peace in Parts.*

22. John W. Sloan and Harry R. Targ, "Beyond the European Nation-State: A Normative Critique," *Polity*, summer 1971, p. 508.

23. Nye, *Peace in Parts.*

24. Haas, "International Integration, The European and the Universal Process," p. 93.

25. Sloan and Targ, "Beyond the European Nation-State: A Normative Critique," p. 503.

26. *Ibid.*, p. 519.

Chapter 6
World Order Perspectives and Alternative World Futures

INTRODUCTION

A discussion of alternative world futures leads to three basic kinds of visions. W. Warren Wagar's conception of *utopia* generally encompasses those theorists who have written of social orders emphasizing face-to-face interaction, shared work, environmental facilities (man-made and natural), and common economic and cultural systems. The *regionalist* vision highlights common political, economic, and cultural interactions among peoples of several states. Usually, these states are geographically contiguous. The language of the regionalists is similar to the language of the utopians. However, the structural prerequisites for regional community more closely resemble those for the federated, industrialized state. The final dominant theme is *world order*. World order refers to those perspectives on problem-solving and human need fulfillment that lead the theorist to define alternative structures, processes, cultures, and interactions solely in global terms. Some kind of *immediate* worldwide organization is central to the world order perspective.

Three major world order orientations are most commonly discussed in the literature: the *political structuralist* conception, the *functionalist* conception, and the *universal cultural* conception. Emphasis on one or another conception does not imply a disregard for other conceptions of world order. However, the literature of each orientation assigns preeminence to a particular set of ideas on creating a "better" world.

The political structuralist argument views its desirable world future in terms of central institutions that wisely organize a system of power. Worldwide political institutions must have sovereign control of certain kinds of political decision-making and the instruments of violence. Most commonly, these institutions form a confederation or a federation that bears resemblance to the stable *domestic* political system. For these theorists, economic planning and a communal consciousness can only be achieved after power and sovereignty are arranged in more suitable configurations.

The functionalist argument is based on the assumption that world peace and universal welfare can only be solved through nonpolitical institutions. Politics stands in the way of cooperation between peoples. The problem, then, is one of circumventing politics and maximizing cooperation on specific economic and technological problems. The functionalist seeks to bring peoples together around common problems and to relegate their political conflicts to a lesser realm of concern.

The universal cultural argument views the process of accommodation and common problem-solving as a by-product of change in human consciousness. Before political structures can be significantly changed and before new institutions designed to solve economic and technological problems can be effective, a common set of global values, symbols, myths, and perceptions must evolve. Institution building that precedes cultural change is bound to fail. Institutions must be built on the foundations of a "universal culture."

POLITICAL STRUCTURALIST CONCEPTIONS OF WORLD ORDER

The history of political structuralist conceptions of world order is quite long. F. H. Hinsley,[1] who undertook an exhaustive examination of this tradition, argues that the large number of world government schemes we have seen since the fourteenth century were motivated by several kinds of goals. World peace or the end of war between states was only one of these. Some schemes were motivated by a desire to reorganize Europe for the mutual benefit of temporal and ecclesiastical authority. Others were concerned with more effective ways of dealing with the non-European world. Still others sought to preserve and protect Christianity around the world. Only a few such plans viewed war in moral terms. Some theorists, however, attempted to distinguish the "just war" from unjustifiable aggression.

Hinsley suggests that after the emergence of the modern state system, considerations of a moral character were decisively overshadowed by "reasons of state." Notwithstanding the diversity of

111

such schemes, their different goals, and their varying ethical implications, all of them can be compared on several critical dimensions. These include the precise character of the proposed scheme, the suggested means of achieving the desired arrangement (coercive or volitional), the degree of universality implied (Europe or the entire world), the historical background of the proposal, the underlying purpose of the proposal, the specific political form of the proposal, the homogeneity of the proposed membership, and the role of great powers in its operationalization.

One of the earliest proposals linking an improved system of world order to a federal distribution of force and sovereign authority is that of Pierre Dubois, the French jurist and politician of the fourteenth century. In 1306, Dubois authored *De Recuperatione Terra Sancta*, a tract proposing the organization of Christian states for the maintenance of peace in Europe. Here, the suggestion is made that peace be regarded as the highest attainable good. As such, it must be so secured among all Catholics that a strongly united and indivisible community of states can be brought into existence.

To organize Europe, a federation of Christian states was needed. And to implement this federation, an appropriate General Council was to be convened by the pope. It was to be made clear to all that Catholics would no longer be permitted to bear arms against Catholics, thereby spilling "baptized" blood. Those peoples that enjoy combat were advised to do battle against the enemies of Christian belief. All disputes between Christian states were to be adjudicated by an international court of arbitration composed of judges elected by the council. In cases where parties might dispute the decisions of the court, appeals could be made directly to the pope. Failure to submit to binding arbitration or to the final determinations of such a process was to be punishable by papal excommunication.

As he was one of the first to propose an international court of arbitration endowed with obligatory jurisdiction over member states, Dubois was a pioneer in the advocacy of more centralized arrangements for the management of power. Moreover, he also urged that the council and its members institute a boycott against a state making war. He further advocated concerted military action against offending states. (To obtain the necessary force, member states were to contribute their armies to the General Council when called upon to do so.) In this sense, Dubois may be regarded as an intellectual precursor of the two great international organizations of the twentieth century. On the other hand, his vision encompassed a far greater degree of centralization than ever actually realized or even contemplated by the League of Nations or the United Nations.

While the primary concern reflected in Dubois's work was the establishment of a federation of states to keep the peace, his underlying concern was for the establishment of French supremacy and for the undertaking of an effective crusade against the infidels in possession of the Holy Land. In conformity with the prevailing conception of universality, his dream was for a worldwide Christian commonwealth. Not to be ignored, however, was the extent to which he tied this conception to the leadership of his mother country. The General Council was to be convened on French soil by a pope who was, in effect, entirely under French influence.

In 1464, Georg Podebrad, king of Bohemia, called for a federation of Christian princes from France, Italy, Germany, and Spain to preserve peace among themselves and to protect Christianity against the Turks. This coalition was to function through an assembly of princely representatives meeting in different cities, a judiciary to adjudicate differences between the princes or between members and nonmembers, and a fiscal officer to receive contributions. The Christian federation was to abolish the use of arms between members. Further, the independent right to wage war was denied. Only the federation itself reserved the right to wage war. In the event that conflict ensued between a member state and a nonmember state, pacific means of settlement were to be applied wherever possible. If, however, such means proved futile, the entire federation was to enter into the matter on the side of its common ally. Where neither of the conflicting parties belonged to their organization, the member states were expected to intervene, with or without resort to arms, as the particular situation required. These provisions resemble those established by the League of Nations.

The pope and the emperor were not to be accorded their usual special place in the Christian world. The emperor was to be consigned to the same position as that of the other princes. The pope, while not a member of the federation, was expected to cooperate with it. Even Dubois, who strongly defended the rights of France as opposed to the Church, had called for the pope to convene the General Council.

The assembly of the federation was to be organized on a nationalistic basis with each nationality accorded one vote. The various political divisions were not to be granted separate votes. Thus, all princes of a given nationality were obliged to reach agreement before voting in the assembly.

Several other proposals for world government were made between the fourteenth and seventeenth centuries. Beginning with the seventeenth century and running through the nineteenth, numerous new schemes were proposed by political theorists and statesmen. Some of these were responses to the emergence of states in Europe, to the growing problem of warfare between states, and to an increasing recognition of the worldwide character of any plan to end violence.

The first truly universal peace arrangement was Emeric Crucé's *The New Cyneas*. Written in 1623, this plan called for a worldwide organization which would embrace both Christian and non-Christian states. Denouncing religious differences as grounds for war, Crucé counseled Christians not to look upon Moslems or Jews as their natural enemies. All religions were to be recognized as fundamentally alike in their common purpose of acknowledging and worshipping God.

To implement his plan for world peace, Crucé suggests a permanent council of ambassadors to settle by majority vote all differences which might arise. Meeting in a neutral city, representatives of monarchs and republics were to be the "trustees and hostages of public peace." Decisions made by majority vote were to be regarded as "inviolable law." Those who undertook to oppose it were to be pursued and forced into submission by force of arms in the event that "gentle means" proved unsatisfactory. For this purpose, a universal police force, "useful equally to all nations and acceptable to those which have some light of reason and sentiment of humanity" was to be created.

While he admits the necessity of securing submission to the decrees of the council through armed force where necessary, Crucé places greater emphasis on the power of moral compulsion than his predecessors. All means of peaceful settlement were to be utilized before the body should resort to war. Moreover, like later attempts at collective security which recognized a special place for the most powerful actors, Crucé suggests that in order to give more authority to the appropriate judgments, "one would take advice of the big republics ... if anyone rebelled against the decree of so notable a company, he would receive the disgrace of all other princes, who would find means to bring him to reason."[2]

In contrast to other proposals like that of Dubois, Crucé seeks no special advantages for his own country. He is not at all anxious to offer France a dictatorial power in the proposed union. Rather, he wishes to see her as merely one of the many members of the organization. Crucé recognizes only one logical claim to his allegiance, the world itself: "What a pleasure it would be to see men go here and there freely, and mix together without any hindrance of country, ceremonies, or other such like differences, as if the earth were as it really is, a city common to all."[3]

Appearing some fifteen years after the publication of *The New Cyneas*, the Duke of Sully's *Memoirs* represent what are perhaps the most celebrated of all major peace plans. Their main purpose was to encourage the states of Europe to unite in a great federation of hereditary monarchies, elective monarchies (to include the empire and the papacy), and republics, thereby dividing Europe "equally among a certain number of powers and in such a manner that none of them might have cause either of envy or fear from the possessions or power of the others." In accomplishing this objective, the number of states was to be reduced to fifteen, and laws and ordinances appropriate to "cementing a union" among them were to be implemented "to maintain that harmony which should be once established."

Nothing worse than "trifling difficulties" were envisaged. As these arose, they would be resolved within the framework of a General Council representing different states. The council was to consist of a certain number of commissionaries, ministers, or plenipotentiaries from "all the governments of the Christian Republic." Constantly assembled as a senate, these representatives were "to deliberate on any affairs which might occur; to discuss the different interests, pacify the quarrels, clear up and determine all the civil, political, and religious affairs of Europe, whether within itself or with its neighbors."[4] While subsidiary local assemblies were also envisaged, only the decisions of the council were to be regarded as final and irrevocable. For military support of the council's decision, the plan also provided for a composite army comprised of armed forces contributed by the princes in proportion to their capabilities. Using such forces, the princes of Europe might undertake missions of conquest in Asia and Africa. Ironically, European peace depended to a large extent upon external war.

Saint-Pierre's *Project for Perpetual Peace* (c. 1714) consists of five fundamental articles. The first of these suggests the formation of a Grand Alliance or European Union to secure a permanent peace between the Christian states of Europe as defined by the frontiers assigned by the Treaty of Utrecht. The second concerns the collection of revenues necessary to sustain the proposed union. The third article involves the renunciation on the part of the Grand Allies of the resort to force:

> The Grand Allies have renounced and renounce for ever, for themselves and for their successors, resort to arms in order to terminate their differences present and future, and agree henceforth always to adopt the method of conciliation by mediation of the rest of the Grand Allies in the place of general assembly, or, in case this mediation should not be successful, they agree to abide by the judgment which shall be rendered by the Plenipotentiaries of the other Allies permanently assembled, provisionally by a plurality of voices, definitely by three-quarters of the votes, five years after the provisional award.[5]

Thus, in the event of a dispute between states, the interested parties would first attempt to reconcile their differences through mediation by several members of the Grand Alliance. Where such efforts prove unsuccessful, arbitration would become necessary.

Article four deals with the contingency that arises when one of the allies refuses to accept either the general rules or particular judgments of the alliance. In such a case "the Grand Alliance will arm, and will proceed against him until he shall execute the said judgments or rules, or give security to make good the harm caused by his hostilities, and to repay the cost of the war according to the estimate of the Commissioners of the Grand Alliance."[6] Authoritative prerogatives given to the federation itself were to be supported by appropriate force.

Finally, the allies were to decide on future federal policy via plurality vote by the representatives in permanent assembly. Such decisions would entail "all articles which may be necessary and important to procure to the Grand Alliance more coherence, more security, and all other possible advantages."[7]

The work of the Abbé de Saint-Pierre was revived by Jean Jacques Rousseau in 1761 as the first part of his essay, *A Lasting Peace Through the Federation of Europe*. Here, by likening the behavior of national actors in the world system to that of men in the state of nature, the powers of Europe are seen as standing against each other in a continuing state of war. All existing treaties binding states represent the fabric not of genuine peace, but of temporary truce. The anarchy of interstate relations stands in sharp contrast to the presumed order of the civil state.

What alteration is required to remove the anarchic element? A federal alteration is needed: The remedy for war is to be found "only in such a form of federal government as shall unite nations by bonds similar to those which already unite their individual members, and place the one no less than the other under the authority of the Law."[8] Rousseau concludes that:

> ... the Federation must embrace all the important Powers in its membership; it must have a Legislative Body, with powers to pass laws and

ordinances binding upon all its members; it must have a coercive force capable of compelling every State to obey its common resolves whether in the way of command or of prohibition; finally, it must be strong and firm enough to make it impossible for any member to withdraw at his own pleasure the moment he conceives his private interest to clash with that of the whole Body.[9]

Yet, looking at the second part of the essay, which represents Rousseau's criticism of Saint-Pierre's project, there is evidence of a notable ambivalence with regard to federation. Most importantly, perhaps, Rousseau expresses little faith in the assumption that federation can be accomplished peacefully. This being the case, it becomes as likely as not that the process of federating Europe will bring about the very forms of violent conflict it seeks to prevent:

> No Federation could ever be established except by a revolution. That being so, which of us would dare to say whether the League of Europe is a thing more to be desired or feared? It would perhaps do more harm in a moment than it would guard against for ages.[10]

Moreover, if we are to assume consistency between the ideas expressed in *A Lasting Peace* and those of *The Social Contract*, additional doubt is cast on Rousseau's advocacy of federation. According to Rousseau, sovereign authority, being no more than the exercise of the general will, is necessarily indivisible:

> But our political thinkers, not being able to divide sovereignty in principle, have divided it in its object: into force and will; legislative power and executive power; the rights of levying taxes, of administering justice, and making war; the internal government and the power of treating with foreigners. But by sometimes confounding all these parts, and sometimes separating them, they make of the sovereign power a fantastical being composed of related pieces; as if man were composed of several bodies, one with eyes, another with arms, another with feet, but none with anything more.[11]

This conception of sovereign authority as indivisible logically precludes a proposal for federation which, by definition, involves a division of sovereign-authoritative prerogatives. The character of federation necessarily conflicts with the character of sovereignty as defined in *The Social Contract*. For these reasons, therefore, it is by no means self-evident that Rousseau seeks the sharing of state power with specially established, European-wide institutions.

Jeremy Bentham wrote his *Plan for a Universal and Perpetual Peace* between 1786 and 1789. He speaks of two prerequisites; first, the reduction and freezing of forces available to actors of the

European state system, and second, the emancipation of dependencies from European control. The first of these propositions suggests that disarmament rather than a transfer of force to federal institutions represents a part of the desired way to peace. While his conception of the means necessary to sustain an effective arrangement for the control of power includes the sharing of sovereign-authoritative prerogatives with newly created, system-wide institutions, no provision is made to support the dictates of these institutions with force. A Common Court of Judicature is proposed, "for the decision of differences between the several nations,"[12] but it was not to be equipped with any instruments of coercive power. Once established, the international tribunal would make war unnecessary: "Just or unjust, the decision of the arbiters will save the credit, the honour of the contending party."[13]

Bentham favors not only the implementation of a Common Court of Judicature, but the creation of a Common Legislature between states as well. Such a Congress or Diet was to be constituted by two representatives from each nation. The proceedings of the Congress were to be made public, and its power was to consist of "reporting its opinion" and "in causing that opinion to be circulated in the dominions of each state." It was to be further empowered to publicly castigate uncooperative nations and to place them under the "ban of Europe."[14] The instrument for sanctions against transgressions was not to be force, but public opinion.

Immanuel Kant's proposals for the realization of perpetual peace rest upon the creation of republican constitutions in every state (see chapter nine, Actors, in Part II). According to Kant, since republican constitutions structure the exercise of authority according to well-defined, publicly accepted laws, their implementation makes the initiation of hostilities obsolete. Newly empowered to make use of their reason, citizens must certainly and immediately recognize the avoidance of war to be in their own interests.

Kant further suggests that the law of nations must rest on a federation of free states (constitutional republics). He calls for a *league of peace* which would not impinge on the liberty of each state. Despite the desirability of a full-fledged world state, reason dictates that only a second best expedient of limited federalism can be achieved.

These and other plans brought to the nineteenth and twentieth centuries a multiplicity of prescriptions designed, among other things, to reduce global conflict. Most plans call for the conclusion of a formal compact among states, setting out rules and regulations to govern their interaction. They usually propose the establishment of some kind of council of powers, either for Europe alone, or for the entire system of states. These schemes often call for decisions based upon majority or plurality rules. Some proposals seek to account for relative power differences by developing weighted voting schemes. Further, the plans try to obligate states to settle their disputes peacefully. Often they are to submit their disputes to binding arbitration. Some plans create economic and military sanctions against recalcitrant states. The application of force by federal authority is to be based upon each state's financial and military contribution to the international army. States are to be obliged to contribute to the financial needs of the organization. In sum, although there is a thread of European ethnocentricity running throughout these schemes, their idea for structural reform ultimately became worldwide. Hinsley argues that twentieth-century peace plans and international organization experiments are direct heirs to these schemes and proposals, from Dubois to Bentham to Kant.

In terms of building political structures to achieve peace and stability, the nineteenth and twentieth centuries saw the movement from theory to action. Inis Claude[15] speaks of three nineteenth-century institutional developments that were direct precursors to the League of Nations and the United Nations. The Concert of Europe established at the Congress of Vienna in 1815 sought to create an informal system of regularized meetings among the European great powers. Its object was to develop common policies of mutual interest to the participants. For much of the century, the Concert system was characterized by periodic conferences among representative diplomats from the great powers.

Until its weakening and final demise near the end of the century, the Concert system interested itself in overseeing European affairs. It decided on new "members" to the European system. It sought to intervene in conflicts in order to maintain the balance of power. It tried to set up viable norms for imperialist behavior. And it was able to "pass" some international "legislation" in reference to river traffic regulation.

Nevertheless, it is not the history of the Concert system that is of interest here. Rather, it is the political structuralist conception of world order that is important. The conception of world order held by foreign policy elites defined a delicate system that could "live" with national self-interest and mutual obligation and support. It was the view of influential leaders that the best one could expect was a tenuous, transitory international system based upon the maintenance of a balance of power. The system was most likely to minimize violence, or to place it within acceptable limits, if it was based upon big power hegemony and big power cooperation. Claude contends that this Concert system perspective strongly influenced the councils of great powers in both the League of Nations and United Nations.

The Concert vision of world order inherited most of the ideas of a balance of power. The Hague Conferences of 1899 and 1907 received their impetus largely from some of the world order writings discussed above. Crucé, Kant, and Bentham are especially notable in this regard. Contrary to the Concert system, the Hague Conferences were broadly representative of states from outside of Europe as well as those within, and of states that were small and weak as well as powerful. The approach of the Hague Conferences was to deal in an abstract way with problems of war and peace and to create a system of law and procedure to minimize conflict. Whereas the Concert powers wished to maintain informality, to address themselves to specific European problems, and to concentrate on the tenuous balance of power, the Hague system wished to create law, to reject balance of power doctrines, and to make the actors which comprised the international system conform to broad principles of peaceful settlement. The Hague approach to world order was more rationalistic and legalistic. Since armed conflicts were deemed a function of misunderstanding and emotionalism, rational debate in regularized assemblies and the application of law to conflict would doubtless end war. Claude contends that the Hague approach was a precursor to the assemblies in both the League of Nations and the United Nations.

The third influence on contemporary international organization, Claude argues, was the increasing number of public international unions that were formed to solve functionally specific problems. These functional bodies provided the impetus for the creation of problem-oriented secretariats in the two twentieth-century organizations. (The functional approach to world order will be treated below.)

Twentieth-century discussion of political organization for peace has taken at least three forms: those theorists who propose adjustments in international law and organization to aid the maintenance of the balance of power; those theorists who make proposals to expand the role and importance of existing international organizations, particularly the United Nations; and those theorists who argue that nothing short of world government or a centrally enforceable world law can bring about peace.

Lassa Oppenheim, a distinguished international legal scholar, wrote his *International Law* in 1905. In this work he discusses five morals that he says can be deduced from the history of international law. First and foremost is the principle that international law can only survive as long as there exists a balance of power among states. This necessitates the existence of a viable equilibrium to eliminate hegemony via disproportionalities of power: "If the Powers cannot keep one another in check, no rules of law will have any force, since an over-powerful State will naturally try to act according to discretion and disobey the law."[16] The balance system is the only viable substitute for the existence of a central sovereign authority over all states which Oppenheim assumes can never be achieved.

Second, tendencies to comply with international law are only enhanced when states act within the context of their national interests. Wars of religion or wars for imperial conquest are antithetical to the maintenance of the equilibrium and hence to law. Third, the only realistic reaction to the question of nationalism and the nation-state is to accept it: "Wherever a community of many millions of individuals, who are bound together by the same blood, language, and interests, become so powerful that they think it necessary to have a State of their own, in which they can live according to their own ideals and can build up a national civilization, they will certainly get that State sooner or later."[17] Fourth, the development of international law and the creation of a peaceful world will take time to achieve. He calls utopian those images of a rapidly emerging world of harmony and peace. Such a world could come about only if people were of one mind, one culture, one set of interests. And that is not to be expected.

Finally, the future success of international law will be a result of both the advancement of public morality and the convergence of economic interests. For Oppenheim, domestic law has developed through an interactive process between common economic concerns and the building of moral standards for the community. He is optimistic about the future in that the progress of economics and morality is seemingly working in favor of international law.

In the abridged version of his classic *A Study of War*, Quincy Wright discusses reforms of the ongoing United Nations system which might enhance the prospects for peace. A more viable conception of international organization is based upon the structural and functional strengthening of the United Nations.

> Structurally they (the United Nations) have inadequately balanced education and investigatory competencies, political and legal jurisdictions, legislative and executive powers, and regional and universal

121

responsibilities. Functionally they have not provided adequate procedures for measuring and changing the representation of peoples and governments, for determining and dealing with basic offenses against a world-order, for assuring popular support to world institutions, and for relating the organization of peace to the basic values of modern civilization.[18]

Structurally, a viable world order requires an international investigatory and educational agency working through the secretariat of the international organization and staffed mainly by scientific experts. This agency should gather data on world opinion through samples of the world press, public opinion polls, and discussions with elites so as to adequately assess ongoing reaction of peoples to the international organization. Knowledge of these attitudes could lead to international organizational policies that would increase loyalties to the organization. Wright suggests that one of the major weaknesses of international organizations is the fact that they lack direct access to national populations. Hence they have only a limited capacity for socializing peoples with a view to creating supranational loyalties.

A second structural change entails the creation of legal and political jurisdictions that would stimulate increasing legitimacy for the World Court and analogous institutions. Currently, states have the option of accepting or rejecting judicial proceedings. He calls for a "judicial monism" that emphasizes the primacy of international law. The World Court could make determinations based upon grievances filed by individuals. Support for international law might be enhanced by providing for state access to the General Assembly and the Security Council when claims have no precedent in existing law. It is through expanding legitimacy for international law and expanding "legislative" rights for nations, that international organization could provide the means for expanding the worldwide political system.

A final structural change would give credence to the realistic claims of regionalism. Since given regions do share common traditions, trade patterns, and strategic interests, they should maintain responsibility for regional problems. Regional semi-autonomy, however, must be clearly based upon the sovereign authority of the world organization.

Wright also speaks of expanded functions. First, the system of representation should be expanded. The international organization, he argues, could institutionalize representation from national parliamentary bodies, increase representation based upon professional and technical expertise, and support representation of various worldwide economic interests. Such functions would expand the capacities of peoples to participate in international affairs, provide for a better reflection of the multiplicity of international interests, and at the same time reduce reliance upon the state as the sole instrument of international policy-making.

Second, contrary to most conceptions of international law that concern themselves primarily with national security, new criminal codes must protect individuals and the international order itself. Generally, Wright contends, only military aggression has been denounced in the past. Other actions might profitably be considered by law as well. These include arbitrary commercial barriers, the mobilization of forces, "warmongering propaganda," and subversive activities.

Wright considers the function international organization could play in defining the concept of *world citizen*. Educational activities of such an organization could disseminate information that increasingly leads people to see the international organization as sovereign and themselves as significant members of the new world order: "Peace requires that the identification of peoples and governments with mankind as well as with the nation be more than verbal. The United States had to go through nearly a century of political controversy and civil war before it was certain that the union was of the people as well as of the states."[19]

Finally, Wright contends that international organization can only succeed if it sets as its task the enhancement of world welfare, broadly defined. The world organization must be perceived by elites and mass publics to be representative of global interests and global responsibilities: "An organization to prevent war must accept the philosophy that institutions are to be judged by the degree in which they advance human freedom and welfare and that the special aims of nation, state, government, or race are subordinate."[20]

Although Wright's proposals would move international organization in the direction of increasing sovereign authority over the member states, they would not take such organization to the point of world government or centralized world law. Other proposals developed in our own century, however, do just that. Perhaps the earliest twentieth-century statement expressing the need for greater global centralization was by Raymond Bridgman.[21] After World War I, the idea of world federal government was revived and advanced by a spokesman of considerably greater public stature. Writing in *The Outline of History*, H. G. Wells is unambiguous in his commitment to worldwide nationality and "the nascent Federal World State to which human necessities point."[22] In a later work, Wells displays the same clear feeling that world peace requires greater centralization. It is the *"sovereign-independence of states,"* says Wells in *The Common Sense of World Peace*, that represents "the cardinal difficulty before us." Only by "pooling sovereignty" can an enduring *pax* be attained.[23]

In the period between the world wars, most writing on behalf of greater centralization was concerned with European or Atlantic union. Easily the most well-known work of this period and in many respects the federalist classic is Clarence K. Streit's *For Union Now: A Proposal for a Federal Union of the Democracies*. Ultimately to become the first chapter of the author's later and larger work, *Union Now: A Proposal for an Atlantic Union of the Free* (1949), this pamphlet proposes a union of the democracies into a federal republic.[24]

The year 1939 was one in which several other federal peace plans were made public. Some of these plans were explicitly tutored by the Streit proposal. W. B. Curry's *The Case for a Federal Union* is such a plan. Like so many others, Curry locates the root cause of interactor conflict in international anarchy. All attempts at abolishing war while retaining full separate sovereignties are considered futile. International anarchy must be replaced by world federal government.[25]

David Hoadley Munroe's *Hang Together: The Union Now Primer* is an attempt to condense, explain, and discuss Streit's *Union Now*. As Munroe points out, the plan of *Union Now* involves the extension of the American system of federal union to the whole world. It entails an executive branch, a legislative branch, and a judicial branch. Like Streit (who was responsible for the foreword and final chapter of this book), Munroe cites adherence to an absolute conception of unrestricted national sovereignty as the principal source of interstate conflict.[26]

The year 1939 was also the year in which Grenville Clark issued his first call for federation, albeit one with strictly limited purposes and with highly restricted powers.[27] These built-in limitations derive more from Clark's concern for a "practical" chance of acceptance than from the conviction that they are desirable from the standpoint of war avoidance. According to Clark, the organs of the proposed federation shall be a Congress and a Supreme Court. No provision is made for the creation of a separate executive department, although appropriate authority is delegated to the Congress to establish such quasi-executive agencies as may be required and to maintain a permanent secretariat.

As regards the use of force, considerable authority is delegated to the Congress. In Clark's own terms, this represents the "stiffest dilution of sovereignty" contained in the entire proposal, and reflects his belief that any effective centralized arrangement for the management of global power must be supported by effective sanctions. The military measures which may be authorized by the Congress include the right to maintain air and naval forces, to fix the contributions of member countries, and to name and remove the commanders-in-chief. It is judged to be an essential feature of the proposal that the federation ought not to be implemented at all unless its strength in armed force is predominant over any other combination that might arise. This implies that military sanctions are to be provided on so great a scale as to do more than simply deter any unauthorized use of force.

Duncan and Elizabeth Wilson are also contributors to the world federalism literature of 1939. In their *Federation and World Order*, the uncontroversial claim is made that the advent of very powerful weapons has made indulgence in war especially costly. What is needed? The answer, we are told, lies in some form of world organization which may partially supercede the state:

> This is the germ of the idea which has come to be known as Federal Union. Can we not, we have asked ourselves, set up a common Federal Parliament for mankind which will be directly representative not of States, but of individual men and women, leaving to the Nation-State the administration of those purely national affairs whose conduct does not threaten, because it does not affect, the nationals of other States?[28]

Searching for a model on which to shape their designs, the authors suggest consideration of the existing federal parliaments which have a long record of success behind them, namely Switzerland and the United States. International federation is selected as the most propitious arrangement for the management of power because it is regarded as the logical "half-way house" between international anarchy, which may or may not be tempered by alliances and leagues, and the kind of super-state which would completely eliminate the existing multiplicity of separate sovereignties.

A few years after the appearance of *Federation and World Order*, Oscar Newfang advanced the case for world federal government.[29] The argument is made that just as the transfer of force to central governments of states is essential to the maintenance of domestic peace, so is this transfer deemed necessary on the more comprehensive global level. The basic conclusions derive from the assumption that what is true for individual state systems is true for the entire world system as well. Whatever the scope of the system involved, central institutions endowed with certain sovereign-authoritative prerogatives must be the repository of force.

In 1943 Ely Culbertson's plan for world federation was made public,[30] but it was the proposals of Emery Reves appearing two years later that received a genuinely large measure of recognition. Indeed, in 1945, Reves succeeded Clarence Streit as the principal figure in the movement for world federation. The crux of Reves's argument may be summed up schematically. There are two principal "observations" that can be made concerning war:

1. Wars between groups of men forming social units always take place when these units—tribes, dynasties, churches, cities, nations —exercise unrestricted sovereign power.

2. Wars between these social units cease the moment sovereign power is transferred from them to a larger or higher unit.[31]

On the basis of these "observations" (presumably functioning as premises or assumptions), says Reves, "we can deduce a social law with the characteristics of an axiom that applies to and explains each and every war in the history of all time":

War takes place whenever and wherever non-integrated units of equal sovereignty come into contact.

One need not be a logician to recognize that this proposition is not necessarily implied by the above premises. Moreover, unless "contact" is tied definitionally to the use of force, in which case the statement is tautological, the proposition is clearly untrue.

In the following year, 1946, the World Movement for World Federal Government was founded in Luxembourg. The United World Federalists of the United States was formed in February 1947 by bringing together various existing organizations: Americans United for World Government, World Federalists (USA), Student Federalists, Massachusetts Committee for World Federation, and World Citizens of Georgia. The plan for world federal government drawn up by the United World Federalists is presented in the books of Cord Meyer.[32]

The appearance in 1949 of Clarence Streit's larger work, *Union Now: A Proposal for an Atlantic Federal Union of the Free*, overshadowed all such efforts.[33] Expanding upon the ideas presented earlier in *For Union Now*, Streit makes plain his contention that universality must be the goal of any plan for world federal government, but that we must begin with the democracies. What is needed is a "nucleus," and this nucleus must be democratic.

In cooperation with Justice Owen J. Roberts and John F. Schmidt, Streit continued to advance his case with publication of *The New Federalist*.[34] Not surprisingly, this book draws its inspiration from *The Federalist*, attempting to apply to the actors in world politics the same federal principles which Madison, Hamilton, and Jay applied to the thirteen states.

A unique event in the history of world federal proposals is the London Parliamentary Conference for World Government which took place in September 1951. Attended by members of parliamentary bodies from all over the world, it was convened on the contention of its organizers that world peace requires the surrender of national sovereignty to the greater sovereignty of a world federal government. The parliamentarians who gathered for the conference began the creation of world government groups throughout the world, and hailed their meeting as a demonstration to governments and to peoples that despite widespread cynicism there existed competent opinion which recognized the solution as possible.

In the decade just past, we may count such figures as Kenneth Boulding, Hans Morgenthau, Arnold Toynbee, Grenville Clark, and Louis Sohn among those who have advanced the idea of world federal government.[35] Of these, the Clark-Sohn proposal has been so widely read that almost all subsequent works on the subject use it as a convenient starting-point. In brief, their *World Peace Through World Law* recommends the creation of a "world authority" which would forbid violence or the threat of violence as a means of settling differences between actors. This world authority would be capable of supporting its dictates with appropriate force. Specifically, the authors envision the creation of a "permanent world police force" for the purpose of forestalling or suppressing the use of force by actors. This plan does not recommend the transfer of *all* sovereign-authoritative prerogatives to the specially created global authority. Only the right to use force is to be transferred to the new agency. There is, then, no suggestion of transmuting the system of separate actors into a single-actor world.

FUNCTIONALIST CONCEPTION OF WORLD ORDER

A number of technological, industrial, and communications changes in the nineteenth century had a dramatic effect upon intrastate and interstate relationships. Increasingly, European

127

economies were tied to overseas markets and resources. International trade was expanding. Concomitant with expanding economies and the construction of an international economic system was the growth of travel and communications. Of necessity there began to emerge what Inis Claude calls public international unions. These were transnational organizations designed to deal with specific functional problems that many states shared in common. Although it would be a mistake to refer to these organizations and their problems as nonpolitical, they were certainly characterized by concerns other than power, balances, and conflict management. In Claude's words:

> It represented adaptation, not innovation; it was less the work of idealists with schemes to advance than of realists with problems to handle ... In the nations most affected by the technological and industrial revolution, central governments were gaining in importance, compared with local and provincial governments, as agencies of administrative regulation, and they were expanding their administrative jurisdiction to cover aspects of economic and social life which had for some time been regarded as outside the province of government. In the international realm, the development of public international unions represented fundamentally similar patterns of evolution: the creation of international bodies to supplement the administrative work of national governments with narrowly limited territorial spheres of competence, and the notable expansion of the subject matter of international relations to include many problems which had been outside the scope of traditional diplomacy.[36]

Various commissions were formed in the nineteenth century to deal with river travel in Europe. The International Telegraphic Union was formed in 1865; the Universal Postal Union in 1874. Other agencies were formed to deal with health, agriculture, tariffs, railroads, standards of weights and measures, patents, copyrights, and drugs. These unions functioned in several ways. They served as information collection points and clearing houses. They became centers for discussing common problems. Some created mechanisms for coordination. They sought to promote uniform standards in several areas. They had limited authority over participating nations, but were able to provide them with useful services. A large number of these organizations were incorporated into the League of Nations and United Nations systems. Many more were also created as common problems increasingly required transnational solutions.

The public international unions added some structural innovations to the international system as well. The bureau of the

International Telegraphic Union became the prototype of the secretariat bureaucracies in twentieth-century organizations. Permanent staffs were created to carry out research and coordinate correspondence. They operationalized the distinction between policy-making bodies representing all states and administrative bodies of representatives that carried out policy. Perhaps most important, these organizations were increasingly populated by nondiplomats, by people who were representative of special kinds of interests or technical experts in given fields. In sum, public international unions expanded the substantive concerns of international relations and created new mechanisms for interstate cooperation. While they were inducing transnational cooperation, they were not markedly affecting state sovereignty in more traditional areas of international interaction.

These nineteenth-century developments in functionally based organizations seem to have been a direct stimulus to twentieth-century functionalist theory. In 1943, David Mitrany wrote *A Working Peace System*, the most thorough articulation of the functionalist position. Here, Mitrany contends that despite the preachings of philosophers and theologians about *human oneness*, the world of the twentieth century remains divided and compartmentalized. Beginning with the industrial revolution, the modern world is characterized on the one hand by intense political and cultural divisions of the globe, and on the other by the coming together of peoples in a "highly integrated organic unity." What has limited unity has been the assertion of individual and later national self-determination. What has brought man together has been "the development of communications, of new sources of power, of new materials, the opening up of new lands, and the rise of mass production . . ." Any solution to the problem of war and unrest must take account of the twin forces of self-determination and material unity, basically "of how to achieve unity in diversity" internationally and "how to have planning without breaking too many individual liberties . . ."[37]

Mitrany says that three kinds of proposals have been made to reduce war and tensions between disparate groups and states. The first is to create a loose association of states that can, given common sentiments of the participants, lead to their cooperation. The League of Nations and the United Nations are examples of this scheme. As suggested above, the second proposal involves the creation of federated systems on a regional or international level. These systems would have considerable sovereignty over national participants; hence, they would provide a cohesiveness that associations lack. The third or functional approach "seeks by linking authority to specific activity, to break away from the traditional link between authority and a definite territory."[38]

Neither the associative nor federal form can successfully grapple with international problems. Like the League of Nations, associations of states are designed to give voice to actors in the international system at the same time that they are to operate efficiently in common enterprises. These goals are mutually incompatible. If international parliaments increase verbal participation, they may hinder the prospects for sophisticated common action. And if they emphasize efficiency in the formulation and execution of policy, they hinder democratic participation of states. Mitrany suggests that viable institutions must organize for stability and for change. The optimum institutions are those that can provide for progressive but evolutionary change. The League experiment was designed to maximize stability; it was ill-prepared to deal with change. It sought to reify national self-determination and great power hegemony in the international system.

Whereas associations are too loose to create a system of evolutionary change, the federalist answer entails too much structure and rigidity to gain wide support. Federalism necessitates a dramatic redistribution of power from sovereign nations to sovereign regional or world bodies. Contemporary resistance to these moves might dramatically escalate hostilities. Further, any successful attempts at regional federation would only exacerbate hostilities and divisions between regions and between regions and nations. Federations that are less than universal in scope would be based upon geographic or ideological principles. Either would be divisive. Finally, both associations and federations are attempts to organize states on the basis of emotionally charged political questions that may only impede success. The functionalist alternative attempts to organize people on the basis of what they have in common rather than what has traditionally separated them.

Although holding to the hope for a system of world authority in the future, it is only through functionalism that such a vision can be achieved. The basic format for a "working peace system" must entail encouraging peoples and states to increasingly cooperate on specific functional problems. If the nineteenth century can be characterized as the Age of the Pursuit of Democracy, the twentieth century is the Age of the Pursuit of Social Welfare. Peoples should organize and participate in cross-national organizations that pursue specific social welfare tasks. The function should guide the organization. And it is the repeated and escalating assignment of responsibilities to functional organizations that would lead to further cooperation and social planning in the international system. Mitrany argues as follows:

Sovereignty cannot in fact be transferred effectively through a formula, only through a function. By entrusting an authority with a certain task, carrying with it command over the requisite powers and means, a slice of sovereignty is transferred from the old authority to the new; and the accumulation of such partial transfers in time brings about a translation of the true seat of authority. If that has been the considered process in the domestic sphere, is it not still more relevant in the international sphere, where even the elements of unity have to be built up laboriously by this very process of patient change?[39]

The process of growth of international-organizational powers will escalate as do the demands for solutions to problems. Mitrany suggests that the depression in the United States underscored the need for common action to increase productivity and wealth. The New Deal, particularly the Tennessee Valley Authority experiment, illustrates an organization of peoples and institutions solving problems without seeking to increase governmental authority through constitutional or structural change.

The New Deal was a natural response to a challenge that circumvented age-old political problems. The natural response to social welfare demands and the need for war prevention entails an increasing web of governmental and group relationships for a host of functional purposes until ultimately, over time, new international planning authorities can emerge.

Inis Claude argues that for functionalists, the problem of maintaining peace relates to three interlocking assumptions. First, functionalists hold to the view that the propensity for violence and war is a function of social and economic conditions in society. Poverty, disease, the great disparity in wealth between rich and poor, these conditions create the frustrations and dissatisfactions that lead to war. Therefore, functional organizations must be designed to alleviate the social ills that breed war. This means programs of support for third world peoples. It also means the formation of organizations that can grapple with the intricacies of social and economic relationships among industrialized states. The problems of both underdevelopment and development call for the application of technical expertise, planning, and other devices that separate the problem from political constraints to action.

Second, functionalists believe that the organization of the world into sovereign actors is no longer commensurate with the character of the problems. Many problems necessitate solutions based on the organic unity of mankind, not on the territorial and vertical distribution of states on the basis of geography and political/economic power: "The state system imposes an arbitrary and rigid pattern of vertical divisions upon global society, disrupting the organic unity of the whole, and carving the world into seg-

131

ments whose separateness is jealously guarded by sovereignties which are neither able to solve the fundamental problems nor willing to permit them to be solved by other authorities."[40]

Finally, functionalists assume that the process of functional cooperation will create a kind of attitudinal and value change that will serve to reinforce cooperation in more and more problem areas. The benefits of cooperation and changed loyalties will ultimately preclude war as a form of human activity. As international organizations provide tangible benefits to people, they will begin to see their utility above and beyond the state. Those who speak of functionalism at the regional level have emphasized the "spillover" effect of such cooperation.

More recently, Ernst Haas, in *Beyond the Nation-State*, revises classical functionalist thought by constructing a complex model which introduces *interest groups, purposive action* on the part of *governments* and *voluntary associations*, specific international *tasks*, international *actions* including *unintended consequences*, and *new actor purposes* based upon *learning*. Central to Haas's argument is the existence of groups motivated by perceptions of interest. Contrary to the idealism of the functionalists, Haas asserts that action by groups and governmental elites results not from altruism but from interest-motivated purposive action.

The activity of national actors leads to pressure for task expansion in the international system. International action, however, is always modified by the demands of the collectivity of actors and the qualities of existing systemic institutions. The systemic responses to national actor demands, the functions, usually encompass consequences unintended by these actors. The unintended consequences are "learned" by the national actors and may change their purposes. Through this process of purposive demand, systemic response, and new purposive demand, the international system can presumably become more integrated.

> Since all functions are understood eventually by the actors, the unintended consequences of their purposes are "learned." Therefore, any function becomes a new purpose at a different systemic level of integration. We must merely distinguish between learning conducive to integration and learning that seeks to block the process.[41]

The Haas formulation adds to functionalism a conception of system transformation that is willed by major national actors. It does not assume the automatic growth of international organization. Haas states that "learning" through functionalism is only effective when actors realize that their interests would be served by adopting new approaches. He also suggests that only those

132

experts who are members of some voluntary association or governmental bureaucracy can successfully receive support for integrative policies. Finally, he discusses several dimensions of existent international organization activity that can cause national actors to pursue further integration or disintegration. In its entirety, Haas's neo-functional model replaces the automatic and sometimes mystical quality of functional thought with an explanation that emphasizes human action, systemic response, and the problematic character of functional integration.

While the functionalist tradition has added important dimensions to international relations theory, its concern for technical tasks and welfare needs makes light of enduring political problems. Even if cooperation spills over from one issue area to another or if unintended consequences lead to new learned patterns of cooperation, the problems of power, narrow national interest, nationalism, and cultural diversity still seem vital. Political structuralist visions of alternative worlds are remiss in their neglect of functional cooperation *and* functionalists are equally remiss in their lack of concern for the needs of political cooperation between states.

UNIVERSAL CULTURAL CONCEPTIONS OF WORLD ORDER

Universal cultural conceptions of world order derive from the premise that there exists (or ought to exist) in the history of man a common set of values, beliefs, symbols, myths, and life patterns. The quest for a peaceful and humane world order requires the coming together of peoples in an organic society much akin to the nuclear family. In *This Endangered Planet*, Richard Falk describes the universal cultural perspective: "The creation of a new system of world order must draw its animating vision from the long and widespread affirmation that all men are part of a single human family, that a oneness lies buried beneath the manifold diversities and dissensions of the present fractionated world, and that this latent oneness alone can give life and fire to a new political program of transformation."[42]

This "animating vision" has a long history. In his *Meditations*, Marcus Aurelius, the Roman stoic, accepts the "connectedness" and "oneness of mankind" as fundamental to any coherent system of thought. Each man's nature is inextricably intertwined with the nature of the whole. There are no unrelated beings in the universe. All men are linked to their fellow men and to the larger universe of which they are a part. The universe itself is seen as one

133

living being with one substance and one soul. Within its inter-connected structure, all things act with one movement, all men act within a web of single texture. The root cause of the oneness of the universe is the coordination of all things by God. The bonds and ties are sacred, and since one God pervades all things, one substance or one common reason unites all intelligent animals.

By the Middle Ages, elements of the idea of universality had fused with the notion of a Christian commonwealth, and St. Thomas Aquinas, John of Salisbury, and Dante were looking upon Europe as a unified Christian community. All three recognized that the Christian community was properly governed by two divinely appointed authorities, the sacred and the imperial. From this division of earthly authority into two parts, a situation of perfect harmony was maintained.

Like the Gothic churches which expressed the idea of unity in their entire structure, the spirit of the Middle Ages created a large hierarchical system in the political sphere. The entire world was conceived as a vertical order extending from the lowest to the highest, and the earthly division of authority was reunited at the level of God, supreme reality, supreme end, supreme genius. Below that level the realm of humanity was to be considered as one. All the world had been created solely for the purpose of providing the background for man's salvation. Humanity was to be regarded as a single and unified whole. Only in its relation to the universe itself was the world to be conceived as a part rather than as a whole. Dante writes, for example:

> Further, the whole human race is a whole with reference to certain parts, and, with reference to another whole, it is a part. For it is a whole with reference to particular kingdoms and nations, as we have shown; and it is a part with reference to the whole universe, as is manifest without argument.[43]

This whole universe was tidy, ordered, and neatly arranged. It was simply conceived as a series of great clocks run by machinery. At its center lay the earth, the microcosm, at once a mere part of this more comprehensive expanse of creation and yet at the same time a single, unified whole unto itself.

Similar conceptions were developed during the eighteenth and nineteenth centuries. Herder, the German romanticist, describes the history of mankind in terms of the life cycles of particular states, yet global culture is described as one unending process in his *Reflections on the Philosophy of the History of Mankind* (1784-1791). The particular cultures of peoples arrive, develop, and disappear; humanity does not. The oneness of humanity is contained in those moral, artistic, and religious features of existence which are common to all peoples. This does not mean that individuation and differentiation among the people are alien to the conception of unity, but that it cannot constitute its final expression. Diversity and unity are part and parcel of God's overall design in the governance of humanity. The divine mind, as prototype of the human intellect, has "stamped the most innumerable multiplicity upon the Earth with unity . . . ."

In the same theological tradition of universal cultural conceptions of world order, the twentieth-century Jesuit Teilhard de Chardin begins with a notion of universality. This is rooted in his concept of "complexification," the process whereby subatomic units pass to extremely elaborate systems of human organization. All matter is part of a fundamental unity. The "stuff" of which all matter is constituted may in the end be reducible to some basic and unique substance; hence, says Chardin, the existence of system in nature is unambiguous. From the recognition that matter is cemented not by haphazard aggregation, but by collective bonds or energy, a unifying power and expression of structure, the interdependence of global parts is understood: "Each element of the cosmos is positively woven from all the others. . . ." There is no way in which the network of cosmic matter can be sliced up into distinct, isolable units. Only one way of considering the universe is really possible, that is, "to take it as a whole, in one piece."[44]

From this it becomes possible to understand the overarching singularity of mankind. Like Herder, Chardin does not deny the creative and enriching function of differentiation. He does insist, however, that the differentiation of groups is maintained only up to a certain point. Once this point has been reached, divergence and differentiation yield to confluence and convergence. This is a movement in which all peoples consolidate and complete one another by cultural cross-fertilization. To properly understand man and his future requires the prior understanding that ethnic, social, and moral ramifications are subordinate to the principal aim of coming together. Man's foremost task is cohesion, "a furling back upon itself of a bundle of potential species around the surface of the earth . . . ." He is confronted with an entirely new phenomenon, human "planetisation." This difficult idea of the worldwide totalization of human consciousness is associated with a closed grouping of people:

> Mankind, born on this planet and spread over its entire surface, coming gradually to form around its earthly matrix a single, major organic unity, enclosed upon itself; a single, hyper-complex, hyper-centrated,

135

hyper-conscious arch-molecule, co-extensive with the heavenly body on which it is born. Is not this what is happening at the present time—the closing of this spherical, thinking circuit?[45]

This "collectivization" of mankind derives from the development by the human mind of a new faculty—the perception of the "conic curvature of Time." It is this radically different temporal view of the world that is responsible for the convulsive drawing together that is now taking place. Unanimity in a common spirit is now possible because of the understanding that time is a continuous flux. There is, says Chardin, only one unity of duration. Just as nothing can exist in space without "something beside it," nothing exists in time without "something before it." Time is an indivisible thread leading back into infinity. Each moment is inextricably tied to its predecessor and successor. Hence, no element in the universe is independent of its neighbor. This is the crux of mankind's "planetisation."

In *The City of Man*, W. Warren Wagar traces the historical and contemporary universal culture themes on world order. He begins by arguing that mankind has reached a point of crisis not only in terms of the sources of planetary danger but because he no longer can accept traditional beliefs about his place in the universe. God is dead and the Enlightenment faith in science is gone. What is needed is a rekindling of Falk's "animating vision" based upon the realities of human potential for creating the world civilization. Rejecting "utopia," Wagar talks about the creation of "cosmopolis"—a universal city reflecting "the quintessence of a civilization, the gathering of all its vital human resources into a living organic city."[46] The choices for mankind are nuclear destruction, dehumanized existence, or world civilization. The latter would be a realistic world civilization drawing upon a synthesis of culture, religion, knowledge, politics, and economics. It represents a "world in a state of optimal integration."

Wagar elaborates on the converging historical roots of cosmopolis. Chinese thought introduced the notion of the "harmonious connectedness of things" or the Confucian ideal of the "great unity." Greek Stoicism presented the vision of a world governed by divine law and the brotherhood of man. Rome added legalism and citizenship to the stoic brotherhood. The medieval world views of Christianity and Islam further presumed a unitary universe; prophets from Dante and Saint-Pierre to Rousseau and Kant described integrated world orders based upon theological unity as well as political confederation.

Wagar then discusses twentieth-century theorists of world

order to illustrate his own conception and appraisal of cosmopolis. He begins by emphasizing the common conceptualization of a world society as an organismic whole in opposition to mechanistic analogues. Mechanical models are purposeless and futureless. They serve to make of man a functional part of a cosmic machine. Wagar describes his organicism:

> Most of the exponents of a world civilization, even those firmly attached to the liberal gospel of the existential uniqueness and freedom of the person, argue that the person cannot realize his potentialities except in a civilization that coheres organically, through the sharing of commonly agreed upon values, goals, symbols, and institutions. That is to say, fullness and wholeness of life in the person requires fullness and wholeness in the common life.[47]

In Pitirim A. Sorokin's terms, a coming world order must be based upon "familistic" rather than "contractual" relationships: "The new rising socio-cultural order promises to give a spontaneous unification of religion, philosophy, science, ethics, and fine arts into one integrated system of supreme values of Truth, Goodness, and Beauty."[48]

For Wagar, the spontaneous movement toward organic unity would proceed in several realms, including syntheses in philosophy, religion, knowledge, the arts, politics, and economics. In the realms of philosophy, religion, and knowledge, the synthesis would involve reconceptions of the mixture of all cultures so that a new synthetic and modern whole might be created to manage the needs of the future.

Wagar's preferred theorists of world order assume that the processes that presage that order first require religious and philosophical syntheses, *then* convergence in the pursuit of knowledge, and *lastly* a synthesis of politics and economics. Wagar assumes that some form of world confederation would be necessary, but views as more central "the meeting of minds which alone can make it viable."[49] Reinhold Niebuhr, says Wagar, expresses the common objection to world government preceding world culture "by insisting that there can be no world commonwealth until and unless a genuine world community grows into full self-consciousness, a world neighborhood in which men feel close enough through ties of common culture and common living to dare to make the leap to political union." World constitutions or police forces or "any of the merely mechanical schemes favored by world government zealots," simply would not be enough to create the kind of world synthesis needed to provide peace, stability, and justice.[50]

Three central issues and challenges to other kinds of world order theorists have been raised by universal cultural conceptions of world order. First, the emphasis on changed states of mind among masses *and* elites seem more important to these theorists than political or economic structural changes. Even though political institutions may be changing while peoples, values, and beliefs are changing, it is the latter that provide the skeletal form for any successful world order. Political institutions built on faulty cultural foundations, these theorists would suggest, are doomed to failure.

Second, the change of consciousness, of values, beliefs, and even of life-styles that is needed to bring about world order manifests an increasing awareness of human *oneness*. In new forms of religion, in hierarchies of values, in ways of understanding human experience, it is the singularity of all mankind that must be stressed. This oneness need not deny the unique in cultural experience; but it must go beyond any cultural pluralism to recognize mankind's common genesis and common set of purposes.

Third, the theorists of cultural conceptions of world order assume not only that such a universal synthesis of religion, culture, and philosophy would provide the optimal conditions for peace and justice, but that the movement of history is actually "pushing" man in that direction. These theories of world order are predictive as well as prescriptive. Technologies, tourist patterns, media, student exchanges, the emergence of nongovernmental organizations—all are pushing mankind beyond the barriers of distinct and mutually hostile civilizations. The role of the activist here is to stimulate and escalate those extant tendencies. In the process, such effort would presumably minimize the divisiveness that still exists among peoples.

STRENGTHS AND WEAKNESSES OF THE WORLD ORDER PERSPECTIVES

The world order perspectives discussed above add several provocative dimensions to the study of alternative world futures. The very fact that they are worldwide in scope is critical. The problems of war, social welfare needs, and divisive cultural nationalism all call for proposals that bring the world together. Wagar may be correct to criticize the utopian position for seeking to create *isolated* pockets of nonviolence, equitable material satisfaction, and common values and beliefs amidst historic strife and injustice.

Some of the world order theorists have not only addressed themselves to meaningful prescription, but they have also derived their perspectives on the future from tangible trends. These theorists are making predictions based upon convincing evidence. In terms of political structures, the international and certain domestic political systems have, in fact, become more centralized and have absorbed certain decisional prerogatives that were formerly left to smaller sociopolitical units. Not only has the state's utilization of persuasion and coercion become more legitimate, but the state itself has increasingly become the central source of personal security and welfare. Beyond this, the state has become a central creator of cultural values and beliefs. But centralization has not stopped with the state. A number of international organizations have begun to function in ways that states used to before the twentieth century. The escalating interaction and partial sovereignty acquired by governmental and nongovernmental organizations of all kinds testify to the increasing centralization of many facets of social life. Perhaps the strongest worldwide integrative forces are those movements which strive toward philosophical, cultural, religious, and social homogeneity. There is considerable evidence to support the view that the plurality of unique and "unblemished" cultures of the past is rapidly declining in the face of dynamic modernization.

The political structuralist and functionalist proposals themselves, given various kinds of critiques of ongoing international and domestic politics, have logical appeal. If the sources of violence and poverty can be attributed to existing structures, then changes in those structures might alleviate the problems they create. If the structural properties of the balance of power system maximize mistrust and violent struggle, then a suitable alteration of that structure is likely to decrease the probability of continued violence. If the fulfillment of welfare needs is inhibited by the pattern of autonomous states engaged in complex economic relationships, then the creation of functional, problem-solving institutions would seem to improve the satisfaction of these needs. Further, these arguments speak to the universal culturalists who assume that peace and prosperity are primarily problems of changing values and attitudes. The universal cultural argument does, however, add an important dimension to the debate. It does so by emphasizing the necessity for changing peoples' consciousness of who they are, where they are going in a broad historical sense, and how much their future goals are the *common goals of all mankind*. For example, it would seem most useful to challenge the kind of American value orientation that MacPherson has called "possessive individualism," and to eliminate the virulent anti-communism that has pervaded the society in the postwar period.

All three world order perspectives also have serious flaws. Despite the argument that security and welfare needs would be met more effectively if their vision were realized, the scope of required organization might dramatically impinge upon the kinds of psychic satisfactions implied in the Maslow need structure (see pp. 11-12). Much of the dissent in industrialized states over the last fifteen years has been a function of alienation and a concomitant sense of powerlessness. Individuals may no longer feel that they fully control their own destinies. From this perspective, any conception of world order seems only to maximize the growing malaise. As suggested by the regionalist vision, a citizen of France who has historically felt helpless in the face of French bureaucracy might only become more anxious in an integrated and federated Europe. The implications of a world order for his sense of control seems obvious. With powerlessness and alienation, some theorists argue, the readiness for mass manipulation increases. Hannah Arendt, William Kornhauser, and Erich Fromm[51] all see precisely this alienation as a precursor to the growth of Nazism in Germany. The implication of this reservation about world order, therefore, is that cultural and political autonomy is needed for people to maintain their identities, their sense of personal efficacy, and their energy for self-actualization.

Not only is the prescription fraught with problems, but the prediction of contemporary movement toward world order is tenuous as well. In her recent book, *The Future of Law in a Multicultural World*, Adda Bozeman[52] argues from the cultural standpoint that disintegration is more characteristic of the contemporary world than integration. Particularly in third world societies, peoples at the tribal or communal levels have become disenchanted with the states that were artificially imposed upon them. As a result, they have sought to reestablish ties with their more provincial past. Africa is not a continent with forty nations, but one with at least one thousand identifiable tribes. Even in the West, she argues, there are indications that localism and cultural renaissance are on the upswing. Bozeman is challenging both the *predictions* and the *prescriptions* of world order theorists. If world order is to become a reality through cultural, religious, or philosophical synthesis, then the multiplicity of revitalized cultural nationalisms would suggest that world order is not even a dim prospect. If world order is to emerge from international law and political or functional organization, third world cultures will be most resistant to such developments. According to Bozeman, the world is not moving toward cultural and political centralization, but toward decentralization. Perhaps an integration of these views is most accurate. *Both* centralizing *and* decentralizing forces are at work in the international system. Therefore, the mix of conflicting forces demands reexamination by students of alternative world futures.

World order perspectives highlight the debate between structural change and change tied to states of consciousness. Structural or institutional change does not necessarily lead to consciousness change. The League of Nations experiment seemed to be an illustration of grandiose expectations as to *value change* with certain minimal but significant institutional changes. Complementary structural and value change seems critical. The universal culturalists tend to ignore the importance of appropriate institutional change in creating sources of authority and distributions of power that can maximize the values sought. Each world order perspective is incomplete without the other.

Finally, the concept of universal homogeneity in cultural, economic, and political terms implies a "sameness" that might inhibit variety and change. Several theorists have linked social change to diversity, cultural cross-fertilization, and to conflict itself. The emergence of a homogeneous world civilization could lead to various forms of stagnation. Theorists like Kenneth Boulding, while recognizing the need for cooperation in political and economic areas, often warn against a unique new danger in the twenty-first century: *boredom.* The analogue to the world society of the future might be represented by today's large international airport. One can stop at almost any such airport in the world and find little indication of difference in cultures, life-styles, or values. If airport culture spills over into cities and countrysides, the vitality of the world's diverse peoples may be lost forever.

NOTES

1. F. H. Hinsley, *Power and the Pursuit of Peace* (London: Oxford, 1963).

2. Emeric Cruce, *The New Cyneas*, Thomas Willign Balch, trans. (Philadelphia: Allen, Lane and Scott, 1909), pp. 102, 104.

3. *Ibid.*, p. 66.

4. Maximilien de Béthune, Duc de Sully, *Grand Design of Henry IV* (London: A Grotius Society Publication, 1921), p. 42.

5. C. I. Castel de Saint-Pierre, *Abrége du Projet de Paix Perpetuelle*, Hale Bellot, trans. (London: A Grotius Society Publication, 1927), p. 27.

6. *Ibid.*, pp. 28-29.

7. *Ibid.*, p. 29.

8. Jean Jacques Rousseau, *A Lasting Peace Through the Federation of Europe*, C. E. Vaughan, trans. (London: Constable & Co., 1917), pp. 38-39.

9. *Ibid.*, pp. 59-60.

10. *Ibid.*, p. 112.

11. Jean Jacques Rousseau, *The Social Contract*, Charles Frankel, trans. (New York: Hafner, 1974), p. 24.

12. Jeremy Bentham, *Plan for a Universal and Perpetual Peace* (London: A Grotius Society Publication, 1927), p. 26.

13. *Ibid.*, p. 27.

14. *Ibid.*, pp. 30-31.

15. Inis L. Claude, Jr., *Swords Into Plowshares* (New York: Random House, 1956).

16. Lassa Oppenheim, "International Law," in *Search for Peace,* David Brook, ed. (New York: Dodd, Mead, 1970), p. 283.

17. *Ibid.*

18. Quincy Wright, *A Study of War* (Chicago: University of Chicago Press, 1965), p. 410-411.

19. *Ibid.*, p. 421.

20. *Ibid.*, p. 425.

21. Raymond L. Bridgman, *World Organization* (Boston: Ginn & Co., 1905), p. 7.

22. H. G. Wells, *The Outline of History, II* (New York: Macmillan, 1920), p. 580.

23. H. G. Wells, *The Common Sense of World Peace* (London: L. & V. Woolf, 1929), p. 18.

24. Clarence K. Streit, *For Union Now: A Proposal for a Federal Union of the Democracies* (Washington: Harper & Bros., 1939).

25. W. B. Curry, *The Case for a Federal Union* (Harmondsworth, England: Penguin, 1939).

26. David H. Munroe, *Hang Together: The Union Now Primer* (New York: Union Press, 1940).

27. See *A Memorandum with Regard to a New Effort to Organize Peace and Containing a Proposal for a "Federation of Free Peoples" in the Form of a Draft of a Constitution for the Proposed Federation* (New York: December 1939).

28. C. E. M. Joad, in Preface to Duncan and Elizabeth Wilson, *Federation and World Order* (London: T. Nelson & Sons, 1939), p. xiii.

29. Oscar Newfang, *World Government* (New York: Barnes & Noble, 1942).

30. Ely Culbertson, *Summary of the World Federation Plan: An Outline of a Practical and Detailed Plan for World Settlement* (Garden City, N.Y.: Garden City Publishing Co., 1943).

31. See Emery Reves, *Anatomy of Peace*, selection reprinted in David Brook, ed., *Search for Peace* (New York: Dodd, Mead, 1970), p. 364.

32. See, for example, Cord Meyer, Jr., *Peace or Anarchy* (Boston: Little, Brown, 1947).

33. Clarence K. Streit, *Union Now: A Proposal for an Atlantic Federal Union of the Free* (New York: Harper & Bros., 1949).

34. Owen J. Roberts, John F. Schmidt, and Clarence K. Streit, *The New Federalist* (New York: 1950). The authors characterize themselves as Publius II.

35. See Kenneth Boulding, *The Meaning of the Twentieth Century* (New York: Harper & Row, 1964); Hans Morgenthau, *Politics Among Nations* (4th ed.; New York: Alfred A. Knopf, 1967); Arnold Toynbee, *A Study of History*, abridgement of Vols. I-VI by D. C. Somervell (New York and London: Oxford University Press, 1946); and Grenville Clark and Louis B. Sohn, *World Peace Through World Law* (Cambridge: Harvard University Press, 1966).

36. Claude, *Swords Into Plowshares*, p. 37.

37. David Mitrany, *A Working Peace System* (Chicago: Quadrangle, 1966), p. 27.

38. *Ibid.*

39. *Ibid.*, p. 31.

40. Claude, *Swords Into Plowshares*, p. 377.

41. Ernst B. Haas, *Beyond the Nation-State* (Stanford, Calif.: Stanford University Press, 1964), pp. 83-84.

42. Richard A. Falk, *This Endangered Planet* (New York: Random House, 1971), p. 296.

43. Dante, *De Monarchia*, Book I, Sec. VII, F. C. Church, trans. (London: 1878), p. 189.

44. Pierre Teilhard de Chardin, *The Phenomenon of Man* (New York: Harper & Row, 1959), p. 44.

45. Pierre Teilhard de Chardin, *The Future of Man* (New York: Harper & Row, 1964), p. 115.

46. W. Warren Wagar, *The City of Man* (Baltimore: Pelican, 1963), p. 15.

47. *Ibid.*, p. 131.

48. *Ibid.*, p. 132.

49. *Ibid.*, p. 200.

50. *Ibid.*

51. Hannah Arendt, *The Origins of Totalitarianism* (Cleveland: World, 1951); William Kornhauser, *The Politics of Mass Society* (New York: Free Press, 1959); Erich Fromm, *Escape From Freedom* (New York: Holt, Rinehart, and Winston, 1941).

52. Adda B. Bozeman, *The Future of Law in a Multicultural World* (Princeton, N.J.: Princeton University Press, 1971).

Chapter 7
Human Needs, the State System, and Alternative World Futures: A Tentative Assessment

INTRODUCTION

The narrator of Kurt Vonnegut's *Cat's Cradle* describes the central premise of his religion, Bokoninism: "humanity is organized into teams, teams that do God's will without ever discovering what they are doing," and "such a team is called a *karass* . . ."[1] Later the narrator explains the idea of a false *karass*.

> Hazel's obsession with Hoosiers around the world was a textbook example of a false karass, of a seeming team that was meaningless in terms of the ways God gets things done, a textbook example of what Bokonon calls a *granfalloon*. Other examples of *granfalloons* are the Communist Party, the Daughters of the American Revolution, the General Electric Company, the International Order of Odd Fellows—and any nation, anytime, anywhere.[2]

Although theorists of alternative world futures may not be familiar with the language of a "karass," many would probably agree with Vonnegut's characterization of the contemporary state as a meaningless "team" in terms of its *definition*, its prescribed *functions*, and its actual *behavior*. More specifically, social-critical theorists and alternative world futures theorists would agree that the state system is not adequately fulfilling the kinds of human needs described by Abraham Maslow. This last chapter in Part I will examine the philosophical bases of the state and the functions it is supposed to perform, in terms of social-critical theory. After further assessment of the three alternative world futures discussed earlier, a community-organized world will be posited as a tentative alternative to the state system. This concluding assessment is not designed to create a new dogma, but to act as a stimulus for continuing discussion by students of alternative world futures.

THE STATE: NATURE, FUNCTIONS, AND BEHAVIORS

Alexander D'Entreves, a political theorist, says in the introduction to his essay, *The Notion of the State*, that "from the hour of birth to the hour of death our life is beset with innumerable forces which obstruct or protect its course and determine its fate" and that some of these forces are "natural" in that they are beyond human control. An extraordinary number of these forces "are those which are commonly associated with the notion of a mysterious but omnipresent entity, of an indefinite but at the same time imperious and irresistible power: the notion of the State."[3]

D'Entreves says that the *notion* of the state has usually been conceived in one of three ways. The *political realists* view the state in the same terms as Max Weber, the German sociologist, as "a human community that (successfully) claims the *monopoly of the legitimate use of physical force* within a given territory."[4] People accept control by the state because they are weak and the state and its agencies are strong. *Legalists*, D'Entreves says, define the state in a different way. It is not a social institution with unlimited power. The state is a system of rules, regulations, laws, and norms that allow it to exercise power in certain specified ways. The law defines the powers and roles of state behavior and the powers and roles of citizens who live within its geographic and legal boundaries. The state is a system of laws and "these 'laws' are made by men, and by men who established, and wished to establish, an 'order' in their relations with each other for the achievement of certain ends, first and foremost that peaceful coexistence which is needed to make further ends attainable."[5]

Political philosophers say that even though force and law are important determinants of what a state is, the most important part of a definition of the state is the *sense of obligation*, or the *authority*, that state decisions command. Force cannot command obeisance nor can the impersonal law. What is central is a "consciousness of a cohesive bond of unity, agreement on purpose, a civic sense, love of country, complete dedication to the common cause."[6] The state is the sum total of the obligations that a collectivity of people voluntarily accept as their own.

The common features of a state, therefore, are force, law, and authority. Theorists have also written about the *functions* states are supposed to perform. John Herz, an international relations scholar, argues that states first emerged to protect people from military attack. In the seventeenth century, kings began to control more land and people, and instruments of warfare became more sophisticated. Both these developments led to the desire to create "hard shell," "impermeable" boundaries within territories. The state began to take on the characteristics of impermeability that once existed in the castle or the walled town of the medieval period. The small military fortresses were replaced by one large fortress that became the boundaries of the new state.[7] "There now was peace and protection within. War became a regularized military procedure; only the breaking of the shell permitted interference with what had now become the internal affairs of another country."[8]

Herz wrote in 1957 that the major task the state was supposed to perform could no longer be fulfilled. Particularly in military terms, the state could not remain impermeable. Air war and the existence of a uniquely destructive nuclear weapons technology meant that no state was impermeable. Further, the increasing economic interdependence of peoples and the global network of communications patterns make the notion of the physically, economically, and psychically isolated state an historical relic. In sum, the central reason for the existence of the state was gone.

Ten years later, Herz reconsidered his entire thesis. He viewed the Cold War and the development of a nuclear stalemate as a source of renewed impermeability. The logic of deterrence (see chapter eight) made the deliberate use of nuclear weapons implausible. If the overwhelming fear and generally recognized abhorrence of nuclear destruction made such weapons effectively unusable, then impermeable boundaries might be restored. And, despite the developing pattern of global integration, third world peoples were increasingly defining themselves along national lines. In effect, Herz concluded that his prediction of the "demise of the territorial state" was premature. In the future, states would continue to provide protection as well as "group identity" and "welfare." Moreover, Herz added:

> *Internal* legitimacy (without which the legitimacy of the unit as such can provide little real solidity) in our day is closely related to

democracy in the broad sense of people having the conviction that they control their destinies and that government operates for their welfare.[9]

Herz called his reconception of national purpose the "new territoriality" of the nation-state. This new territoriality implied three state functions: physical protection under conditions of nuclear stalemate; modernization, development, and the equitable distribution of economic resources; and psychological identification with the state based primarily upon certain kinds of mass participation in domestic political processes.

Analyses of the implications of the *notion* of the state and considerations of its presumed failure to fulfill assigned functions stimulate a concern for alternative world futures. If the realist definition is broadly accepted, the major focus of state activity concerns the efficient use of physical force in the name of control and obeisance to sovereign authority. The application of force becomes particularly intense when individuals within the state seek to bring about social change and challenge the legitimacy of various state institutions or elites in the process.

Although the legalist conception offers the prospect of constraints on unchecked state behavior, the rule of law presumes a uniformity of values and life-styles that may hinder individual autonomy. Law may be one of several important forces that stimulate the standardization of behavior. If this standardization is resisted, the use of force is justified in terms of legal redress. Further, state law may be more a reflection of the values or interests of particular elites, or classes, or ethnic groups than of an entire population.

Where it is defined in terms of "consciousness of a cohesive bond of unity," "agreement on purpose," "love of country," or "complete dedication to the common cause," the state and its primary institutions are reified. Elites create a series of affect-laden symbols that are used to achieve consensus and conformity in support of any goals the state pursues. This conception of the state lends itself to the manipulation of peoples under the guise of "nationalism."

These images have definite international ramifications. If the state is defined as the "human community that (successfully) claims the monopoly of the legitimate use of physical force within a given territory" and it has the capacity to use that force, international violence becomes more self-fulfilling. While this monopoly is actually restricted to its own borders, the absence of any controlling authority in the world system leaves each state in the position to effectively extend its jurisdiction to an extent

147

coincident with its power. Quincy Wright cites Arnold Brecht, a political theorist, on this point: "there is a cause of wars between sovereign states that stands above all others—the fact that there are sovereign states, and a very great many of them."[10]

Finally, the state viewed as a collectivity of obligations leads its leaders to mobilize masses of peoples through the dissemination of nationalistic symbols. Quincy Wright hypothesizes a relationship between state authority, symbolism, and war:

> The larger the group and the less accessible all its members to direct sensory contact with all the others and their activities, the less available are instinct, custom, or universal acceptance as bases of group behavior, and the more symbols and opinions about them are the stimuli and guides for behavior. In the large groups which make war in modern civilization, symbols have been responsible for initiating and guiding that particular behavior.[11]

Coupled with the dangers inherent in its conceptualization, the state may not be performing its basic functions. States are still subject to the threat of nuclear war (primarily the great powers) and domestic intervention (primarily third world and Eastern European nations). In the seventeenth-century state system, military defenses could be amassed that would preclude offensive successes. The post-world war state system is characterized by such overwhelming potential for nuclear and conventional destruction that the idea of impermeability seems totally implausible. Offensive weapons technology continues to outdistance attempts at defense.

In terms of welfare and participation, differences between rich and poor, powerful and weak, continue to be dramatic. It was recently estimated that 20 percent of the peoples of the third world are "undernourished" and 60 percent "malnourished."[12] These estimates did not include the lower economic strata in the developed nations. In reference to participation, over one-half of the population of Latin America, for example, is subject to military rule. This brings into question the role of the state supporting democracy.

The social-critical theorists discussed in chapters two and three address themselves to the actual *behavior* of the state domestically and internationally. Theories of *balance of power* and *political realism* imply the perpetuation of interstate violence; they assume that the international system is a system of constant struggle. Theories of *stratification* and *rank disequilibrium* illustrate the mechanisms of interaction between rich and poor, powerful and weak, that are deleterious to community and self-determination. Theories of the *endangered planet* and *future shock* emphasize problems of ecology, technology, and violence as they relate to uncontrolled change.

Domestic social-critical theories speak to the obstructions of human need fulfillment by the state. The *statist critique* points to the continued limitations of personal control, efficacy, and the means of sustenance which derive from the existence of large, centralized states. The *organizational/technocratic critique* analyzes the loss of control of human organization. This results from the continued expansion of organization and technology, and from the dehumanizing implication of scientific expertise. The *economic critique* warns of the disparity between rich and poor in terms of wealth and power. This is seen as a result of the expansive characteristics of capitalist economic systems. The *political elitist critique* warns that the emergence of small groups of elites coupled with the continued impotence of unorganized masses yield certain preconditions for dictatorial societies. Finally, the *cultural critique* points to potentially destructive societal norms and values that reinforce or create dynamics of struggle, dominance, and ethnocentricity.

In short, a careful examination of the concept of the state, an evaluation of the success of functions it traditionally performs, and a survey of social-critical literature that deals with domestic and international ramifications of state behavior leads the student of alternative world futures to question the capacity of the state system to satisfy human needs.

REGIONALISM, WORLD ORDER, AND ALTERNATIVE WORLD FUTURES

Our discussion of alternative world futures began with a checklist of human needs originally formulated by Abraham Maslow. In his early work, Maslow speaks of needs for food, sex, shelter, and security: what were referred to as *self-preservation needs*. He then indicates that man desires love and a sense of belonging: *community needs*. Much of Maslow's later work concerns itself with self-esteem and self-actualization: considered here as *self-determination needs*. It has been argued that despite the universality of these instinctual needs, they provide a useful checklist from which one can evaluate various alternative forms of social organization. It has also been argued that a viable, humane society ought to provide (at a minimum) for self-preservation, community, and self-determination.

149

Three predominant alternative world futures literatures were then discussed. A long tradition speaks of *utopia*, either as isolated communal forms (*microcosmic forms*), or as communal forms with some concern for intercommunal interaction (*macrocosmic forms*). A more recent perspective studies how national groupings may be formed into *regional* systems. These are designed to organize productive capacities and scientific expertise for broader distribution of goods and services and to minimize violence between contracting states within the region. Finally, three world order traditions were discussed: the *political structuralist*, *functionalist*, and *universal cultural* orientations. These alternatives seek to organize all of humanity around new political institutions, new welfare institutions, or a new cultural synthesis.

The regionalist vision draws much of its insight from the properly functioning nation-state. The neo-functionalist positions of theorists like Ernst Haas seek to create in one region, like the Europe of the common market countries, a set of supranational institutions that efficiently organize production and distribution of resources to the regional population. Since politics and welfare cannot be separated, integration theorists view viable groups within regions and recognized institutional elites within countries as sources of support for integration. The interaction of groups, elites, and technocrats will yield workable policies for the region. Integration theorists view future regions as technocratic states with food, shelter, goods, and services provided for all, and conflict between national groups successfully managed.

The most unfortunate aspect of the regionalist perspective is its conscious adaptation of the industrialized state as its microcosmic analogue. Even though the state has not usually been defined in terms of welfare, and even though the regionalist organizing principle *is* welfare, it is by no means clear that regional organization can more successfully reduce the disparities between rich and poor and more adequately meet the welfare needs of its population. It also remains to be seen whether the region can adequately manage conflict within its bounds and between itself and other actors.

A glaring difficiency in the regional vision is its lack of concern for the needs relating to community. Even though integration theorists often use the rhetoric of community, the kind of community they envision is similar to the system of authority characteristic of the nation-state. National symbols are merely replaced by regional symbols. Frenchmen and Germans become Europeans. The scope of nationalism may be increased rather than substantially changed. Finally, in reference to self-determination needs, little or no reference is made to individuals in the new regional system. It may be that the more successful the regional effort is in welfare and political terms, the less likely it will be to create the environment for self-realization and self-actualization.

World order perspectives raise similar doubts. The political structuralist vision may successfully deal with the management of power (see chapter ten for a more detailed discussion) but the overriding emphasis upon eliminating interstate violence leads it to ignore questions of poverty and powerlessness. The functionalists are correct to suggest that violence is in part a function of poverty and disease, particularly if there are great and visible disparities between haves and have nots. As chapter six suggests, several proponents of world government schemes were primarily interested in enshrining the status quo generally and their own countries' international positions in particular. The single-minded emphasis on war avoidance leaves many other needs unattended.

The functionalist world vision is analogous to the regionalist concern at the global level. Mitrany's ultimate hope is to create a world of centralized institutions that deal primarily with economic and technical problems for the planet's population. Even though the emphasis on welfare is commendable and the hypothesized linkage between violence reduction and the elimination of poverty and marked stratification quite accurate, the functionalists also ignore the community and self-determination needs so vital to affiliation and individual autonomy.

The universal cultural perspective goes beyond narrow political and welfare concerns to posit a world in unity and harmony. Values, beliefs, and life-styles will come together in a new synthesis that will create a common culture for the planet's population. Even though most of these theorists would not deny the relevance of centralized political institutions and a common concern for eliminating poverty and uncontrolled change in industrial and technological development, a commitment to changed consciousness remains central to their argument. The debate between those who view a change of consciousness as a precondition for institutional change and those who view a change in institutions as a prerequisite to consciousness change is an important one. Even though the debate remains unresolved, the powerful impact of institutions on altering the way people perceive reality cannot be understated.

One important reservation that emerges from an analysis of the cultural position can be seen in the demand by these theorists for cultural homogeneity. The existence of isolated pockets of unique cultures or even of whole civilizations is seen as a continuing source of conflict in an age of technological integration and unplanned change. Only through philosophical, religious, and intellectual syntheses can man expect to survive.

What remains disturbing about this position is its implicit potential for loss of community and individual autonomy. Many states have created unified cultures out of disparate subcultures. With the destruction of unique heritages and cultures, man seems to slip into a commonality of purpose and desire that borders on conformity. Couple the destruction of cultural pluralism with potent political and economic institutions and what is created is the manipulation of the many by the few. It may be that diverse cultures preserve what is best in man, his own spontaneously created uniqueness. Although poverty, war, and ecosuicide appropriately capture most of our attention, serious consideration should be given to the image of the future postulated by Kenneth Boulding, a world civilization that looks like the social organization of an international airport *any place* in the world.

Despite the negative consequences discussed above, an alternative world future must utilize the positive features of world order and regionalist perspectives. Global problems require global solutions. War and ecological spoilage do not lend themselves to local decision-making. Conflict between peoples still necessitates some overarching system of influence and control. The equitable distribution of goods and services is a world problem as well as a community problem. Tentatively, therefore, an alternative world future is posited below that draws extensively upon the spirit of utopian and anarchist thought in the context of a regional and world network of communities organized in commonwealths. Essentially, each alternative vision is incomplete without some features of the others.

ALTERNATIVE FUTURES AND ORGANIC COMMUNITY

Common to most of the alternative futures discussed above is the spirit of organic community. Organicism suggests a way of conceptualizing social organization that draws parallels between the human organism and a given social system. Contrary to the mechanical analogy that likens society to a well-oiled machine, the organic model implies a living, growing, and purposive entity. Organic models presume that "disease" in any part of society is a reflection on the entire social system. Growth among the parts and total organismic growth are complementary. Consequently, both individuals and social systems are subject to growth and decay, pleasure and pain, toil and leisure. Given this conception of society, the fundamental community task is to fulfill the needs of its members. This achievement makes the community grow and prosper.

The achievement of human need fulfillment in the organic community would require several community characteristics. First, the question of *size* becomes critical. It would seem that the spirit of organicism demands social organizations of small size or microcosmic utopias to provide the knowledge from which mutual responsibility can grow. In terms of mutual awareness, one cannot expect organic community beyond the bounds of face-to-face relationships.

Once a community is of the size whereby people can be truly aware of each other, then a second criterion of organic community becomes relevant, *intimacy*; to grow, to create a life in common, people must be able to tangibly experience each other. Those others with whom one interacts must not be known primarily as functions or objects. The modern state, however, has destroyed the intimate personal relationships that people might have with each other.

In *The Symbolic Uses of Politics,*[13] Murray Edelman argues that people relate to politics through two kinds of symbols, "referential" and "condensational." *Referential* symbols are those mental images that bear close relationship to "reality." *Condensational* symbols are emotive in character and hence less likely to accurately reflect "reality." Most people appear to experience politics through condensational symbols. Small communities of a size whereby people can *know* each other may experience politics and social life through referential symbols. The potentially stereotyped, emotional, and often hysterical reactions to unknown and distant peoples are reduced as people become *aware* of each other and live together in more intimate social relationships.

An organic community requires a *sense of commitment* among its members to the community itself and to the potential of its individual members. Some theorists have argued that an ideology, a specific purpose, or an external enemy are needed to bind together all potential members. Irrespective of the values and purposes for which it was formed, the members must see the complementary individual and collective needs of the community. Each individual must significantly commit himself to the life of the community and to all of its members.

Since organicism requires the willing intimacy and commitment of community members to each other, it must also create the conditions whereby individual *autonomy* can thrive. Organic notions presume the growth of individuals and the community in parallel directions. However, the common evolution occurs in the context of spontaneity, creativity, and individual action. It is the community that creates the context in which human freedom can thrive. Freedom is not the negative sort that pits collectivity against individual, but the positive kind of freedom that conceives of the collectivity as a stimulus for individual action.

An organic community also provides its members with *psychic and social predictability*. Such a community is the embodiment of norms and values that guide human behavior and create expectations about the future. Robert Lifton, a psychiatrist, talks about man's "compelling, universal urge to maintain an inner sense of continuity, over time and space, with the various elements of life."[14] If the community is to function, Lifton would suggest, five modes of a "sense of immortality" must exist. The biological mode of immortality requires a belief in "living on through" past death by way of the transmittal of tradition. The theological mode involves a "spiritual conquest of death." The creative mode provides men with the belief that they live on in the community through their works. The natural mode involves the belief that man will be "survived by nature, the sense one will live on in natural elements, limitless in space and time." Finally the mode of experiential transcendence involves the feeling that one is expanding beyond one's limitations. Lifton contends that the five modes "are constantly perceived inner standards, though often indirect and outside of awareness, by which we evaluate our lives, by which we maintain feelings of connection, significance, and movement so necessary to everyday psychological existence."[15]

Finally, organic models imply the existence of *physically healthy members*. This means an equitable distribution of resources and services. Since the health of the community is reflected by the health of its individual members, the fulfillment of self-preservation needs provides a necessary (if not sufficient) condition for the existence of organic community.

Theorists of alternative futures often pay homage to organicism, but not all of their visions can satisfy the criteria for its achievement. Given the criteria of *size, intimacy, sense of commitment, autonomy, psychic and social predictability,* and *physical health*, the ideal is most likely to be met in the microcosmic utopia. The criteria for the creation of an organic community seem to satisfy the conditions for the fulfillment of human needs as well. Self-preservation needs, community needs, and self-determination needs are almost certainly satisfied in the organic model. A commitment to human need fulfillment and organic community suggests the applicability of the utopian tradition.

Although many would look favorably at the utopian vision, they would also raise several well-founded objections to its lack of feasibility. Some might argue that the world is entirely too complex to move in the direction of decentralized, semi-autonomous communities. The scientific and technological benefits of the modern age seemingly require the kind of centralized administration that can optimally deal with mass production and the division of labor. They would further raise the specter of the necessity of marshaling expertise in the pursuit of social progress. And the kinds of planetary dangers that Falk and Wagar describe require planetary solutions: centralized planning in reference to population control, resource utilization, and distribution of the world's wealth. Finally, it might be argued that the world has in fact come together; that people are now organized in socioeconomic units above and beyond the state. Community life can offer no more than a fond remembrance of a pre-industrial past.

What these objections suggest is that attainable communities cannot be as autonomous as the microcosmic-utopian literature would prefer. Perhaps the optimal concepts of alternative world futures must begin with the community, always seeking to retain political, economic, and cultural control to the fullest extent possible at that level. Larger and larger relationships among people should be built only when needed. If the organic ideal affords the greatest opportunity for human need fulfillment, and if that model requires community rather than regional or world order plans, then every attempt should be made to revitalize community in the life of man. This means adjusting technology, expertise, planning, and economic growth to fit patterns of worldwide networks of communities. The working principle should be to decentralize as much as possible, always remembering the maximum utility found in the organic community model.

Some "operating rules" for prospective "architects" of alternative world futures now suggest themselves:

1. Begin at the base. Encourage and increase structures and processes that maximize community.

2. Offer as much autonomy as possible to community control of political

decision-making, cultural affairs, decentralized technologies, and economic self-sufficiency.

3.   As problems and needs require, encourage intercommunity interaction. Such interaction ought to proceed on a functional basis in a way that trade and an appropriate division of labor is maximized. With every attempt to maintain community integrity, such interactions need not be viewed as a move to create homogeneity among peoples, except as they share common interests and needs. From intercommunity interaction, regional authorities with some measure of sovereignty may be justified. Community representatives might meet to form regional councils and make region-wide decisions. Again, such regional cooperation need not be encouraged to break down diversity or to incrementally build larger and larger sovereign units. It should be a device to increase mutually beneficial interchange. If the norm of cultural and political pluralism is broadly respected, functional efforts need not become a force for more and more centralized authority.

4.   Collectivities of representatives from regions of the world might organize worldwide bodies to tackle problems of global concern. These world bodies could serve as policy-makers in some realms, information dispersing agencies in others, and as role models for future collective action. Further, the world centers could also assume some responsibility for redistributing wealth or for encouraging voluntaristic efforts in this direction.

The essence of this plan, therefore, is a synthesis of all three visions for a viable alternative world future. The organic community may afford the best opportunity for human need fulfillment, but the complexities of the modern world and the extensive potential for social progress through macrocosmic cooperation make community, regional, and world visions complementary. As long as community is the foundation of such an alternative, one might expect few negative by-products of regional or world order models.

These arguments are admittedly tentative. Students of alternative world futures must study the varied models in detail, giving further thought to the prospective correspondence between organic community, loose federalism, and human need fulfillment. The proposals above are not yet blueprints; they are skeletal forms needing continued examination and elaboration.

It should also be clear that community revitalization need not be viewed in opposition to the organization of today's world. Communities, regions, and world organizations exist that might provide the basic form for a new global order. The changes that organic community requires are as much changes of consciousness, values, beliefs, and purposes as they are changes of structures. As Kropotkin and Buber point out, people have historically formed and reformed in communities of common purpose. Even in the face of strong central authority, they have sought to maintain organic ties with those close to them. What is needed are (1) sustained and visible attempts to broaden community construction and maintenance, and (2) serious educational or propaganda efforts to restore the sense of hope that building community might entail.

The conception of a viable organic world community, as well as the encouragement of secondary regional and world bodies, ought to be conceived of not as an "end state," but as a *process of growth and humanization of the social and physical environment.* An alternative global future is both a *striving for* and an *achievement of* certain goals. The positing of alternative world futures is the first step in a process that leads man to narrow the gap between what actually exists and what potentially can be. Only when the visions are left unproposed and the commitments to *move* are left unsaid does man experience stagnation.

NOTES

1.   Kurt Vonnegut, *Cat's Cradle* (New York: Dell, 1969), p. 11.

2.   *Ibid.*, p. 67.

3.   Alexander Passerin d'Entreves, *The Notion of the State* (London: Oxford University Press, 1967), p. 1.

4.   H. H. Gerth and C. Wright Mills, eds., *From Max Weber* (New York: Oxford University Press, 1958), p. 78.

5.   D'Entreves, *The Notion of the State*, p. 3.

6.   *Ibid.*, p. 6.

7.   John H. Herz, "The Rise and Demise of the Territorial State," in James N. Rosenau, ed., *International Politics and Foreign Policy* (New York: Free Press, 1961), p. 82.

8.   *Ibid.*, p. 82.

9.   John H. Herz, "The Territorial State Revisited: Reflections on the Future of the Nation-State," in James N. Rosenau, ed., *International Politics and Foreign Policy* (rev. ed.; New York: Free Press, 1969), p. 83.

10.   Quincy Wright, *A Study of War*, abridged by Louise Leonard Wright (Chicago: University of Chicago Press, 1964), p. 188.

11.   *Ibid.*, p. 258.

12.   Paul R. and Anne H. Ehrlich, *Population, Resources, Environment* (San Francisco: Freeman, 1970), p. 67.

13.   Murray Edelman, *The Symbolic Uses of Politics* (Urbana: University of Illinois Press, 1964).

14.   Robert Jay Lifton, *Boundaries* (New York: Vintage, 1969), p. 22.

15.   *Ibid.*, p. 3.

Some Analytic Models
of World Order
and War Avoidance

Chapter 8
The Dynamics of Power Management in the Present World System

INTRODUCTION

Part II of this volume is concerned with the creation of new systems of world order with particular reference to war avoidance. Everything in this part derives from the assumption that the existing system of world order is unsatisfactory; that only a new configuration of global forces can yield peace and security. Before proceeding to consider alternative systems, however, it will be instructive to consider the dynamics of power management or war prevention *in the present system*. The following chapter offers such a consideration. In effect it is a look at the internal logic of the system we seek to transform or supplant.

THE STATE OF NATIONS AS STATE OF NATURE

> *The officer, surrounded by these noises, was moved and a little embarrassed. He turned away to give them time to pull themselves together; and waited, allowing his eyes to rest on the trim cruiser in the distance.*

> William Golding, *Lord of the Flies*

At the conclusion of William Golding's nightmarish novel, *Lord of the Flies*, there is an ironic twist that suggests a basic fact about world politics. Although the naval rescue puts an end to a period of unimagined savagery between groups of schoolboys left stranded on an island, the global society to which they are returned bears close resemblance to their former condition. The state of nations is the state of nature. Like boys abandoned on an island, the actors in world politics coexist in a condition of natural liberty. There is no common power, no common authority to keep them in awe. Each actor is a law unto itself. Hence, it is upon "the trim cruiser in the distance" (i.e., military force) that all actors must ultimately rely for satisfaction of wants.

ON THE HISTORY OF THE STATE OF NATIONS

How did this condition develop? What are the origins of the anarchic character of world politics? To answer this question we must turn back the pages of history to that great peace settlement which ended the Thirty Years' War and consecrated the emergence of the modern state system—the Peace of Westphalia.

The Thirty Years' War was the last of the religious wars sparked by the Reformation. Its cessation signalled the destruction of the medieval Holy Roman Empire and the creation of a new global system. After 1648, force and sovereign authority were no longer concentrated in the hands of the Hapsburg emperor, but were decentralized among the imperial princes. Instead of the unity of the Christian world, the Peace of Westphalia offered a system of independent states.

But independence does not imply equality of strength! While the new states were all perfectly equal in law, their capacities for action on the world stage varied considerably. The consequence of this discrepancy between sovereign equality and power was a pattern of world politics that persists through the present day: international order maintained not "from above" by some overarching central authority, but "horizontally" from other actors. The sustaining attributes of this pattern may be summarized in terms of credible deterrence postures, viable alliances, and—if need be—measured acts of retaliation.

As mechanisms for the management of power, these attributes received express recognition in 1713 in the treaty of peace at Utrecht. By the terms of this treaty, no provision was made for the establishment of system-wide institutions, and the doctrine of a balance of power (see Part I) was formally established between states. In the text of the treaty between Great Britain and Spain, one of the foremost objects is stated to be "the establishment of a peace, for Christendom, by a just equilibrium of power."

At the Congress of Vienna in 1815, the principle of a power balance which had achieved formal recognition at Utrecht more than one hundred years before was effectively sustained. No iconoclastic reaction to the decentralized world system manifested itself. Indeed, no drastic revision of the international system was even contemplated. The resultant Concert system did not produce a transnational institution politically superior to the system's constituent state units. The later Hague system also pointed to changes *within* the global system. It did not address itself to the basic transformation of the system itself.

After World War I, the feeling was widespread that the balance of power had failed. Understandably, a cry went up for a "community of power" to replace the "balance of power." The Covenant of the League of Nations became the institutionalized form of this "community of power." Nevertheless, the sovereignty-centered idea of consent that had served as the basis of authority since Westphalia continued to operate, and the management of power was still an operation to be undertaken by individual states, acting alone or in groups. The global sphere was not yet to lose its distinctive character.

After the total collapse of world peace that arrived in the wake of World War II, the diplomats once again resolved to achieve an improved system for managing power. To this end, a revised version of the League was established. Like the League, the creation of the United Nations represented a new effort to manage power through international organization. The decentralized distribution of force and sovereign authority was preserved, and with it the framework of the state system bequeathed at the Peace of Westphalia. As each member remains fully sovereign, the United Nations has no competence in matters within the domestic jurisdiction of a given state. Article 2(7) provides the following:

> Nothing contained in the present Charter shall authorize the United Nations to intervene in matters which are essentially within the domestic jurisdiction of any state or shall require the Members to submit such matters to settlement under the present Charter . . . .

Nevertheless, although the organization is founded upon "sovereign equality," the United Nations goes much farther than its major predecessor *in principle.* The Charter goes beyond the Covenant in formalizing the replacement of self-help conceptions of security with ones which call for centralized determination and application of sanctions. Yet, this greater degree of centralization has in no way equipped the United Nations with sanctions against delinquencies generally or aggressive wars in particular. Like the

League, the United Nations has left the basic contours of the global system unimpaired. Individual states remain in possession of force and sovereign authority, and the management of power continues to rest upon foundations of "deadly logic."

THE LOGIC OF DETERRENCE

What are these foundations? In the first place, they are foundations of *fear*. Assuming that actors (1) always value self-preservation more than any other preference or combination of preferences, and (2) always choose rationally between alternative courses of action,[1] it follows that they will always refrain from initiating the use of force against other actors who are believed to possess a *credible deterrence posture*. Hence, the use of force between actors may be limited by "deadly logic" to the extent to which actors can convince other actors that they possess the ability and the resolve to deliver an annihilating (or unacceptably destructive) response.

What are the ingredients of such communication? First, in terms of *ability* there are two essential components: *payload* and *delivery system*. It must be successfully communicated to the potential user of force that the firepower and the means of delivering that firepower are capable of wreaking unacceptable levels of destruction *after a first-strike attack*. This means that retaliatory forces must appear sufficiently *invulnerable* and sufficiently elusive to *penetrate* the would-be attacker's active defenses. It need *not* be communicated to the potential user of force that such firepower and/or the means of delivery are *superior* to his own. The capacity to deter need not be as great as the capacity to win. In the present nuclear age in particular, an admittedly inferior store of firepower and delivery systems may have great potential deterrence value.

The second ingredient of communication is one of *willingness* or *resolve*. How may actors convince potential antagonists who contemplate the use of force that they possess the resolve to deliver an unacceptably destructive response? The answer to this question lies in the demonstrated strength of the commitment to carry out the threat. Actors must often demonstrate that escape from the commitment to act is extremely difficult if not physically impossible. Thus the stationing of American troops in Europe as a "trip wire" served to convince the Russians that war in Europe would necessarily involve the United States. The United States sought to enhance the credibility of its threat by getting itself committed to its fulfillment.

It should not be supposed from the language used here that credible threats of deterrence date back only as far as the first guns or bombs (gunpowder was first used militarily during the fourteenth century). A glimpse at Herodotus, for example, provides an idea of what probably constituted unacceptable destruction in ancient times. According to the Greek historian, when the Persians instructed their ambassadors to resort to threats, their import was hardly more pleasing than modern threats of nuclear destruction: "Tell them . . . that when they are beaten (in ancient times, victory *was* a requirement of unacceptable damage) they will be sold as slaves, their boys will be made eunuchs, their girls carried off to Bactria, and their land confiscated." Such threats were always coupled with the promise of *no* disagreeable action in return for compliance.[2]

These, then, are the basic features of "deadly logic," the system of security through fear upon which we depend. Needless to say, it is a system which provides little cause for complacency. The ingredients of a credible deterrence posture are extraordinarily complex. It is no mean task for actors to successfully communicate both the ability and the resolve to unleash unacceptably damaging retaliation.

Moreover, the crucial assumption of rationality itself raises many questions. Clearly, the actual behavior of actors cannot always be expected to conform to a given set of rules. As the Italian dramatist Luigi Pirandello reminds us in Act II of *Henry IV*, constructions which rest upon the foundations of logic necessarily crumble before madness,[3] and madness is not unknown in world politics. Even if we are able to accept the assumption of rationality, erroneous information may be used in the calculations of actors. Rationality refers only to the *intention* of maximizing specified values or utilities. It need not imply that only "correct" information is used in the decisional calculus.[4] Similarly, rational actors may make errors in calculation which lead to radical instability.

Finally, let us not forget the danger of war by mechanical accident. However rational, well informed, and skilled in techniques of calculation, actors are still subject to the threat of enormous destruction via mechanical failure or breakdown. All things considered, the present system of global security can certainly stand alteration. Alternative systems must be explored.

COLLECTIVE DEFENSE AND DETERRENCE

The foregoing discussion has described only the most basic contours of our global "threat system." In fact, credible deterrence postures cannot always be achieved single-handedly. As a result, the use of *alliances* or collective defense arrangements has been of enormous importance throughout history. Actors who are themselves unable to demonstrate such postures look to alliance agreements with other actors as a way of achieving the desired image in the world system.

Belief in the alliance as a viable technique of projecting the image of a credible deterrence posture is widespread in the literature of international relations theory. Indeed, it has even been suggested that membership in an alliance is *always* essential to the maintenance of a credible image in terms of deterrence; that no *single* actor, however "powerful," can always successfully persuade other actors that it possesses the ability and the resolve to deliver an unacceptably destructive response. To Lord Bolingbroke, for example, who had been intimately involved in the delicate negotiations leading to the Peace of Utrecht in 1714, "occasional union, by alliances with other states ... is so necessary to all the nations on the continent, that even the most powerful cannot subsist without it . . . ."[5]

Somewhat less convinced than Bolingbroke that membership in an alliance is always necessary to an image of credible deterrence, Emmerich de Vattel, the eighteenth-century Swiss theorist of natural law, is still optimistic about alliances insofar as they may assist the *lesser* powers. In this respect, his position more closely resembles that of British statesman Robert Walpole, who refers to alliances as a means by which "the weak are defended against the strong."[6] Thus, we have Vattel's statement that "force of arms is not the only expedient by which we may guard against a formidable power. There are other means, of a gentler nature, and which are at all times lawful. The most effectual is a confederacy of the less powerful sovereigns, who, by this coalition of strength, become able to hold the balance against that potentate whose power excites their alarms. Let them be firm and faithful in their alliance; and their union will prove the safety of each."[7]

Such optimistic pronouncements notwithstanding, however, it is by no means self-evident that alliances always succeed in making individual members appear to other actors as possessors of a credible deterrence posture. Indeed, the history of international political theorizing is replete with skeptical utterances concerning the "proven" capacity of alliances to provide an image of credible deterrence not otherwise attainable. Most often, the key element of such skepticism lies in what is believed to be the demonstrated unreliability of actors when called upon to act in a fashion thought to be contrary to their own judgments of self-interest.

Perhaps one of the earliest and best-known doubters of alliance reliability was Sir Thomas More. Describing the foreign policy of his Utopia, More explains why the Utopians do not enter into alliances:

> Treaties, which all other nations so often conclude among themselves, break, and renew, they (the Utopians) never make with any nation. "What is the use of a treaty," they ask, "as though nature of herself did not sufficiently bind one man to another? If a person does not regard nature, do you suppose he will care anything about words?" They are led to this opinion chiefly because in those parts of the world treaties and alliances between kings are not observed with much good faith.[8]

Not unlike More in his assessment of alliance reliability is Francis Bacon. Linking security to power position, this great thinker of the seventeenth-century Age of Reason has serious reservations about the efficacy of alliances in the achievement of a favorable power position. No matter how solemn or sanctimonious the oaths which confirm treaties of alliance, such treaties are little to be depended upon as "they seem used rather for decorum, reputation, and ceremony, than for fidelity, security, and effectuating."[9]

Similarly, the eighteenth-century Whig philosopher of conservatism Edmund Burke has stated that in the interaction between nations, "we are apt to rely too much on the instrumental part. We lay too much weight upon the formality of treaties and compacts."[10] Thomas Paine, too, has commented upon the flagrant disregard for treaties of alliance which characterizes the behavior of states:

> Perhaps there is not a greater instance of the folly of calculating upon events than are to be found in the treaties of alliance. As soon as they have answered the immediate purpose of either of the parties they are but little regarded. Pretences afterwards are never wanting to explain them away, nor reasons to render them abortive. And if half the money which nations lavish on speculative alliances were reserved for their own immediate purpose, whenever the occasion shall arrive, it would be more productively and advantageously employed.[11]

Finally, let us consider the opinion of Alexander Hamilton:

> There is nothing absurd or impracticable in the idea of a league or alliance between independent nations . . . . With a view to establishing

167

the equilibrium of power and the peace of that part of the world, all the resources of negotiations were exhausted, and triple and quadruple alliances were formed; but they were scarcely formed before they were broken, giving an instructive but afflicting lesson to mankind, how little dependence is to be placed on treaties which have no other sanction than the obligations of good faith, and which oppose general considerations of peace and justice to the impulse of any immediate interest or passion.[12]

In the close of Hamilton's argument we have the crux of the case for alliance unreliability. Being axiomatic that actors always act in a self-interested manner, it follows that actors will on occasion fail to honor their alliance obligations. In terms of John Locke's principle of the supremacy of rights, actors feel no obligation to honor treaty commitments once the inducement of expected benefits has been replaced by the expectation of injury or loss. Actors therefore deem Frederick the Great's well-known question concerning violation of treaties ("Must the people perish, or must the Prince violate a Treaty?")[13] unworthy of serious or extended consideration.

Treaties of alliance, then, are obeyed where obedience is judged to be most desirable and disobeyed where disobedience is deemed to be most desirable. Whether treaties of alliance are reliable or unreliable depends upon the extent to which adherence to their stipulated conditions conforms to an actor's judgment of self-interest. Taken by themselves, formal treaty commitments are not enough to ensure compliance. It must also be that the interests of the partners are in close conformity with one another; indeed, that they are inextricably intertwined. In this regard, Frederick the Great is surely guilty of understatement when he postulates as "a known truth in politics" that "the most natural and consequently the best allies are those who have common interests. . . ."[14] Men, says Edmund Burke, are tied to one another not by papers and seals, but "by resemblances, by conformities, by sympathies. It is with nations as with individuals."[15] Stronger yet is the language of Francis Bacon: "There is . . . one true and proper confirmation of faith . . . Necessity; or the danger of the State, and the securing of advantage."[16]

Thus, actors can look forward to promised support from alliance partners only when the latter deem such support to be in their own interests. This fact concerning the precarious status of alliance support must be borne in mind above all others when we consider whether or not membership in an alliance provides the capacity for making individual member actors appear to other actors as possessors of a credible deterrence posture. We recall that where an actor enters into an alliance as a means of making other actors believe that it possesses a credible deterrence posture, its success will be largely contingent upon the extent to which it can convince potential aggressors that it is in the interests of its alliance partners to deliver an unacceptably destructive response on its behalf.

But if alliances are of questionable value in enabling actors to project the image of a credible deterrence posture, what of the oft-quoted advice that security-seeking actors may at least look to treaties of alliance as a means of reducing the number of their potential enemies? Is it not true that by entering into an increasing number of alliance agreements, actors necessarily decrease their number of potential enemies? Even if an actor fails to honor its treaty obligations by actively intervening on behalf of its alliance partner, has the partner not at least succeeded in *neutralizing* that actor? The position has been aptly summarized by Frederick the Great, perhaps the best example of the enlightened despot of the eighteenth century:

> It is often said—and often repeated without much reflection—that treaties are useless because they are never observed in all points, and that the present age is no more scrupulous in keeping faith than any other. I answer that although many examples may be produced, ancient, modern, and some very recent of princes who have not fulfilled all their engagements, yet it is always prudent and necessary to make alliances, for your allies otherwise will be so many enemies, and if they refuse to send you supplies when you need them, you may at least expect them to observe an exact neutrality.[17]

The problem with Frederick's analysis, however, is that it is based on the mistaken assumption that actors will never act *against* their alliance partners. While he recognizes that the self-interest assumption necessarily implies that actors will at times fail to honor their alliance commitments, Frederick fails to recognize as a corollary of this same assumption that actors may at times take an active position *against* their allies. If formal treaty commitments are insufficient to ensure compliance with duly recorded obligations, they are also insufficient to ensure a position of passive friendship or neutrality. It is fallacious, therefore, to conclude with Frederick that actors may, at the very least, expect the observance of "an exact neutrality" on the part of their alliance partners. Among the many known historical instances which lend empirical support to this point is the situation which came to prevail between Corinth and Athens during the

Peloponnesian War. According to Thucydides, despite a treaty of alliance in force between them, "a situation inevitably came about where Corinthians and Athenians were openly fighting with each other."[18]

COLLECTIVE SECURITY AND DETERRENCE

Another collaborative arrangement for managing power within the decentralized framework of the extant world system is collective security. Unlike alliances, which are characterized by the advance identification of friend and (usually) of foe, collective security arrangements rest upon a presumption of impartiality and flexibility until an aggressor has been identified. Such arrangements stipulate means for settling disputes among *all members of the system* while alliance agreements are concerned only with opposing threats which originate from *outside the alliance*. The collective security agreement, then, is concerned with the general limitation of inter-actor violence *within* the system while the alliance agreement is concerned with offering a collective response to actors external to that agreement.[19] Summing up, Robert Osgood correctly suggests that the principal difference between an alliance and a collective security agreement is that

> such an agreement obligates its members to abstain from recourse to violence against one another and to participate collectively in suppressing the unlawful use of force by any member. It may also obligate its members to resist aggression by a non-member against any of them, but what distinguishes it from a mere collective defense agreement is that it presupposes a general interest on the part of all its members in opposing aggression by any of them and entails procedures for the peaceful settlement of disputes among the members.[20]

Such differences aside, however, it is clear that collective security arrangements suffer the very same deficiencies as treaties of alliance insofar as the management of power is concerned. While such arrangements substitute the principle of "all for all" for the notion of "some for some," the obligations incurred still derive only from an actor's consent. What an actor has conceded on the basis of such obligations an actor may, if it chooses, revoke.[21] There is, then, no reason to suppose that actors will be any more reliable in honoring the obligations which derive from commitments to collective security than they will be about obligations stemming from commitments to *selective* security.[22]

As in the case of treaties of alliance, the reliability of collective security arrangements in a decentralized world system will depend upon the extent to which adherence to their requirements corresponds to particular judgments of self-interest.

COLLECTIVE DEFENSE AND COLLECTIVE SECURITY

There are various factors to be considered which affect an actor's determination of whether or not the honoring of alliance or collective security agreements conforms to its own judgment of self-interest. We may briefly consider the alternative courses of collaboration as factors *themselves*. That is, let us consider how the reliability of each is affected by the other insofar as they coexist within the same system.

At first glance, it may appear that the simultaneous presence of two different types of collaborative arrangement for managing power in the world system is more propitious for deterrence than the presence of one alone. This is because the likelihood of particular actors assisting other actors in projecting an image of credible deterrence may look greater where two separate and distinguishable frameworks for such assistance exist side by side. As the number of opportunities for mutual identification of self-interest increases, it is argued, so does the potential for augmenting individual deterrence capabilities.

On closer examination, however, we reach a very different set of conclusions. Despite the widely held idea that collective defense and collective security can only *supplement* one another as arrangements for limiting the use of force between actors, it is clear that any harmony between the two types of arrangement may be ended whenever a situation of contradictory commitments develops. In such an event, the reliability of one particular arrangement may be decisively *undermined* because of the presence of the other. For example, an actor may be faced with a choice in which satisfying the requirements of a collective security arrangement means defaulting on an alliance agreement or vice-versa. Whatever the choice made, one actor or another in the system may suffer in terms of the credibility of its deterrence posture because of the dual presence of arrangements for collective defense and collective security. As Arnold Wolfers has suggested, the cases in which the two alternative forms of collaboration are complementary and helpful to each other "are largely a matter of happy coincidence."[23]

LEGAL ORDER IN THE STATE OF NATIONS

Finally, let us consider the distinctive character of *law* in the extant system of world politics. Unlike law in most modern domestic systems, international law functions within a system that lacks government. As the actors in world politics coexist without an authority above them, there can be no hierarchy of institutions and officials to apply rules in a relationship of superordination and subordination. Hence, international law is a law of *coordination*. Otherwise stated, the global system is characterized by a "horizontal" rather than "vertical" legal order. As Richard A. Falk has pointed out, the analytic distinction between horizontal and vertical legal orders serves to classify legal systems according to the degree of centralized authority and force.[24]

Let us consider this distinction in greater detail by comparing the two forms of legal order in terms of four basic dimensions: (1) *sources* (where legal norms are created); (2) *agents of discovery* (where delinquent behavior is determined); (3) *agents of judgment* (where the character of sanctions is determined); and (4) *agents of application* (where sanctions are applied).

In the absence of the kinds of specialized institutions which characterize vertical legal systems, the *sources* of international legal norms cannot be legislatures and courts. Pursuant to Article 38 of the Statute of the International Court of Justice, such sources include international conventions or treaties, international custom, the general principles of law recognized by civilized nations, and (subject to the provisions of Article 59 of the Statute which states that the decision of the court has no binding force except between parties and in respect of that particular case) judicial decisions and the teachings of the most highly qualified publicists.

With respect to *agents of discovery*, the determination of delinquent behavior in vertical legal systems is centralized in specific officials and institutions, namely police and courts. In the international legal order, however, such determinations are decentralized. That is, they are left up to the individual actors. There exists no centralized determination of delinquent behavior.

As to the third basic dimension, *agents of judgment*, the determination of what threatened evil or punishment ought to be applied is typically centralized in courts under domestic or vertical law. In the international legal order, however, such decisions are left up to individual actors.

Finally, the *agents of application* in vertical systems are basically courts and penal institutions while in the international

172

legal order they are the actors themselves. Just as in primitive domestic legal systems, the execution of sanctions is undertaken by the offended actor or its allies rather than by agents of specially established central institutions. Security is maintained by self-help.

Does all of this imply that international law is not *really* law? Clearly, there is no "correct" answer to this question. The answer depends entirely upon one's particular definition of law. Where law is tied definitionally to a social system *with* government, international relations are necessarily *excluded* from the realm of law. This is the position of the nineteenth-century legal theorist John Austin and the seventeenth-century philosopher Thomas Hobbes. For Austin, international law is not "true" law because there exists no world sovereign to enforce it. What we call international law Austin describes only as "positive morality." *Real* law always requires a central sovereign whose commands are supported by force. Similarly, Hobbes argues that law is definitionally incompatible with a condition of natural liberty, either among individual men or among the actors in world politics. In the state of nature "the notions of right and wrong, justice and injustice, have no place. Where there is no common power, there is no law . . . ."

Alternatively, where law is more broadly defined, one might argue that international law is "really" law. So long as it is defined in terms of particular rules and procedures which need not necessarily be tied to government or hierarchic relationships among actors, the global order may be properly described as a legal one. Most modern theorists of international law (e.g., Kelson, McDougal, Falk, Fisher) favor this broader form of conceptualization.[25] As a result, these writers are perfectly willing to recognize that lawful relationships may exist horizontally as well as vertically or hierarchically. For them, the international order *is* a legal order.

So much for the "problem" of international law as law. What really ought to concern us about the distinctive quality of international law is not its structural dissimilarity to domestic law per se, but rather the implications of its uniqueness for world order. On this issue there are essentially three major positions. The first of these is a decidedly pessimistic one. Known variously as "cynicism" or "realism," depending upon the writer's own preferences and perceptions, this position argues that in a world system that lacks government, international law is bound to be inadequate in the regulation of coercion and violence among states. Proponents of realism reflect a very basic concern for the

173

social-political context of international law. According to Myres S. McDougal and Florentino P. Feliciano, this attitude,

> expressed in the accents of ultra-sophistication and disenchantment, affirms that man's destructive impulses and instruments of violence have escaped all bounds and that little or nothing can be done by law either to control international coercion or to minimize the destruction of values once violence erupts.[26]

Observable at the opposite pole are proponents of "utopianism" or "idealism," a position characterized by an excess of faith in the viability of legal management. Those who identify with this outlook tend to appraise the efficacy of legal rules apart from their political context. In so doing, they neglect to realize that the importance of international law in the management of world power is inextricably tied up with a variety of other variables. It does not function autonomously in the pursuit of peace. According to McDougal and Feliciano, the utopian attitude,

> manifested in continuing high deference to certain inherited terms of art, affirms an excess of faith in technical concepts and rules, divorced from contexts and procedures, as determinants of decision and exhibits much too little concern for the clarification of policies in detailed contexts and for the search for new principles and procedures.[27]

The third position lies somewhere in between these polar positions. Proponents of this position recognize law as a more or less dependent variable in explaining world order; yet they do not regard this fact as a sweeping denial of its effectiveness. While acknowledging the dominant role of power in world politics, they do not draw the conclusion that law is entirely unimportant. Indeed, representatives of this "middle" position might even understand law as a particular form of power itself.

In any event, as a vehicle of restraint and stability, international law is not without very serious problems. And it is probably in more trouble today than at any previous time in its history. To mention just one source of difficulty, the growing number of modernizing or revolutionary non-Western actors with divergent cultural backgrounds has heightened global mistrust and inhibited opportunities for global legal cooperation. International law itself is often regarded by these actors as a reactionary instrument of oppression designed to keep them in a continuing condition of subservience. Moreover, the fear on the part of status-quo actors concerning revolutionary acts of subversion and infiltration sometimes leads *them* to undermine legal norms and procedures. The result is an attack on international law on two fronts, by the revolutionary or modernizing actors and by status-quo actors in response to them. It is a condition of considerable ironic proportions.

THE CONTEMPORARY INSTITUTIONALIZATION OF INTERNATIONAL LAW

Although the horizontal system of international law which we recognize today is basically unchanged from its early, post-Westphalian form, there have been some major attempts at institutionalization. Even though state actors still coexist within a legal system that lacks government, this system has undergone some significant structural changes. These changes may affect the ability of international law to cope with an increasing variety of urgent planetary dangers.

At the present time, the single most important instance of institutionalization is the United Nations. While its creation did not signal the beginnings of international government or "vertical" law, it did indicate the addition of an important institution to the prevailing "horizontal" pattern. Article 13 of the Charter instructs the General Assembly to "initiate studies and make recommendations for the purpose of . . . encouraging the progressive development of international law and its codification." Pursuant to this article, the General Assembly created the International Law Commission to assist in its task.

The practice of the political bodies of the United Nations is also concerned with the development of international law. As a result, the body of international law concerning such matters as statehood, domestic jurisdiction, recognition, and the use of force is continually evolving. Taken as a whole, such evolution reflects an important new source of *customary* international law. This is the case even though the Charter is itself a *treaty*, a fact giving rise to the argument that any new rules of international law which derive from United Nations activities are attributable to a treaty as source.

Compared to its major predecessor, the United Nations Charter goes much further than the Covenant of the League of Nations in formalizing the replacement of self-help with the centralized determination and application of sanctions. While League procedures regarding the application of enforcement measures were fully decentralized, the Charter has centralized decisions concerning threats to peace and the application of enforcement measures.

This greater centralization has not, however, equipped the United Nations with sanctions in the strict sense. After all, punitive action against a permanent member of the Security Council is effectively ruled out. This is the case because such action is subject to the veto of that member. Without its consent, there can be no punitive action. This means that to the extent that the United Nations is assigned a preeminent role in the international legal order, there are really *two* such orders: one that applies to the powers which comprise the permanent membership of the Security Council and one that applies to the rest of the system. For all intents and purposes, such a system renders law coincident with power and the United Nations organization an institutional reflection of the prevailing pattern of influence.

Indeed, the greater centralization of decisional authority in the United Nations is not particularly crucial to the operation of the "second" international legal order. Even for this overwhelming majority of the earth's states and peoples, there is nothing about the United Nations that suggests a genuine removal of the state of nations from the state of nature. This is the case not only *in fact* (i.e., in terms of the actual life history and performance of the organization) but also *in principle* (i.e., in terms of the instrument of incorporation). The decentralized system of international law is strongly reaffirmed in Article 2 of the Charter, which states that the organization rests upon the "sovereign equality" of its membership and recognizes that certain matters "are essentially within the domestic jurisdiction of any state. . . ."

This is not to mention that some states are not even members of the United Nations and even *less concerned* with its authority and influence. While Article 2.6 of the Charter states that "The Organization shall ensure that States which are not members of the United Nations act in accordance with these principles so far as may be necessary for the maintenance of international peace and security," this is not an instance of objective lawmaking. While this clause charges members to carry out important decisions, even against nonmembers, there is no obligation on the part of nonmembers to submit. The clause does not make law for them.

Summing up our discussion, it should not be forgotten that the role of law must also be examined from the standpoint of *different kinds of global systems*. Even the idealist or utopian thinker must realize that the character of world political relationships is constantly changing, and that the contextual background of world law is changing as well. Consequently, even satisfaction with the current status of world law is no reason for complacency. The present configuration of world politics represents only one case in an infinite variety of possible configurations, and legal theorists must learn to recognize the implications of system change for legal order. This will require the imaginative conceptualization of alternative world systems that can be examined from the standpoint of international law as well as the general dynamics of power management. Appropriate "guidelines" for such conceptualization will be discussed in the following chapters.

NOTES

1. Actors behave *rationally* when (1) they evaluate alternatives on the basis of their preferences among them; (2) they order these preferences in consistent and transitive fashion; and (3) they always choose the preferred alternative. Moreover, where risky situations are involved, rational actors make selections in terms of expected-gain calculations. That is, in order to reach a decision, actors determine the product of subjective utility and subjective probability for each of the acts under consideration and compare the products. These products represent the expected gain for these acts.

2. See Herodotus, *The Histories*, Aubrey de Selincourt, trans. (Baltimore: Penguin, 1954), p. 362.

3. *Henry IV:* Do you know what it means to find yourselves face to face with a madman—with one who shakes the foundations of all you have built up in yourselves, your logic, the logic of all your constructions? Madmen, lucky folk, construct without logic, or rather with a logic that flies like a feather.

4. On this point, see Phillip Green, *Deadly Logic: The Theory of Nuclear Deterrence* (Columbus: Ohio State University Press, 1966), p. 157.

5. See "Remarks on the History of England," *The Works of Lord Bolingbroke* (4 vols.; London: Cass & Co., 1844, reprinted 1967), vol. I, p. 386.

6. Hansard, *Parliamentary History*, XII, pp. 168-169, cited in Edward Vose Gulick, *Europe's Classical Balance of Power* (Ithaca, N.Y.: Cornell University Press, 1955), p. 61.

7. Emmerich de Vattel, *The Law of Nations*, Book III, Chapter III, sec. 46, Joseph Chitty, ed. (Philadelphia: T. & J. W. Johnson, 1861), pp. 310-311.

8. Sir Thomas More, *Utopia*, Book II, Edward Surtz, S. J., ed. (New Haven: Yale University Press, 1964), p. 116.

9. Francis Bacon, "The Wisdom of the Ancients," in A. Spiers, ed., *Bacon's Essays and Wisdom of the Ancients* (Boston: Little, Brown, 1884), p. 331.

10. Edmund Burke, "Three Letters to a Member of Parliament on the Proposals for Peace with the Regicide Directory of France," Letter I, in *The Works of the Right Honorable Edmund Burke* (5th ed., 12 vols.; Boston: Little, Brown, 1877), Vol. V, p. 317.

11. Thomas Paine, "Prospects on the Rubicon," in Moncure Daniel Conway, ed., *The Writings of Thomas Paine* (New York and London: G. P. Putnam's Sons, 1906), Vol. 2, p. 196.

12. *The Federalist*, No. 15.

13. See "The History of My Own Times," in Jay Luvass, ed., *Frederick the Great on the Art of War* (New York: Free Press, 1966), p. 38.

14. See "An Essay on Forms of Government and on the Duties of Sovereigns," in Luvass, ed., *Frederick the Great on the Art of War*, p. 37.

15. See "Three Letters to a Member of Parliament on the Proposals for Peace with the Regicide Directory of France," Letter I, in *The Works of the Right Honorable Edmund Burke*, Vol. V, p. 317.

16. See "The Wisdom of the Ancients," in Spiers, ed., *Bacon's Essays and Wisdom of the Ancients*, p. 332.

17. See *Anti-Machiavel* (1740), cited in Luvass, ed., *Frederick the Great on the Art of War*, p. 37.

18. See Rex Warner, trans., *The Peloponnesian War*, Book I, Chapter 4 (Baltimore: Penguin, 1954), p. 40.

19. See Wolfram F. Hanrieder, "International Organizations and International Systems," in Richard A. Falk and Wolfram F. Hanrieder, eds., *International Law and Organization* (Philadelphia: Lippincott, 1968), p. 279.

20. Robert E. Osgood, *Alliances and American Foreign Policy* (Baltimore: Johns Hopkins University Press, 1968), pp. 17-18.

21. See F. H. Hinsley, *Power and the Pursuit of Peace* (Cambridge: Cambridge University Press, 1963), p. 319.

22. The use of the term "selective security" to denote an alliance system is attributable to Inis L. Claude, Jr., *Swords Into Plowshares* (New York: Random House, 1959), p. 275.

23. See Arnold Wolfers, "Collective Defense versus Collective Security," *Discord and Collaboration* (Baltimore: Johns Hopkins University Press, 1962), p. 183.

24. See Richard A. Falk, *Legal Order in a Violent World* (Princeton, N.J.: Princeton University Press, 1968), p. 52.

25. While these four theorists share a commitment to a "broad" definition of law, this is not to imply that they are in agreement on the subject generally. There are, for example, some notable differences between Hans Kelsen and Myres McDougal concerning the study of international law.

26. Myres S. McDougal and Florentino P. Feliciano, *Law and Minimum World Public Order* (New Haven: Yale University Press, 1961), p. 2.

27. *Ibid.*

Chapter 9
Actors

INTRODUCTION

Studying about world order and war avoidance means studying about alternative world systems. Steeped in a long and distinguished tradition, such study recognizes that the existing world system is only one case in an infinite variety of possible world systems. Hence, guided by an overarching commitment to peace, the student must define his task in terms of the imaginative conceptualization of different global futures.

None of this is to be regretted! From the time of the pre-Socratic Greek philosopher, Heracleitus of Ephesus, men have understood time as universal flow, as the continual newness of all things. So long as one recognizes time as a process of deterioration and renewal, the world appears in a continuing state of transformation. It is to understand this state and to render it subject to purposeful control that the world order scholar must dedicate himself. He must define his subject in terms of the development and transformation of world systems.

In so doing, the selection of alternative global configurations must be informed by considerations beyond mere inventiveness. While an awareness of future possibilities is certainly desirable, it must also be coupled with a well-reasoned investigation of an hypothesis. Inquiry must begin with suggested explanations, and "models" must be selected accordingly. Whatever models or descriptions of alternative world futures are chosen for investigation, they must be constructed so as to permit the examination of particular connections that are expected to obtain between precisely defined variables. Known as hypotheses, these "connections" guide the search for *theoretic order* among the facts of *world order*. The former is necessarily antecedent to the latter. In those exercises where no hypothesis is offered to tutor the selection of interesting models, there is no reason to favor the derived conclusions over any others that might be advanced. In such cases the mode of "explanation" is backward.

This is because an hypothesis is a guide. It does not emerge spontaneously as inquiry is concluded; rather, it functions throughout the entire process, integrating and organizing sets of empirical findings into a single coherent system. Without a tentative answer in the form of an hypothesis, there exists no criterion in terms of which the considered empirical facts may be judged logically relevant or irrelevant.

Different hypotheses tutor the description of world system models in terms of different dimensions. Our concern in these remaining chapters of Part II will be with hypotheses that lead to the examination of systems conceptualized along (1) an *actor* dimension, (2) a *process* dimension, (3) a *contextual* dimension, and (4) a *structural* dimension.[1] This examination will treat only the war-avoidance features of the systems.

In this chapter, therefore, we will consider the war-avoidance qualities of several systems[2] described in terms of *actors*. These systems are (1) systems that are homogeneous as to a particular type of state government; (2) systems that are homogeneous *or* heterogeneous as to *any* particular type of state government; (3) systems comprised of all state actors or systems of mixed actors; (4) systems in which the size and number of actors vary; (5) systems comprised of status-quo or revolutionary-modernizing actors; and (6) systems in which actors have undergone various forms of "behavioral" transformation. By developing a wide variety of interesting models that derive from hypotheses emphasizing actor variables, chapter nine offers the student a special measure of creative promise for investigating alternative world futures.

1. HYPOTHESES LINKING WAR AVOIDANCE TO WORLD SYSTEMS THAT ARE HOMOGENEOUS AS TO A PARTICULAR TYPE OF STATE GOVERNMENT

Perhaps the best known of these hypotheses is found in the pages of Immanuel Kant's *Perpetual Peace*. Resembling the earlier project of Saint-Pierre (*Projet de paix perpetuelle*), Kant's proposal of 1795 rests on the hypothesis that viable foundations for world peace require the creation of republican institutions in every state. What is needed, says Kant, is a world system that is uniformly republican as to type of government.

Upon what form of reasoning does this claim for republican constitutions rest? According to Kant:

> If (as is inevitable in this form of constitution) the sanction of the citizens is necessary to decide whether there shall be war or not, nothing is more natural than that they would think long before beginning such a terrible game, since they would have to call down on themselves all the horrors of war. . . .whereas in a constitution in which the subject is not a citizen, i.e., one which is not republican, war is the least considerable matter in the world, because the Sovereign is not a member in the State, but its owner.[3]

True to that spirit of Enlightenment which rests upon the freedom to make use of one's reason in all matters, Kant freely assumes that by letting men decide for themselves whether or not they wish to make war, all such conflict will cease. Newly empowered to make use of their reason, citizens will certainly and immediately recognize the avoidance of war to be in their own interest. This requirement of homogeneity as to republicanism found in Kant's First Definitive Article is explicitly embodied in Article IV, Section 4 of the Constitution of the United States, which guarantees to every state a republican form of government. A similar clause was contained in the Covenant of the League of Nations, but to no meaningful effect.

What might we say about Kant's argument? In the first place, it should be recognized that even though it is internally consistent, i.e., the conclusion is necessarily implied by the premises, the premises themselves may be subject to doubt:[4]

> *Major Premise:* If granted the right to decide for themselves whether or not the state should engage in warfare, individuals will certainly choose peace.

At first glance, this seems to be an eminently reasonable assumption. Can anyone deny that war is an unhappy interruption of the blessings of peace? What else could have been intended by the strong sense of the tragedy of war that one finds behind the tales of heroism in the ancient Epic? How else may we interpret the tone of such classics as Tolstoy's *War and Peace* or Erich Maria Remarque's *All Quiet on the Western Front*? More recently, can there be any question about the kinds of sentiments that gave rise to *MASH* or *Catch-22*? How else may we characterize the feelings and frustrations of Vietnam?

Such judgments notwithstanding, it might also be noted that a great many human societies have regarded warfare as an established and *enjoyable* social rite. As Michael Howard, the military historian, has pointed out, "In Western Europe until the first part of the seventeenth century, warfare was a way of life for considerable sections of society, its termination was for them a catastrophe, and its prolongation, official or unofficial, was the legitimate objective of every man of spirit." Even in Kant's own century, war was widely accepted as an almost indispensable part of the pattern of society.[5]

Another problem, perhaps, lies in Kant's failure to distinguish between views of war held by those who have experienced it—the mutilated veteran, the crippled child—and those held by general populations. For those who have had no part of warfare, its perceived costs need *not* outweigh its perceived benefits. In terms of the poetry of the Classical Age, the poetry of Pindar: "Sweet is war to him who knows it not, but to those who have made a trial of it, it is a thing of fear."

> *Minor Premise:*   In republican states, individuals have the right to decide for themselves whether or not the state should engage in warfare.

Here we have another assumption that is by no means self-evident. Kant's dismissal of any doubt by definitional fiat (republican systems of government are tied *definitionally* to citizens' rights to make decisions concerning war) is a less than satisfactory measure. Clearly, even if republican *constitutions* do structure the exercise of sovereign authority according to laws requiring citizen consent, there is no reason to suppose that such laws are always obeyed. Witness, for example, the American republic's decision to make war in Southeast Asia vis-a-vis the American Constitution. Major differences often exist between constitutional instruments and behavioral actuality. Such differences cannot be underestimated. Kant did just that. This conclusion is certainly corroborated by an empirical inspection of republican governments. Contrary to Kant's investigations, republican states have not been immune to involvement in warfare.

One last word about this important philosopher: Kant recommends the creation of republican institutions in *all* states. Anything less than a *completely* republican system of actors would presumably result in the victimization of republican actors by nonrepublican ones. Thus, even if we were able to discount our earlier criticisms of Kant's principal assumptions, his recommendation would probably fail on the *feasibility* level. Even if his proposal for a homogeneously republican world order were desirable from the standpoint of war avoidance, it would stand precious little hope of implementation.

Indeed, even if *every* state valued a homogeneously republican world system more than the existing one, it does not necessarily follow that they would *all* agree to "republicanize." This is the case because (1) each actor may feel that the cost of such transformation may exceed the benefits unless every other actor also transforms, and (2) each actor may feel that every other actor feels the same way. Hence, even where a completely republicanized world system is the preferred outcome of every actor, such a system may not be implemented *because each actor will always fear that its own transformation will not be universally paralleled.* This problem is often referred to in terms of "the tragedy of the commons."[6]

2. HYPOTHESES LINKING WAR AVOIDANCE TO WORLD SYSTEMS THAT ARE HOMOGENEOUS OR HETEROGENEOUS AS TO ANY PARTICULAR TYPE OF STATE GOVERNMENT

A. Homogeneous

Logically, several hypotheses may be offered relating war avoidance to world systems composed of any single type of state government. While they have not yet been widely advanced, such hypotheses would reflect the assumption that certain patterns of "behavior" distinguish different types of government from each other. Hence, sovereign-authoritative decision-makers in homogeneous systems will operate with a better understanding of the "rules of the game" than will their counterparts in heterogeneous systems. Freed from the ambiguities of heterogeneous or mixed-government systems, these decision-makers are believed less likely to fall victim to the misperceptions and misunderstandings which cause war. If it is further assumed that certain kinds of homogeneous systems (e.g., homogeneously republican,[7] homogeneously monarchical, etc.) are preferable to others in terms of common bases of action, it follows that such systems are especially worthy of endorsement.

If, however, a great deal of importance is assigned to the role of idiosyncratic or personality factors in the making of foreign policy decisions, these hypotheses lose their persuasiveness. This is the case insofar as such factors invalidate the assumption that different patterns of action are distinctive to different types of

183

government. Indeed, *any* factors which lead to such invalidation will bring about the demise of these hypotheses.

In any event, whatever one's feelings about the connection between war avoidance and homogeneous government systems, the extant system of world politics appears irremediably heterogeneous. In empirical terms, there is little reason to suspect a shift toward a system characterized by one type of state government. A system of mixed-government actors seems likely to continue for some time to come.

B. Heterogeneous

Alternatively, hypotheses may be advanced which relate war avoidance to heterogeneous or mixed-government systems. One such hypothesis represents a reversal of the homogeneity argument: that is, that the greater variety of actor behavior which characterizes mixed-government systems is *favorable* in world order terms. Such reasoning derives from the assumption that ambiguity and uncertainty about "rules of the game" and other actors' decisional calculi inspire caution and restraint in foreign policy formulation.

Another hypothesis may relate war avoidance to systemic heterogeneity in terms of *likelihood of alignment*. Insofar as it is assumed that (1) collective defense or alliance bonds are more easily formed in systems that are homogeneous as to type of actor than in heterogeneous ones, and (2) alliances are "latent war communities"[8] and counterproductive to peace, it follows that mixed-government systems are preferred. If, however, alliances are judged to be a means of augmenting particular deterrence postures and thus *productive* of peaceful behavior, this conclusion must be reversed. This means that homogeneous systems rather than heterogeneous ones should be preferred. This is also the case where it is assumed that *collective security* arrangements are more easily formed and sustained in homogeneous systems and that such arrangements are conducive to peace.[9]

3. HYPOTHESES LINKING WAR AVOIDANCE TO WORLD SYSTEMS COMPOSED OF ALL STATE ACTORS OR SYSTEMS OF MIXED ACTORS

The kinds of hypotheses considered thus far only concern variations in *types of government*. No basic departure from the state as actor has been assumed. This section will consider certain hypotheses which actually vary the *type of actor*.[10]

A. Systems of All State Actors

Several hypotheses link war avoidance to world systems composed entirely of state actors. These hypotheses may stem from a variety of different assumptions, including the balance of power "rules" discussed earlier. For example, in systems composed entirely of state actors there can be no repository of authority *above* the actors. The resultant condition of *formal* equality serves to protect individual actors from termination by administrative decree or authoritative fiat—actions which are likely to inspire conflict and warfare.

Furthermore, in systems composed entirely of state actors power may be more or less effectively managed by methods of "balancing" and the related logic of deterrence. Since all state actors share a primary commitment to self-preservation, all state actors will refrain from undertaking warlike action when such action is judged likely to evoke an unacceptably destructive counterstrike. While there may be some doubt concerning the continuing success of peace through deterrence, the creation of nonstate actors may aggravate the situation further. This is the case insofar as such actors may rank some preferences ahead of security and self-preservation, thereby rendering their decisional calculi insensitive to threats of retaliatory destruction. Historically, of course, the twin notions of "balance" and "deterrence" in the modern state of nations derive from the various consequences of the Treaty of Westphalia in 1648.

B. Systems of Mixed Actors

Now for the other side of the coin. Several hypotheses may also link war avoidance to world systems composed of different types of actors. For example, one such hypothesis derives from the argument that the condition of natural liberty which characterizes the homogeneous state system is an actively unstable one. With all actors coexisting without a controlling authority above them, each actor is impelled to behave selfishly and often violently in order to satisfy wants. The resultant condition is one where right is coincident with power. While *formal* equality in the international state of nature may protect actors from dissolution or dismemberment by superior authority, it may also permit such happenings at the hands of other actors. *Formal* equality has no bearing on *de facto* inequalities of power—inequalities which yield a variety of "horizontal" if not "vertical" hazards (i.e., hazards initiated by other actors rather than central agents of general authority).

In a system of mixed actors, then, the condition of sovereign equality which characterizes the state system is replaced by one of partial inequality. Actors relate to one another not only on the horizontal level of "coordination," but on the vertical level of "subordination" and "superordination" as well. In terms of existing institutions, it is as if the United Nations were suddenly endowed with an appropriate measure of sovereign authority and force; as if it became a *supranational* actor. Such hierarchic relationships, it is often argued, would inhibit global violence by placing limits on the external sovereignty of state actors.

How are these limits imposed? This depends upon the precise character of the mixed-actor system involved. If it is a system of several different kinds of actors engaged in various different relationships of subordination and superordination, then limits on external sovereignty are imposed on each level of actors by each succeeding level. This is possible because each actor is ranked hierarchically in terms of authority. Alternatively, if it is a system comprised only of states and some specially established world government actor, then limits on external sovereignty are imposed solely by appropriate agents of the world government. From the standpoint of war avoidance, either kind of mixed-actor system presumably represents an improvement over a system composed entirely of state actors.

Occasionally, proposals for world government contain an additional stipulation concerning type of constituent state governments. Differences in "type" are felt to bring about parallel differences in efficacy. In this capacity, "type of constituent state government" figures importantly as an *intervening variable*.

Among the twentieth-century proposals for world government discussed in Part I, several have included the requirement that state actors must have republican or democratic institutions (typically, the two terms are used interchangeably). For example, Clarence Streit's *Union Now: A Proposal for an Atlantic Federal Union of the Free* is solidly founded upon the principle of democratic actors. World government, of course, is certainly needed, but such government would have to be comprised of democratic subgroups. According to Streit:

To organize world government soundly we must turn to the peoples most advanced and experienced politically, and this turns us to the democracies. Peoples that accept dictatorships must be classified, politically, among the immature or retarded, or inexperienced, high as they may rank otherwise.[11]

To this point we have assumed that systems of mixed actors are ordered hierarchically, i.e., that such systems are comprised of different types of actors whose interactions conform to certain settled patterns of dominance and submission. Nevertheless, there is no *necessary* reason why mixed actor systems must be so ordered. Indeed, such systems may be characterized by the same condition of formal equality that we ordinarily associate with systems composed entirely of state actors. It follows that systems of mixed actors may also represent a condition of natural liberty at the global level. The state of nations is *always* the state of nature in systems composed exclusively of state actors; it *may* be the state of nature in systems of mixed actors (see chapter eight on state of nature).

Where mixed-actor systems are characterized by "horizontal" relationships between actors, they are susceptible to the same variety of "horizontal" hazards as systems of state actors. Just as in the latter configuration, such systems are comprised of actors whose ultimate locus of "appeal" must be to a viable power position vis-à-vis would-be antagonists. With no controlling power to keep them in awe, these actors must rely upon their own devices for protection and satisfaction of preferences.

Yet, this does not mean that the twin notions of balance and deterrence which serve to manage power in systems of state actors are necessarily operative here. The heterogeneity of actor types may have a deleterious effect on the logic of deterrence. Since different types of actors may assign different values or utilities to self-preservation, the ability of certain actors to protect themselves via threats of retaliatory destruction may be seriously undermined. Moreover, heterogeneity of actor types may occasion various ambiguities and misunderstandings concerning "rules of the game." The consequences of such conditions may be extremely destabilizing.

In short, it appears that systems of mixed actors are favorable in war-avoidance terms only where the actors are organized hierarchically. Where they are organized horizontally, the consequent condition of natural liberty presents even greater difficulties than are encountered in a system of state actors. If the coexistence of state actors without an authority above them represents a precarious arrangement for managing power, the coexistence of different types of actors in natural liberty may be even more precarious.

In empirical terms, however, it appears that the world system may be moving decisively toward this mixed-actor form of natural liberty. Such a development would not be entirely new or uncommon. According to Oran R. Young:

> Interactions among the political units in the Mediterranean arena during the sixth through fourth centuries B.C. and during the fourth and fifth centuries A.D. exhibited the fundamental characteristics of mixed-actor systems. There are, moreover, relevant examples of systems of this kind in the history of more recent periods. The European system that prevailed from approximately the tenth through the fourteenth centuries was a mixed-actor situation of almost classic proportions.[12]

Such things considered, it appears that students of world order must begin regular investigations of conditions wherein *several qualitatively different types of actors* (e.g., states, regional blocs, collective defense or collective security arrangements, international organizations, multinational corporations) *interact*. Assuming that these conditions will have important implications for the character of world politics, students will need to recognize that the prevailing state-centric world view must be revised. Failing this, world order studies may repeat the errors of "pure" mathematics, deriving theorems from first principles that are no longer consistent with experimental findings or systematic empirical observation.

4. HYPOTHESES LINKING WAR AVOIDANCE TO SIZE OR NUMBER OF ACTORS IN THE WORLD SYSTEM

A variety of testable propositions may be generated linking war avoidance to the size or number of actors. For example, while so-called ministates may be seriously disadvantaged in a world system that is comprised of states of all sizes, a system that is comprised entirely of ministates may have some distinct advantages.[13] As such states are likely to have a less expansive range of concern than their "big brothers," a ministate system may be untroubled by certain forms of forceful conquest.

Moreover, since a system composed entirely of ministates would have a greatly increased *number* of actors, it would also be a system with a greatly increased number of interaction opportunities. As a result, actors will be increasingly likely to become subject to a variety of cross-loyalties. From the standpoint of classical international relations theory, an increased variety of cross-loyalties is certainly *conflict mitigating*.[14]

On the other hand, there are also persuasive reasons for arguing that the increased number of actors in a total ministate system may be deleterious to peace and security. Many such reasons derive from the assumption that reliable alliance agreements are crucial to protecting certain actors in world politics. For example, the increased number of interaction opportunities which accompany the shift to a ministate world system would tend to render any given alignment more impermanent and unreliable.

For those who are unhappy with the prospects for world systems comprised of a large number of small actors, the logical alternative may be to recommend "maxistate" or regional bloc systems. One interesting configuration in this connection is the multibloc model proposed by Roger Masters.[15] According to Masters, this model is best described as Kaplan's "balance of power" model with five or more regional blocs as actors. So long as regional bloc actors are tied definitionally to larger units of territory than state actors, the effective result is a smaller number of larger actors.

From the standpoint of alliance reliability, such an arrangement would be uniquely favorable. At the same time, the large actors in such a system are even more likely to exhibit hegemonial tendencies than are the leading actors in the extant system. Confronted with a very small number of similar sized actors, each one would be apt to keep a continuing watch on the chances for becoming "top dog." This conclusion derives from the assumption that the power-maximizing behavior of actors characteristic of our present system would persist unimpaired in a multi-bloc system.

5. HYPOTHESES LINKING WAR AVOIDANCE TO THE NUMBER OF STATUS QUO OR REVOLUTIONARY-MODERNIZING ACTORS IN THE WORLD SYSTEM

Yet another set of hypotheses emphasizing actor variables may relate war avoidance to the extent to which status quo or revolutionary-modernizing actors comprise the system. The first sort of "happy guesses" might derive from the assumption that the former category of actor is less likely to undertake destabilizing kinds of activities than the latter. There can be little doubt that the attitudes and activities of revolutionary and modernizing actors place special strains on existing arrangements for the management of world power. When its basic tenets appear serviceable elsewhere, revolutionary action tends to engender not only further internal war, but international war as well. Sometimes the external expansion of revolutionary ideology yields war in the Hobbesian sense of protracted enmity rather than continuous actual fighting. The Cold War is a case in point.

Furthermore, so long as it is assumed that stability increases as the system becomes more centralized,[16] we may also assess the effects of these kinds of actors on stability by examining their effects on centralization. If the effect of revolutionary or modernizing actors is to further decentralize or maintain the current distribution of force and sovereign authority in the world system, such actors would appear *destabilizing*. They would continue reliance upon self-help as the prevailing arrangement for managing power. Alternatively, if the effect of revolutionary or modernizing actors is to bring about increasing centralization, such actors would seem to exert a *stabilizing* effect.

It seems apparent that the most basic prerequisite to increasing centralization is the establishment of general or system-wide trust. In this respect, the effect of revolutionary or modernizing actors has been an inhibiting one. The growing importance of such actors has intensified the self-interested character of actor behavior. Actual revolution has reinforced already existing ideological rifts. The inclination of revolutionary actors to "export" revolution to status quo actors has induced the latter group to respond in kind. This frequently means the support of anti-democratic governments as well as the initiation of counterrevolutionary movements.[17] The system-wide consequences of all this are unambiguous: the competitive struggle for appropriate values is accentuated, polarization continues to harden, and general trust becomes increasingly difficult to achieve.

While the terms "revolutionary" and "modernizing" are often used interchangeably,[18] one might also choose to distinguish between them. Where such a distinction is made, one might settle upon additional reasons for arguing that modernization is counterproductive to peace and international stability. In the search for capital needed to sustain rapid industrialization, modernizing actors may resort to control or confiscation of private property. The risks assumed by investors in modernizing societies—expropriation, confiscatory taxation, or laws prohibiting repatriation of profits—are often capable of generating international tensions and strains. Moreover, the process of modernization poses notable challenges to the inhibitory capacities of international law.[19] And if it is assumed that a prominent connection exists between internal disorder and global disorder, one might also emphasize some of the more disruptive features of modernization: rising tensions, mental illness, violence, divorce, juvenile delinquency, and racial, religious, and class conflict.[20]

Alternatively, if modernization is tied definitionally to an enduring capacity to deal with change and transformation, an argument can also be made for linking modernizing actors with *stability and war avoidance*. By transforming all systems by which men organize themselves within states, the process of modernization may have a decidedly stabilizing effect on the character of international relationships. As Manfred Halpern has pointed out, "The revolution of modernization ... is the first revolution in the history of mankind to set a new price upon stability in any system of society; namely, an intrinsic capacity to generate and absorb continuing transformation."[21] Achieving this capacity *within particular societies*, one might argue, is bound to strengthen the fabric of international society as well. According to this argument, a world system comprised of actors demonstrating a persistent capacity for coping with change and transformation will itself exhibit such capacity.

Today, one's position on the relationship between revolutionary or modernizing actors and world order is apt to parallel one's position on the link between communist revolution and world order.[22] Where it is felt that the degeneration of competitive capitalism into exploitative imperialism presents a more serious and enduring challenge to peace than the forcible socialization of private property in the means of production, one is likely to regard communist revolution as *stabilizing*. Alternatively, where one does not accept the assumption relating capitalist development to imperialism and war, ongoing movements for national liberation and socialist revolution may appear decidedly *destabilizing*. This is especially true if one believes that the conduct of communist *cadres* is strongly influenced by communist *theories* of violence which extol the systematic use of force within a pattern of worldwide revolution.

Moreover, one's position on the relationship between communist revolution and war avoidance is apt to parallel one's position on the link between revolutionary nationalism and world order. This is the case because of the extremely close connection between revolutionary nationalism and revolutionary communism. In the process of winning power, communist revolutionary movements identify with and encourage revolutionary nationalism. Although classical Marxism has generally been identified as a movement with professedly internationalist leanings,[23] later modifications of doctrine include the conscious fostering of nationalism.

Current strategies of communist revolution view national liberation as the sole immediate objective. Other more distant objectives are deferred until this one is achieved, giving the appearance that national liberation is the only goal. Whatever differences exist between revolutionary nationalism and revolutionary communism, they do not concern the desirability of achieving national liberation. Communists should not be accused of "using" the forces of national liberation to further their own objectives because their commitment to the notion of national self-determination is genuine. It is an integral part of their revolutionary credo. National liberation *is* one of their objectives, however intermediate.

6. HYPOTHESES LINKING WAR AVOIDANCE TO ACTORS WHO HAVE UNDERGONE VARIOUS FORMS OF "BEHAVIORAL" TRANSFORMATIONS

Finally, hypotheses may also link war avoidance to world systems comprised of actors that have undergone appropriate "behavioral" transformations, i.e., changes in the characteristic behavior of actors in the world system. Such transformations would revise the characteristic preference-maximizing behavior of actors either by (1) creating a condition wherein actors identify their own preferences with the well-being of the entire global community, or (2) creating a condition wherein the preference-maximizing activity of actors has been removed entirely. Before examining these conditions, however, let us first consider what is meant by the extant character of actor behavior—the character which our hypotheses seek to transform.

Like individual men whose private affections are always stronger than their sympathetic or social feelings, the actors in world politics are "egoistically" motivated. The principal obligation of an actor is always to itself. Each always acts to maximize its own particular preferences.

Now, what are the consequences of such a self-seeking mode of conduct? Interestingly enough, they are roughly the same for individual men as they are for the actors in world politics. Hence, John C. Calhoun's account of the consequences of *individual* selfishness sheds a great deal of light on our own subject:

But that constitution of our nature which makes us feel more intensely what affects us directly than what affects us indirectly through others necessarily leads us to conflict between individuals. Each, in consequence, has a greater regard for his own safety or happiness than for the safety or happiness of others, and, where these come in opposition, is ready to sacrifice the interests of others to his own. And hence the tendency to a universal state of conflict between individual and individual, accompanied by the connected passions of suspicion, jealousy, anger, and revenge—followed by insolence, fraud, and cruelty—and, if not prevented by some controlling power, ending in a state of universal discord and confusion which it is ordained.[24]

As Calhoun's assessment ultimately points to the need for some "controlling power" or government, we may suppose by analogy that what is needed at the more comprehensive world system level is also some common power or authority. Yet, the hypotheses with which we are concerned favor a reorientation of actor preferences over a change in world political institutions. These hypotheses emphasize changes of the actors themselves rather than structural alterations of their environment.

And what might such changes entail? Basically, two principal kinds of transformation may be considered. The first of these would reorient attitudes in such a way that actors might begin to identify their own preferences with the well-being of the entire global community. Here, self-interest and community interest would become one.

Notwithstanding the great difficulty involved in implementing these new attitudes, the second kind of "behavioral" transformation is even more far-reaching. This kind of transformation would reorient attitudes in such a way that the private preference-maximizing activity of actors would disappear entirely. Unlike the previous kind of transformation, which involves the identification of private interests with systemic ones, this type would end the private preference-maximizing character of actors altogether. Rather than seek to create a condition wherein actors believe that what is best for the system as a whole is also best for themselves, this proposal calls for a world in which the fusion of private and collective interests is so complete that the idea of "self" interest is no longer meaningful. Just as in the previous recommendation, the actors in such a world would act in the interests of the system as a whole. They would do so, however, not because they view such behavior as self-interested, but because they value community well-being for its own sake.

193

CONCLUSION

The foregoing chapter has set forth a variety of world order models that are described in terms of *actors*. These models offer only the tip of the iceberg; they are by no means exhaustive. Their basic properties have been presented and explored so that students of alternative futures may be apprised of a generally neglected reservoir of world order scholarship. A much larger number of additional models remains to be developed. The surest road to success in this venture involves a creative understanding of actor variables in the process of explanation. We require new prologues for global drama. These might begin with imaginative student hypotheses linking various qualities of actors to war avoidance.

NOTES

1. The four-dimension scheme of classifying world systems according to actors, structure, process, or context is borrowed from Oran R. Young, *A Systemic Approach to International Politics*, Research Monograph No. 33, Center of International Studies, Princeton University, June 30, 1968. Needless to say, this four-fold manner of classification is for purposes of emphasis only. Actual systems of world politics concern various combinations of *all* relevant variables.

2. Our examination of these systems will center around the following criteria of evaluation: logical consistency, character of premises or assumptions, historical accuracy, comparative judgments (vis-à-vis other conceivable systems), and feasibility (likelihood of achievement).

3. Immanuel Kant, *Perpetual Peace*, Helen O'Brien, trans. (London: Sweet & Maxwell, 1927), pp. 26-27.

4. These premises are distilled from Kant's argument; they do not represent his own words.

5. Michael Howard, "Military Power and International Order," in John Garnett, ed., *Theories of Peace and Security* (London: St. Martin's, 1970), p. 42.

6. On this point consider Garrett Hardin, "The Tragedy of the Commons," *Science*, 162 (December 1968), 1243-1248; Thomas Hobbes, *Leviathan*; and Richard A. Falk, "Statist Imperatives in an Era of System Overload," paper presented to the 139th meeting of the American Association for the Advancement of Science, December 28, 1971.

7. Note the Kantian hypothesis discussed earlier.

8. This term is taken from the subtitle to the following work: Francis A. Beer, *Alliances, Latent War Communities in the Contemporary World* (New York: Holt, Rinehart & Winston, 1970).

9. The differences between the two alternative forms of collaboration are discussed in chapter eight.

10. Differences in "type of government" figure as primary or independent variables in section 1 hypotheses.

11. Clarence Streit, *Union Now* (New York: Harper & Bros., 1949), pp. 63-64.

12. Oran R. Young, "The Actors in World Politics," in James N. Rosenau, Vincent Davis, and Maurice A. East, eds., *The Analysis of International Politics* (New York: Free Press, 1972), p. 137.

13. Examples of ministates in the extant world system include Iceland, Monaco, Liechtenstein, San Marino, and Vatican City. For an interesting treatment of the ministate idea, consider Patricia Wohlegemuth Blair, *The Ministate Dilemma*, Occasional Paper No. 6., Carnegie Endowment for International Peace, June 1968.

14. As they tie their definition of multipolarity to the number of actors, Karl Deutsch and J. David Singer's advocacy of multipolarity signifies their preference for a system of many actors. See Karl Deutsch and J. David Singer, "Multipolar Power Systems and International Stability," *World Politics*, XVI (April 1964), 390-406.

15. See Roger Masters, "A Multi-Bloc Model of the International System," *American Political Science Review*, LV (December 1961), 780-798.

16. Such an assumption is by no means uncontroversial. Indeed, one might also advance a convincing argument to the opposite effect, i.e., that stability *decreases* as the system becomes more centralized. From *this* standpoint, if the effect of revolutionary actors is decentralizing, such actors would appear *stabilizing*. And if their effect is centralizing, these actors would seem to exert a *destabilizing* effect.

17. Richard A. Falk, "Revolutionary Nations and the Quality of the International Legal Order," in Morton Kaplan, ed., *The Revolution in World Politics* (New York: Wiley, 1962), p. 314.

18. For example, the *communist* modernization models are essentially the same as the communist *revolution* models. This is the case insofar as communist revolution is viewed as a modernizing revolution.

19. Richard A. Falk, "Historical Tendencies, Modernizing and Revolutionary Nations, and the International Legal Order," in Richard A. Falk and S. Mendlovitz, eds., *The Strategy of World Order*, Vol. 2 of *International Law* (New York: World Law Fund, 1966), p. 182.

20. See, for example, Myron Wiener, *Modernization* (New York and London: Basic Books, 1966), p. 3. Modernization also typically involves (1) an increased centralization of power within states; (2) an increased differentiation and specification of political institutions; and (3) an increased amount of popular participation in politics. Depending upon one's views on these characteristics, they may be used to support the contention that modernization is stabilizing *or* destabilizing.

21. Manfred Halpern, "The Revolution of Modernization in National and

International Society," in Carl J. Friedrich, ed., Nomos VIII, *Revolution* (New York: Atherton, 1966), p. 179.

22. This position itself depends upon one's particular conception of communist revolution.

23. See Alfred G. Meyer, *Leninism* (New York: Praeger, 1957), p. 145.

24. John C. Calhoun, *A Disquisition on Government*, C. Gordon Post, ed. (New York: Liberal Arts Press, 1953), p. 5.

Chapter 10
Processes

INTRODUCTION

Perhaps the most widely known hypotheses concerned with world order and war avoidance lead the student of alternative futures to describe systems in terms of the *process* dimension (i.e., particular patterns of power management). Linking war to the decentralized nature of the world system, these hypotheses rest upon the argument that the actors in world politics are unable to coexist peacefully without a suitable authority above them. As in the case of individual men living outside the civil state, the absence of such authority in the world system constitutes anarchy, and anarchy breeds war. The required remedy is tentatively explained to be an alteration in the form of a world federation or world state.

To actually investigate the hypothesis, the student will have to consider configurations of world politics that are characterized by at least three basic kinds of *processes* or arrangements for the management of power. Described in terms of the distribution of force and sovereign authority,[1] such configurations might be represented as follows:

S A = Sovereign Authority
F   = Force

System 3	S A	F		MOST	EFFECTIVE
	shared	shared			
System 2	S A	F	EFFECTIVENESS	POWER	MANAGEMENT
	shared	decentralized			
System 1	S A	F		LEAST	EFFECTIVE
	decentralized	decentralized			

Where sovereign authority is decentralized, the world system is homogeneous as to type of actor. There exist no specially established central institutions of sovereign authority. As to the instruments of interstate violence, these are distributed among all of the separate actors.

Where sovereign authority is shared, the world system includes a specially established federal center. Here, force may be decentralized or shared. Where force is decentralized, all instruments of interstate violence are distributed among all of the actors alone. Where it is shared, the instruments of interstate violence reside both within the appropriate institutions of the federal center and within all of the actors.

Systems 1, 2, and 3 are easily identified with balance of power, collective security, and world government processes respectively. Regrettably, while the history of political thought is replete with hypotheses linking the effectiveness of war prevention to increasing global centralization,[2] these hypotheses have never been subjected to careful and rigorous examination. The following discussion offers a way to remedy this situation.

SYSTEM 1: THE STATE OF NATIONS AS STATE OF NATURE

System 1 is represented by a decentralized distribution of force and sovereign authority. Each actor is itself a self-contained unit of sovereign-authoritative decision, and each actor is endowed with a measure of force. How is power managed in such a system? What manner of limiting inter-actor violence prevails where actors coexist without an authority above them? How may the use of force between actors be restricted with each actor the sole judge of its own conduct? We will begin to answer these questions by drawing out the implications of certain assumptions pertaining to the characteristic behavior of actors in System 1.

The Logic of Competition

Like Hobbesian men, the actors in world politics are selfishly motivated. The primary obligation of an actor is always to itself. Confronted with a choice between what it deems best for the system as a whole or for any other single actor or group of actors and what it deems best for itself, an actor will always choose the latter alternative. This brings us to

Assumption 1:   Actors act to maximize their own particular preferences.

Moreover, if we assume further that

Assumption 2:   Each actor believes that every other actor is preference maximizing.

Assumption 3:   Each actor believes that the amount of preferences in the world system is fixed.

We may conclude that in acting to maximize their own particular preferences, actors come into competition with one another.

Our conclusion stipulates that actors assume a competitive stance vis-à-vis one another. Does this mean that actors coexisting without an authority above them are always conflictful? Certainly not! True, Hobbes suggests that the state of actors in a world system without superior authority constitutes a condition of war. But this need not imply the use of force, for "the nature of war, consisteth not in actual fighting, but in the known disposition thereto, during all the time there is no assurance to the contrary."[3] While the restraining influence of government is absent where each actor functions as the sole judge of its own conduct, restrictions on the use of force between competing actors are still imposed in such a system by the overarching commitment to self-preservation. This may be demonstrated by the following argument:

Assumption 1 specifies that actors act to maximize those factors which yield a measure of satisfaction, i.e., preferences or wants. This does not mean, of course, that actors always act to maximize *all* preferences. The maximization of one preference may conflict with the maximization of another, and actors may have to choose between them. How is such selection accomplished?

In the most general terms, we may suppose that actors choose between alternative courses of action on the basis of perceived or anticipated consequences. These consequences have two dimensions. The first of these dimensions is the level of the measure of satisfaction or *subjective utility* which accrues from each conceivable outcome. The second of these dimensions is the *subjective probability* that each conceivable outcome will occur. By combining the judgments which it makes along both of these dimensions, an actor determines its choice of action. This involves determining the product of subjective utility and subjective probability for each of the acts under consideration and comparing the products. These products represent the *expected value* or *expected gain* for these acts. We may thus state

Assumption 4:   The principle for deliberation of actors is to choose a course of action which has the highest expected value.

Conjoined with

Assumption 5:   The utility of self-preservation is always higher than the utility of any other preference or combination of preferences.

We are led to conclude that actors always pass up preference-maximizing activity which involves initiating the use of force against other actors which are believed to possess a credible deterrence posture. It follows that the use of force between actors in System 1 may be limited to the extent to which actors can successfully convince other actors that they possess the ability and the resolve to deliver an unacceptably destructive or annihilating response. We reach this conclusion by drawing out the implications of five major assumptions concerning the characteristic behavior of actors in System 1 world politics.

SYSTEM 2: BETWEEN STATE OF NATIONS AND FEDERATION

In the System 2 world, the *right* to use force is transferred from the actors to a specially established center of sovereign-authoritative decision (concretely, such a center might be formed if the United Nations were endowed with the ultimate right to use force), while the *instruments* of inter-actor violence remain decentralized among the actors alone. We are confronted, then, with a condition of sovereign-authoritative prerogatives unsupported by force.

How is power managed in such a system? What manner of limiting inter-actor violence prevails where actors coexist with an appropriate authority above them, but where they alone are the possessors of force? How may the use of force between actors be limited where the actors are no longer the sole judges of their own conduct, but where the weapons of war remain exclusively in their own individual repositories? Is there any reason to suppose that power would be more effectively managed in such a situation than in one where both force *and* sovereign authority reside solely with the separate actors? Indeed, must we not suffer a violation of logic by positing a condition of sovereign authority unsupported by force? And even if we do not suffer such a violation, what possible advantage can such an analytic separation afford the study of alternative world futures? It is with these questions in mind that we begin the following discussion.

The view that sovereign authority requires force may be traced to the notion that obligation derives from the assurance of protection. Without such assurance there can be no sovereign authority. And as such assurance requires force, sovereign authority and force are necessarily intertwined. Conceptually, no characterization of the former without the latter can be recognized.

Thus, according to Hobbes, "The obligation of subjects to the sovereign, is understood to last as long, and no longer, than the power lasteth by which he is able to protect them."[4] Similarly, the theorist Jean Bodin argues that to speak of sovereign authority unsupported by force is to create a logical monstrosity. Obligation to sovereign prerogatives derives exclusively from the ability to provide safety:

> The word of protection in generall extendeth unto all subjects which are under the obeysance of one soveraigne prince or seignorie; As we have said, that the prince is bound by force of armes, and of his lawes, to maintaine his subjects in suretie of their persons, their goods, and families: for which the subjects by a reciprocall obligation owe unto their prince faith, subjection, obeysance, aid, and succour.[5]

An inseparable link between sovereign authority and force may also be found in the twentieth-century work of Robert Lansing, Secretary of State in President Wilson's cabinet. According to Lansing, sovereign authority is "the fundamental authority which controls, restrains, and *protects* man as a member of society."[6] Like Hobbes, Bodin, and Lansing, the German theorists Fichte, Hegel, Ranke, and von Treitschke strongly contend that right derives from might. This meaning of sovereign authority is implied by the conceptions of Lord Bryce and T. H. Green as well.[7]

Alternatively, there are several notable figures in the history of political thought who feel that sovereign authority need not be tied to force. The distinction between power and authority was already laid down by Cicero in *The Laws* while the Platonic conception of authority is certainly founded upon obedience without force. Indeed, it has even been contended that force *cannot* be the sovereign basis of securing compliance. In this view, not only *can* sovereign authority emanate from sources unsupported by force; it *must* secure obedience *without* the threat or use of force. Where force is threatened or used, sovereign authority has failed. As Hannah Arendt points out, the authoritarian relation between those who command and those who obey does not rest on the force at the former's disposal. Rather, what they have in common is the hierarchy itself, "whose rightness and legitimacy both recognize and where both have their predetermined stable place."[8] Similarly, Bertrand de Jouvenel emphasizes the volitional core of the authority concept: "Authority is the faculty of inducing assent. To follow an authority is a voluntary act. Authority ends where voluntary assent ends."[9] It follows that that margin of obedience which is won only by the threat or use of force demonstrates the *failure* of authority.

For our own usage, sovereign authority need *not* be tied to force. There is, then, no *logical* reason why our conception of sovereign authority ought to be rejected. But what of the value of such a conception for inquiry? Even if it raises no logical objections to posit the condition of sovereign-authoritative prerogatives emanating from sources which lack force, is there any reason to suppose that such prerogatives will actually be capable of securing compliance? Clearly, the analytic distinctness of the two concepts does not deny their close connection in decision-making. Even the most cursory look at international affairs reveals that authority is closely interwoven with force. The former is not usually found apart from the latter.

Let us look to Plato for guidance. Plato seeks to discover a "forceless" principle of obligation. He realizes, however, that such notions as Truth and Reason are inadequate to assuring widespread compliance. What, then, does he regard as the appropriate basis of authority? In terms of the well-known analogies which occur again and again in the great political dialogues, the basis of authority is *special knowledge* or *expertise*. In the relations between the captain of a ship and the passengers, or between the physician and the patient, for example, special knowledge or expertise provides the basis for compliance. Force is unnecessary! The compelling element inheres in the relationship itself.

Now, what might this suggest for the situation under discussion, i.e., the effectiveness of power management where those who possess the right to use the instruments of violence are themselves deprived of such instruments? Is the separate center (e.g., an authoritative United Nations) able to secure compliance on the basis of some special claim to knowledge or expertise? Clearly, the basis of authority here is *not* expertise, but some *commonly felt need for centralized management*. It is this "need" which must be the compelling element in the relationship between actors and the separate center if sovereign prerogatives unsupported by force are to be capable of securing compliance. The principal question, then, concerns the "rank" of this need in the actors' preference orderings. Just how high a position is assigned to the need for centralized management? And just how "commonly felt" is this need? Needless to say, the presence of even a small number of powerful actors who do not believe that centralized management is important might have serious consequences for the other actors.

Let us first consider the position which actors assign to the need for centralized force management in their preference orderings. If actors regard such management as essential to their survival, it would certainly appear that this "need" ought to be assigned a very high rank. Indeed, as we assume that the value assigned to self-preservation by actors is always higher than that which is assigned to any other preference or combination of preferences, it would appear that the need for centralized management of force ought to be assigned the *highest possible* position in actors' preference orderings.

To make such an assumption, however, would be foolhardy because it would suppose that actors identify their own prospects for survival with the prospects for the system as a whole. While such an identification might appear eminently reasonable in the view of an "outside" observer, from the point of view of individual actors no such identification is justified. Actors do not form their own preferences by referring to organizational/ decisional requirements for the security of the entire system. They do not, therefore, order their preferences in accordance with what they consider these requirements to be. The actors in System 2 world politics almost always prefer the prospect of security advantage accruing to them alone to the prospect of such advantage accruing to them by virtue of their membership in the system.

Actors "behave" in this way because of the lack of confidence each has in the others' willingness to work toward realization of the common objective. Even if *each* actor in the system favors a situation in which *every* actor complies with central management, it does *not* necessarily follow that they will all comply. This is because each actor will always be uncertain about the willingness of the other actors to comply. So long as the instruments of violence are denied to the central managers of this truly authoritative United Nations-type institution, there is no reason for actors to believe that central management can assure their safety. Hence, the expected benefits of seeking security "privately" almost always seem to exceed those of "collective" security. This behavior describes a truly central dilemma of achieving an improved arrangement for war avoidance via System 2 world politics: even rational, self-interested actors who stand to gain from general cooperation will not act cooperatively.

Needless to say, more optimistic conclusions about war avoidance in System 2 world politics might be obtained by substituting a different set of assumptions for the ones implied in the foregoing argument. It ought to be noted, however, that these assumptions require far more of actors than we can prudently accept. There is simply no denying that Assumption 4 below severely strains the limits of credibility:

Assumption 1:   Each actor believes that the cost of compliance for each actor must be less than the benefit to it if at least some critical number of actors comply with the dictates of centralized management.

Assumption 2:   Each actor believes that the cost to an actor of complying is greater than the benefit to it of complying if less than some critical number of actors comply.

Assumption 3:   Each actor believes that each actor does better if at least some critical number of actors comply than if none comply.

Assumption 4:   Each actor believes that each actor knows that what it knows about the other actors is paralleled by what the other actors know about it, and each actor believes that each actor knows that the other actors are rational.

The conclusion is quite clear. Although it has sometimes been denied by certain writers and thinkers who have consistently confused their own preferences with those of actors,[10] the transfer of right without force is ineffective in the management of world power. There is little reason to suppose that power would be more effectively managed in a System 2 situation than in one where *both* force *and* right reside solely with the separate actors. Like Vladimir and Estragon, the two enigmatic Beckett creations of *Waiting for Godot* who came to realize that they have been waiting by a dying and scraggly shrub when they ought to have been waiting by a robust and healthy tree, the spokesmen for System 2-type centralized management must also learn to recognize that they have "come to the wrong place."

SYSTEM 3: FEDERATION

In the System 3 world system, both force *and* sovereign authority are shared with a specially established global center. Unlike the configuration described by System 2, therefore, sovereign-authoritative prerogatives which emanate from the separate center in the System 3 world system are supported by force.

How is power managed in such a system? What manner of limiting inter-actor violence prevails where actors coexist with an appropriate authority above them, and where this authority is also in possession of force? How may the use of force between actors be limited where the actors are neither the sole judges of their own conduct nor the exclusive repositories for the weapons of war? Is there any reason to suppose that power would, of necessity, be more effectively managed in such a situation than in one where (1) both force and sovereign authority are decentralized among the separate actors (System 1), or (2) sovereign authority is shared while force remains decentralized (System 2)? These are the questions which guide us in the following discussion.

As the actors are deprived of the ultimate right to determine for themselves when the weapons of war may be properly resorted to, the critical factor in the investigation of System 3 appears to concern the particular manner in which *force* is shared. Depending upon the particular distribution of force between the actors and the separate center, we may suppose that the management of power in System 3 configurations will be more or less effective.

Just *how much* force must be possessed by the separate center if it is to be capable of securing regular compliance? Must it possess a *preponderant* share? Or is the only requirement that it possess enough force to appear able to unleash unacceptably destructive sanctions upon recalcitrant actors? And if the latter, what about the ability to *appear willing* to invoke such sanctions? Is *perceived willingness* a necessary concomitant of the separate center's possession of such a measure of force?

Moreover, what of the relationship between the amount of force required and the amount actually possessed by the separate center? Maybe the amount of force actually possessed by the center need not be characterized by preponderance *or* by the appearance of being able to inflict unacceptable damage. Whether it is preponderance *or* the appearance of being able to inflict unacceptable damage that is required, perhaps the separate center—while it generally requires *some* force—actually requires

205

"personal" possession of a lesser amount. That is, to secure compliance with its dictates, the separate center need not have the total amount of force necessary to the task in its own repositories. These problems will now be considered in some depth.

Let us consider the last question first: Does the separate center (concretely, some form of greatly strengthened United Nations-type institution) generally require a smaller amount of force in its own repositories than the total amount actually needed? An affirmative answer to this question requires acceptance of the following assumption: Actors considering noncompliance with the dictates of the separate center generally feel that the center's own force will be augmented by contributions from other actors.

How convincing is this assumption? In effect, it asks us to believe that actors will appear more willing to render force contributions to a separate center possessing some force, however inadequate, than to a separate center without any force. We are asked to believe, therefore, that unlike the actors in System 2, the actors in a System 3 world express confidence in the separate center, however small its own force repository. Even where the separate center's "personal" measure of force is below that measure which is required, it is suggested that actors in System 3 assign a higher preference ordering to compliance with the dictates of centralized management than do the actors in System 2. Is this a reasonable suggestion?

It is indeed *if* we accept the following assumptions:

Assumption 1:   Each actor believes that each actor will gain by complying with the requests for additional force by the separate center if at least some critical number of actors comply.

Assumption 2:   Each actor believes that each actor will lose by complying with the requests for additional force by the separate center (i.e., each actor believes that the cost of complying will exceed the benefit of complying) if less than some critical number of actors comply.

Assumption 3:   Each actor believes that each actor will fare better if at least some critical number of actors comply than if none comply.

Assumption 4:   Each actor believes that at least a critical number of actors are rational and that what it knows about the other actors is paralleled by what the other actors know about it.

But why accept these assumptions? Are they any less unwarranted than those described in connection with System 2? Why should we feel differently about compliance with centralized management in the investigation of a System 3 world where the separate center does not itself possess an adequate supply of force?

We look immediately to the separate center. There we recognize a significant difference between System 2 and the System 3 model described. In the latter configuration, the separate center possesses some force *of its own*. Unlike System 2, the System 3 situation involves a request for *additional* force. It follows that a smaller number of actors is required for cooperative behavior in System 3. Moreover, while System 2 entails a "bell on the cat" problem (no one wants to go first because the separate center has no force of its own), the System 3 world has no such problem. There the separate center already possesses the force with which to take the first step. These reasons suggest that we may be more optimistic about compliance with the dictates of centralized management in System 3 than in System 2. As regards such compliance, the actors consider a *gainful situation* more likely in the *former* configuration.

Let us now turn to the second question which has been raised: Just *how much* force must the separate center possess if it is to be capable of securing regular compliance? All that is required is that measure of force which, in the eyes of the actor involved, appears capable of inflicting unacceptable damage. From the standpoint of the individual actor, supremacy or preponderance by the separate center in terms of force is clearly unessential to successful deterrence.

But this assumes that each actor sees itself vis-à-vis the separate center as the only offending actor in world politics. It assumes that each actor contemplating an unauthorized use of force views the separate center's *entire* force repository when calculating the center's ability to inflict unacceptably damaging punishment. Depending upon the prevailing state of actor satisfaction and the conditions of inter-actor rivalry and competition, such an assumption may be more or less warranted.

If, for example, individual actors contemplating the unauthorized use of force perceive that several other actors are contemplating similar activity, it is likely that these actors will evaluate their prospective retaliatory costs in terms of some

207

measure of force less than the separate center's total allotment. In such cases,[11] the ability of the separate center to appear able to respond with unacceptably damaging strikes may indeed require the appearance of preponderance or superiority. Specifically, as perceived by each would-be aggressor, it may require the appearance of being able to deliver as many (or more) unacceptably damaging strikes as the expected number of offending actors.

On the other hand, such an appearance may not be required if the separate center is believed to possess an arsenal of strategic nuclear weapons. This is the case so long as it is assumed (1) that actors do not have any increased doubts concerning the separate center's *willingness* to make good on its threats where strategic nuclear weapons are involved; (2) that actors believe that the number of separate weapons in this arsenal is at least as large as the expected number held by offending actors; (3) that actors believe that this minimum number of weapons will not be reduced by first-strike attack; and (4) that actors judge the expected damage of any single strategic nuclear weapon to be within the unacceptable range. In effect, this last assumption specifies that actors believe that the greatly increased yield of strategic nuclear weapons is such that the breakdown of even a less than superior arsenal in response to a multiplying number of conceivable targets has no debilitating consequences for the ability of each resultant force to wreak unacceptable damage.

To this point, our discussion of power management in System 3 has been concerned solely with the separate center's *force* requirements. No mention has yet been made of the separate center having to appear *willing* to use this force. As we know, however, for an actor to be deterred by the separate center it must believe that the center not only possesses the *ability* to deliver an unacceptably damaging strike, but that it is also more or less *willing* to do so.

Upon what factors will such perceived willingness depend? Much depends on individual actor perceptions of the separate center's own image of its proper purpose. In other words, how do the actors contemplating the unauthorized use of force feel about the separate center's conception of itself in terms of global management and regulation? If the actors feel that the decision-makers of the separate center consider the actual execution of a threatened sanction to be abhorrent, perhaps because such execution would appear inconsistent with the very objectives to which the separate center's existence is dedicated, then *willingness* to carry out the threat of unacceptable damage may understandably be doubted. This may be all the more so if the separate center has (implicitly or explicitly) referred to nuclear weapons use in its threat to respond.

On the other hand, if actors feel that the decision-makers of the separate center regard the preservation of their perceived resolve above all else, then *willingness* to carry out the threat of unacceptable damage may be widely believed. Just what effect the reference to nuclear weapons will have on the extent to which the center is believed willing to carry out its threat will depend upon the actors' view of just how strongly the decision-makers of the separate center value their image of uncompromising resolve.

Perceived willingness may also depend in part upon the structural configuration of the world system. It might be argued, for example, that in the view of actors, the extent to which the decision-makers of the separate center value their perceived resolve increases as the system moves from multipolarity to bipolarity. This is the case where it is assumed that actors believe that (1) the extent to which the decision-makers of the separate center value their image of resolve varies in accordance with the perceived consequences of failed resolve in number-of-actor terms, and that (2) the perceived consequences of failed resolve in number-of-actor terms worsen or deteriorate as the system moves from a multipolar to a bipolar state. This second assumption is itself derived by the joining of two other assumptions: (1) the perceived consequences of failed resolve in number-of-actor terms worsen or deteriorate as the actors in the system become more and more aligned with fewer and fewer "blocs" (each bloc has a leading actor which forms a pole of the system), and (2) the actors in the system become more and more aligned with fewer and fewer blocs as the system moves from a multipolar to a bipolar state.

And finally, even where it is assumed that actors believe that the forces of the separate center are sufficiently invulnerable, perceived willingness may also depend in part upon actor perceptions of (1) the disutility which the separate center attaches to whatever destruction it might still suffer (to forces or otherwise) as a consequence of making good on a threat, and (2) the likelihood that the separate center will feel forced to anticipate incurring such disutility as a consequence of making good on a threat. If, for example, actors believe (3) that the separate center has defined a specified level of destruction which it deems unacceptable, and (4) that the center feels that such a level of destruction would be incurred if it chose to make good on a threat to use force, then actors will very likely believe that the separate center would be unwilling to carry out its threat. Perceived willingness, therefore, will depend in part upon the center's ability to convince actors *not to believe* 3 and/or 4 above. As it is difficult to conceive of a situation in which the separate center does not consider a certain level of destruction to be unacceptable, it will be incumbent upon it to convince would-be offending actors of its conviction that by making good on its threat to use force it does not feel that it will be inviting an unacceptably damaging counterstrike.

In view of the foregoing discussion, we may note that even in a world system where the separate center is endowed with the ultimate right to make decisions concerning the use of force between actors, and where this right is supported by an amount of force deemed sufficient to inflict unacceptably damaging punishment, the management of power need not necessarily be effective. This is the case because such effectiveness also requires the belief on the part of actors (1) that the separate center is *willing* to make good on its threats to use force, and (2) that the separate center's capability of yielding unacceptable damage is not vulnerable to first-strike attack or to active defense efforts. Interestingly enough, these extraordinarily complex requirements are generally overlooked by advocates of world government. Undaunted by their omissions, these enthusiastic spokesmen for global centralization feel certain that the logic of their proposed configurations is beyond question and that their only proper efforts concern problems of feasibility and achievement.

SYSTEM 3 TRANSFORMED: A DYNAMIC VIEW

Let us suppose for a moment that the System 3 model has been transformed. No longer is force *shared* with a specially established global center. Rather, this center now has not only the *right* to use force, but it is the *exclusive* repository of force itself. It follows from our basic framework of concepts that inter-actor violence is eliminated by definition in such a system. It is a single-actor world. Hence, so long as we assume a "frozen" or static conception, the investigation of this system has nothing to do with our inquiry-guiding hypothesis. Where our model is dynamically oriented, however, a different conclusion may be in order.

But why consider such an orientation? Is there any reason to suppose that the separate center would consider the voluntary surrender of some measure of force to agents of what were formerly actors? Indeed, having achieved a distribution of force and sovereign authority which makes inter-actor violence a thing of the past, should it now risk such violence on its own volition?

An affirmative answer to this question will not be out of order if we assume that (1) the strains and tensions which customarily arise between actors in world politics continue to exist even after their relinquishment of the instruments of violence; (2) the decision-makers of the separate center recognize this and believe that such strains and tensions must find the most effective means of alleviation; and (3) the decision-makers of the separate center believe that by risking the possibility of violence between actors (i.e., by relinquishing some force), they are providing for the most effective release of such strains and tensions. Clearly, exactly what measure of risk ought to be taken (i.e., just *how much* force ought to be relinquished) will depend upon the separate center's considered evaluation of various perceived combinations of inter-actor violence, disorder, and/or oppression.

We have seen, then, that even in a world system which leaves only the separate center in possession of force, inter-actor violence may still occur. This is the case because the total effective and authoritative blockage of such violence may occasion the onset of other forms of undesirable behavior, thereby inducing the decision-makers of the separate center to deliberately permit the possibility of actors using force against one another. What this means is that the decision-makers of the separate center are unwilling to pursue the objective of inter-actor war avoidance without considering the accompanying impact on other sought after values. The prevention of war cannot be accomplished in a manner which avoids other center goals. Finely intertwined and delicately interwoven, these goals—together with that of war prevention—must be weighed one against the other in the subtle process of deciding which course of action is to be followed.

CONCLUSION

The creation of a working "peace system" for the world requires great care. It is not enough to justify proposals for alternative world futures on the basis of disaffection with prevailing arrangements for managing power. More centralized alternatives are not *necessarily* more desirable. Alternative configurations may or may not prove more suitable, and each must be painstakingly examined on its own merits.

Our own analysis has illustrated this clearly. We have discovered that there is no necessary connection between the extent to which force and sovereign authority are transferred to

211

system-wide institutions and the effectiveness of power management. Where a variety of other important conditions are not met, [12] it may well be that increasingly centralized distributions do not provide successively more effective arrangements for the management of power. In short, the hypothesized link upon which a significantly large number of proposals for world federation are founded cannot stand the test of sustained investigation. This being the case, it follows that the sizable measure of time and effort currently being expended on behalf of greater global centralization via "world peace through world law" may be misguided. [13] Such misguided expenditure stems from the widespread failure to recognize that the careful examination of proposed configurations from the standpoint of desirability is necessarily antecedent to concerns for *feasibility* and *achievement*.

What does all of this mean for those who have placed their faith in some form of world government arrangement for managing global power? Should believers in the virtues of greater global centralization regard our findings as cause for consternation and dismay? This depends upon the extent to which the other conditions necessary to the viability of world government configurations are judged capable of fulfillment. Where it is believed that meeting these conditions poses no major obstacle, continued optimism about the value of greater centralization need not be unwarranted. If, however, the achievement of these conditions is thought to be unrealistic, world government is certain to be viewed with declining favor.

What path remains open to the latter group? What must remain as their picture of the world? Does it bear resemblance to Teilhard De Chardin's ephemeral metaphor?

> A rocket rising in the wake of time's arrow that only bursts to be extinguished; an eddy rising on the bosom of a descending current . . . .

It need not; a more hopeful picture may still be conceived. What is required is a shift in orientation. Dismayed with the prospect of seeking solutions within the classic framework of assumptions concerning actor behavior, the student of alternative world futures may focus instead on the creation of certain different frameworks. Rather than seek to understand ways in which conditions may be met in a system where certain extant forms of actor behavior are assumed, he may begin by specifying alternative forms of behavior (see chapter nine). Thereafter, the resultant world systems may be explored in terms of their power-management consequences. The new emphasis is on affecting changes in the very conditions of actor behavior which give rise to pessimistic conclusions about the desirability of world government.

What might such changes entail? Aristophanes offers an answer in *Lysistrata*, likening the process of unification to the act of weaving:

> Then you should card it and comb it, and mingle it all
>   in one basket of love and unity,
> Citizens, visitors, strangers, and sojourners—all the
>   entire, undivided community.
>
> These to one mighty political aggregate tenderly,
>   carefully, gather and pull;
> Twining them all in one thread of good fellowship
>   thence a magnificent bobbin to spin,
> Weaving a garment of comfort and dignity, worthily
>   wrapping the people therein.[14]

Clearly more is involved here than simple transfer of right augmented by force. Unification requires *love*. It requires *good fellowship*. It requires *comfort* and *dignity*. And it must be accomplished *carefully* and *tenderly*. In short, unification requires a *fundamental reorientation of attitudes*. To realize a working peace system, the actors in world politics must do more than establish common system-wide institutions, even where such institutions are properly endowed with authoritativeness and force. As suggested in the preceding chapter, they must learn to identify their own preferences with the well-being of the entire global community. Self-interest and community interest must become one.

Peace, then, may wait for us beyond the line where actors are pitted against other actors in fear and competitive disharmony. It may wait for us at the point where we are able to witness a "totalisation of the world upon itself, in the unanimous construction of a spirit of the earth."[15]

How is this point to be reached? The answer may lie in some *new* version of the outlook which dominated medieval Christendom. Comprehended as a great allegory, the hierarchically ordered world of Thomas Aquinas and Dante was inspired throughout by aspiration to fulfill the will of God. In such aspiration lay the foundation of world unity and world peace. Today, the peculiar urgency of planetary danger offers an unambiguous humanistic ideal to replace Divine Will as an object of universal aspiration. We refer to *survival*. Peace may come when survival sits where once God reigned.

NOTES

1. By *force* we mean the weapons of war—guns, battleships, missiles, etc. By *sovereign authority* we mean the ultimate *right* to make decisions and enforce obedience in the world system.

2. Among the most widely known of these proposals in the history of Western political thought are the following. Several of these proposals are discussed in Part I: Pierre Dubois, *De Recuperatione Terra Sancta*; Dante, *De Monarchia*; Francois de la Noue, *Discours politiques et militaires*; Emeric Crucé, *Nouveau Cynée*; Sully, *Le Grand Dessein*; William Penn, *An Essay Towards the Present and Future Peace of Europe*; John Bellers, *Some Reasons for a European State*; C. I. Castel de Saint-Pierre, *Projet de paix perpetuelle*; Jean Jacques Rousseau, *A Lasting Peace Through the Federation of Europe*; Jeremy Bentham, *Plan for an Universal and Perpetual Peace*; Immanuel Kant, *Perpetual Peace*.

   A vast literature advancing the case for world government has its origins in our own century. Among the most notable are the following: Raymond L. Bridgeman, *World Organization* (1905); H. G. Wells, *The Common Sense of World Peace* (1929); Clarence K. Streit, *For Union Now* (1939); W. B. Curry, *The Case for a Federal Union* (1939); David H. Munroe, *Hang Together: The Union Now Primer* (1940); Grenville Clark, *A Memorandum with Regard to a New Effort to Organize Peace* (1939); Duncan and Elizabeth Wilson, *Federation and World Order* (1939); Oscar Newfang, *World Government* (1942); Emery Reves, *Anatomy of Peace* (1945); Norman Cousins, *Modern Man Is Obsolete* (1945); Cord Meyer, *Peace or Anarchy* (1947); Crane Brinton, *From Many One* (1948); Vernon Nash, *The World Must Be Governed* (1949); Grenville Clark and Louis B. Sohn, *World Peace Through World Law* (1966).

3. *Leviathan*, Chapter XIII, Part I.

4. *Leviathan*, Chapter XXI.

5. Jean Bodin, *The Six Books of a Commonweale*, K. D. McRae, ed. (Cambridge: Harvard University Press, 1962), p. 69.

6. Robert Lansing, *Notes on Sovereignty: From the Standpoint of the State and of the World* (Washington: The Endowment, 1921), p. 2.

7. See James Bryce, *Studies in History and Jurisprudence*, Vol. II (Oxford: Clarendon, 1901), p. 64; and T. H. Green, *Lectures on the Principles of Political Obligation* (London: Longman's, 1941), pp. 136-137. See also Sigmund Freud and Albert Einstein for their contention that sovereign-authoritative prerogatives cannot emanate from sources which lack the support of force. See Freud's letter to Einstein of September 1932, in David Brook, ed., *Search for Peace* (New York: Dodd, Mead, 1970), pp. 17-26; see also the large collection of Einstein's letters in Otto Nathan and Heinz Norden, eds., *Einstein on Peace* (New York: Schocken, 1968).

8. See Hannah Arendt, "What Was Authority," in Carl Friedrich, ed., *Authority*, Nomus I (Cambridge: Harvard University Press, 1958), p. 82. In terms of the literature on international law, Gerhart Niemeyer is most prominently associated with the idea that "an international order which

depends on force as its *ultima ratio* is a permanent source of international struggle rather than a medium of order." [See Gerhart Niemeyer, *Law Without Force* (Princeton, N.J.: Princeton University Press, 1941), pp. 21-22.] We may trace this idea back to Grotius, who states that authority in the world system necessarily derives from the claims of Christian morality on the minds of men. It cannot rest upon a base of organized force.

9. Bertrand de Jouvenel, *Sovereignty: An Inquiry into the Political Good* (Chicago: University of Chicago Press, 1957), p. 33.

10. See, for example, Jeremy Bentham's *Plan for an Universal and Perpetual Peace* (1843); William Ladd, "Essay on a Congress of Nations," *Prize Essays on a Congress of Nations* (1840); and Lassa F. L. Oppenheim, *The Future of International Law* (1921).

11. In this connection, there are several ways in which actors contemplating the unauthorized use of force can influence the expected disutility of the separate center's threatened response. These ways include: (1) collusion with other actors contemplating the unauthorized use of force; (2) exercise of furtive pressure on other actors to undertake the unauthorized use of force; and (3) "buying off" the separate center.

12. As determined in the foregoing discussion, such conditions concern matters including perceptions of the *value of authoritativeness* in securing compliance; the *amount* of force; the *nature* of force; the *vulnerability* of force; and the *willingness* to use force.

13. The reader will recognize that the criticism being offered of "world peace through world law" is not the usual one. The point here is not that the "world law" approach is unsatisfactory because it is naively conceived, but that it may be unsatisfactory even where it is not so conceived. That is to say, it may be unsatisfactory *even where a preponderant measure of force is provided to encourage compliance with legal dictates.*

14. Aristophanes, of course, intends this passage to refer to the unification of the subject city-states of the Athenian Empire.

15. See Pierre Teilhard de Chardin, *The Phenomenon of Man* (New York: Harper Torchbooks, 1959), p. 253.

Chapter 11
Context

INTRODUCTION

Several hypotheses relating nuclear weapons and world order may lead to systems described along the *context* dimension. The best known of these hypotheses link the proliferation of nuclear weapons to increasing global instability. With the continuing spread of nuclear weapons, it is observed, the secure existence of actors in world politics becomes more and more precarious, more and more akin to the dangerous condition wherein individuals coexist without an authority above them. The basic contours of such reasoning will be described in this chapter.

ANOTHER LOOK AT THE STATE OF NATIONS AS STATE OF NATURE

Hobbes tells us that although the state of nations is the state of nature, it is still more tolerable than the condition of individual men in nature. This is because with individual men "the weakest has strength enough to kill the strongest." With the advent of nuclear weapons, however, there is no longer any reason to suppose that the state of nations is more tolerable. As a growing number of actors in world politics come to possess nuclear weapons, they also come to share the equality of Hobbesian men. The state of nations thus draws closer and closer to the true Hobbesian state of nature. No longer does the state of nations lack those inconveniences which are attendant upon a pure state of nature. The "dreadful equality" which accompanies the proliferation of a nuclear weapons technology has frightfully destabilizing implications for the world system. As the system

216

approaches the point where any actor is able to "kill" any other actor, war becomes increasingly likely.

But does it really? Does not a proliferating nuclear weapons technology provide an increasing number of actors with a *credible deterrence posture*? And is not such a posture a critical condition of international stability? (See chapter ten.) According to Morton Kaplan, a system in which all actors are in possession of weapons of such a character "that any actor is capable of destroying any other actor that attacks it even though it cannot prevent its own destruction" (the "unit veto" system) is likely to be highly unstable *unless* "all actors are prepared to resist threats and to retaliate in case of attack."[1] Presumably, the hypothesized link between the proliferation of nuclear weapons technology and instability is reversed where such proliferation provides each actor with a credible deterrence posture.

On this basis, the appearance and spread of uniquely destructive weaponry need not require a correction of Spinoza's contention that "a commonwealth can guard itself against being subjugated by another, as a man in the state of nature cannot do." So long as credible deterrence postures are regarded as basic to international security and nuclear weapons are judged capable of ensuring such postures, there is no reason to suppose that the breakdown of protective defense necessarily implies a higher incidence of inter-actor conflict. Quite the contrary! The proliferation of a nuclear weapons capability is associated with the *more effective* management of power in the world system. This is certainly what Churchill had in mind when he made the following statement before Commons on November 3, 1953:

> When I was a schoolboy I was not good at arithmetic but I have since heard it said that certain mathematical quantities when they pass through infinity change their signs from plus to minus—or the other way round. It may be that this rule may have a novel application and that when the advance of destructive weapons enables everyone to kill everybody else nobody will want to kill anyone at all.[2]

From this standpoint, a great many analyses must be deemed defective because they fail to distinguish *capabilities* from *intentions*. The argument goes something like this: Surely the breakdown of unilateral national defense and the consequent vulnerability of "heartlands" may be attributed to the greatly increased destructive capabilities of nuclear weapons. But such increased capabilities need not, of necessity, enhance the likelihood of war. The element of *deterrence* must not be overlooked. Theorists like Kenneth Boulding have seemingly failed to consider that would-be attackers will refrain from attacking vulnerable heartlands where the prospect of cost and risk is judged to exceed prospective gains.[3] Where the situation which unilateral national defense attempts to establish—"unconditional viability"—is no longer possible, one need not conclude that "irretrievable disaster" is imminent. An actor which is only "conditionally viable" might still be able to effectively *deter* an attack on its territory. This is the case where the actor's post-attack retaliatory capacity is judged by the potential attacker to be sufficient for wreaking an unacceptably destructive or annihilating response and where the actor is judged willing to unleash such a response.

The point is, then, that even though *defense* is exceedingly difficult to achieve in the nuclear age, the new technology may still inhibit the use of weapons between actors via *deterrence*, i.e., by threatening to inflict terrible costs.[4] The threat of retaliatory destruction is a replacement for protective defense.

Such reasoning is sorely ill founded. It is ill founded because it derives from the assumption that a *nuclear weapons capability* brings with it the means for projecting the image of a credible deterrence posture.[5] There exists no automatic connection between the possession of one and the projection of the other. This will be demonstrated below.

In terms of Stanley Hoffman's metaphoric representation of world politics as a game of roulette, a proliferating nuclear weapons technology means an increasing likelihood that the game is to be played with a nuclear "ball."[6] What does this mean in terms of particular deterrence postures? Or in Raymond Aron's words, "Where does the novelty of deterrence lie in the nuclear age?"[7] The answer comes immediately to mind: it lies in the material or physical consequences of carrying out the threat. In one form or another, this point has been made repeatedly in the body of professional literature. The advent of a nuclear weapons technology, we are told, represents a revolutionary progression—a quantum jump—in the destructive capacity of weaponry.[8] The potential of nuclear war is peculiarly destructive and peculiarly rapid in its destructiveness.[9] Thus, Glenn Snyder has told us that since the development of the atomic bomb, the enormous magnification of the capability to inflict punishment has fundamentally altered the traditional notions of a power balance.[10] And in a similar vein, Arthur Lee Burns has claimed that nuclear weapons have qualitatively changed the nature of affairs between actors in the world system.[11]

The special essence of nuclear deterrence is, then, the excessive cost of retaliation. It is *this* feature of deterrence by nuclear threat which has prompted broad acceptance of the Churchill remark describing safety as "the sturdy child of terror" and survival as "the twin brother of annihilation."[12] F. H. Hinsley, for example, claims that nuclear weapons "constitute for the first time a true deterrent, one that will never have to be relied upon so long as it exists—and this is likely to be forever."[13] Confident in the virtues of a *pax atomica*, Hinsley regards nuclear weapons as "absolute" and differences of nuclear strength between actors as insignificant.[14]

But is the argument well taken? Does the enormous magnitude of damage which nuclear weapons are capable of inflicting necessarily imply that threats to use them are persuasive in the deterrent sense? The answer to this question must certainly be "No." The persuasiveness of a threat rests not only on the anticipated level of destruction, but also on the perceived willingness or resolve to carry it out. And there is no apparent reason to suppose that the much higher levels of destruction implied by nuclear threat are believed by actors to be accompanied by a heightened willingness to make good on that threat. Indeed, in a considerable number of cases there are good reasons for supposing just the contrary to be true, i.e., that threats to retaliate by nuclear response are decidedly *less* credible. President Kennedy's abandonment of his predecessor's policy of "massive retaliation" reflects this recognition.

For example, it has often been pointed out that the threat of nuclear reprisal can only be used to deter a nuclear attack. It is extremely doubtful that a conventional or non-nuclear attack on an actor would be likely to evoke a nuclear response. In terms of a doctrine of massive retaliation which is intended as a response to less than massive (i.e., non-nuclear) aggression, the prospective attacker may find the threat of nuclear reprisal difficult to believe. This is especially so when the prospective attacker knows that it is believed to possess a nuclear second-strike capability.[15] As John Herz has pointed out, in view of the likelihood of effective nuclear counter-retaliation where nuclear weapons are used in response to non-nuclear attack by a nuclear power, the threat to use nuclear weapons in response to non-nuclear attack is rather implausible.[16] We recognize, then, that despite the immensely destructive consequences of nuclear retaliation, the threat of such retaliation might not provide for a credible deterrence posture where it is not believed likely to be resorted to.[17] Thus, it may be that in order to limit the use of conventional force between actors in the nuclear age, credible deterrence postures will ultimately have to rest upon conventional modes of firepower: *Si vis pacem, para bellum non-atomicum.*[18]

We have just seen that despite the enormously debilitating consequences of nuclear retaliation, an actor possessing a nuclear weapons capability need not necessarily be endowed with a credible deterrence posture. This is because an actor endowed with such a posture must also be *believed willing* to carry out the threatened response. And such perceived willingness or resolve is in no way a *necessary* concomitant of the nuclear threat.

Yet another reason why a nuclear weapons capability does not necessarily imply a credible deterrence posture centers on the vulnerability of retaliatory forces. A secure retaliatory force is indispensable to deterrence. A deterrent force must be judged capable of inflicting unacceptable reprisals, and this requires being judged able to survive a first-strike attack by the actor contemplating such a strike.[19]

Where an actor believes that a would-be deterrer's retaliatory force is vulnerable to its first-strike attack, the incentive to preempt may be great. Nuclear weapons capability notwithstanding, the deterrence posture of the would-be deterrer is hardly credible. On the other hand (assuming perceived willingness), where potential antagonists judge each other's retaliatory forces to be capable of inflicting unacceptable damage after a first-strike attack, the deterrence postures on both sides are deemed credible.[20]

How, then, can retaliatory forces be made to appear secure? What means may actors employ to convince potential antagonists that a first-strike attack would leave unimpaired a sufficient offensive capacity to deliver an unacceptably destructive response? There are several alternatives available to an actor. One of these involves protection of missile launching sites by means of *hardening.*[21]

There are several reasons why hardening of retaliatory forces is not a very desirable means of ensuring invulnerability. The principal case against the so-called fortress method is that a hardened, immobile launching site can be destroyed once sufficient striking power is achieved. Hardening can never render launching sites capable of withstanding direct hits or near misses, and modern guidance systems make such hits or near misses increasingly likely. Moreover, the attacker will always be able to increase yield and blast effect in order to stay ahead of the hardening process. According to J. David Singer, "The harder the site, the bigger the warhead it will attract, and the more fallout, heat, and blast destruction the environs will probably receive."[22] Harder bases, then, merely draw heavier attacks. It is both easier and cheaper to launch an additional missile and/or increase yield than it is to increase hardening to the point which nullifies the offensive adjustment. According to Oskar Morgenstern, "Hardening imposes a greater burden on a country than the burden the opponent has to assume in order to raise his striking power with which to offset the effects of hardening."[23]

Let us pursue this matter in somewhat greater technical detail. By keeping the "exchange ratio" high, actors may preclude any advantage to other actors in attempting a disarming first-strike attack against their retaliatory forces. One means of increasing the exchange ratio is thought to be hardening. Where improvement in warhead yields and guidance accuracies of intercontinental missiles outdistances growth in silo hardness, however, the stability of the exchange ratio is shaken. That is, it moves precariously close to unity.

Now, in recent years we have seen the development of multiple independent re-entry vehicles (MIRV). With the development of such vehicles, each warhead can be independently guided to a specific planned target. This is accomplished by providing each warhead mounted on the upper stage of a missile with its own guidance and control mechanism to seek out its programmed target. Such independent targeting for individual warheads (the product of improved computer technology resulting from electronic miniaturization) clearly represents a much more effective power of destruction.[24]

The development of MIRV missiles is, therefore, a potentially destabilizing situation of enormous consequence. Such development puts land-based deterrent forces in particular jeopardy. Where missiles are equipped with such vehicles and where the accuracy of each one is high, the hardening of deterrent missile silos becomes less effective as a means of assuring retaliatory force survival.[25] Indeed, the development of MIRV missiles may well drive the exchange ratio below unity. Assuming equal cost, it becomes cheaper to destroy retaliatory forces in this situation than to build them.[26]

But what of the use of anti-ballistic missile systems to supplement hardening? If successful development of MIRV missiles (one missile carries a significant number of independently guided warheads capable of attacking separate targets) can lead to a situation where the would-be deterrer is no longer believed to possess a credible deterrence posture, might not the deployment of an anti-missile missile system reverse this situation and remove the attacker's incentive for a first-strike?[27] By putting into operation

221

an active defense of retaliatory missiles, would not the first-strike psychology fostered by MIRV-type weapons be effectively countered? Is it not clear that while anti-ballistic missile (ABM) systems are not very helpful as an active defense measure to protect cities, such systems may still be helpful in the defense of retaliatory forces?[28]

There can, of course, be no single answer to these questions. Any answer must be tutored by careful examination of the particular offensive and defensive missile capabilities in question. From what we know of the current and developing state of offensive missile technology, however, there are compelling reasons to doubt the effectiveness of an ABM defense of retaliatory forces. Aside from the implementation of such systems being very costly, the development of MIRV-type weapons means that a separate anti-ballistic missile is needed for each individual *warhead*. This is because the separation of re-entry vehicles in such weapons takes place well before ABM interception is possible. So long as it does not become technically possible to achieve ABM interception prior to separation, and so long as separate anti-ballistic missiles cannot be successfully directed against each separating warhead, then partition into several separate warheads greatly reduces the chances for ABM intercept of all the incoming warheads.[29] It appears, therefore, that the achievement of a secure retaliatory force might require more than hardened silos, even where hardening is reinforced by anti-ballistic missiles.

What might this something "more" be? One oft-discussed means centers on the sea-based deterrent. As a dispersed and mobile delivery vehicle, the atomic submarine might be a suitable replacement for (or supplement to) a fixed, land-based intercontinental ballistic missile (ICBM) retaliatory force. As submarine-launched missiles are not readily pinpointed, a mobile sea-based ballistic missile system is unlikely to be subject to the destabilizing effects of MIRV-type weapons. Moreover, if all strategic forces were at sea, the necessity to pre-target cities for retaliation would probably be eliminated[30] while the possibility of pre-targeting strategic forces would be precluded. In these circumstances, says Frank Bothwell, "an accidental launch would have far less probability of catastrophic damage, and a counter-force war would be fought largely at sea."[31]

There are, however, several important questions which must be raised. First, just how difficult is it to pinpoint missile-carrying submarines? Are such seagoing vehicles really invulnerable to first-strike attack? The concern has frequently been expressed that it is certainly conceivable for one actor to be able to locate, identify, and trail another actor's submarines "on station." This means that it might be possible to destroy them all at once.[32] Second, what about the appropriate land-based command posts which must *also* be able to survive an attack if submarines bearing retaliatory missiles are to be able to act?[33] Clearly, even if we assume that the submarines themselves cannot be located, identified, and trailed, there is no reason to suppose that essential land-based command posts share such a favored position. And third, where a proliferating nuclear weapons technology results in an increasing number of actors basing their retaliatory forces on submarines, how will it be possible to identify the actor-source of a particular attack?[34] Where a polaris-type missile is fired at a given city, how will the attacked actor be able to determine precisely who it was that initiated the attack? With this problem in mind, it has even been suggested that actors clear all of their atomically armed submarines from the sea so as to prevent a case of mistaken identity.[35] All things considered, it appears that sea-basing of retaliatory forces also suffers serious defects as a means of rendering such forces "invulnerable."

Up to this point we have had little cause for optimism as regards the protection of a credible retaliatory capacity. This does not mean, however, that there are other *separate* means which, as *alternatives*, offer more viable prospects of achieving such protection. And it does not mean that retaliatory forces are necessarily doomed to "vulnerability." It does mean that an actor interested in making its retaliatory forces appear invulnerable must in all likelihood rely on an approximate *mix* of land-based and sea-mobile[36] launch systems.[37] Moreover, such systems must also be *protected, concealed, multiplied,* and *dispersed* to the greatest extent possible. While a mixed-systems force need not appear invulnerable per se, its creation is certainly a critical step toward projecting the desired image.[38]

In sum, we have just considered another important reason why a nuclear weapons capability does not necessarily imply a credible deterrence posture. An actor with a nuclear weapons capability may or may not be judged the possessor of such a posture. This judgment depends (among other things) upon whether or not a prospective attacker deems the would-be deterrer's retaliatory forces capable of inflicting unacceptable damage after a first-strike attack. It follows that even a primary emphasis on credible deterrence postures as the critical condition of international stability need *not* lead us to conclude that the proliferation of nuclear weapons results in the more effective management of world power. And as such proliferation may also enhance the likelihood of nuclear war by mechanical accident or errors in information as well as by escalation from conventional conflict, it is unfavorable to effective power management on all counts.

Indeed, even if it were concluded that a nuclear weapons capability does always imply a credible deterrence posture, and even if the dangers of accidental war and inadvertent escalation were overlooked, a strong case might still be made for nonproliferation. This case would rest upon the assumption that a nuclear weapons capability is developed slowly. It does not emerge full-grown overnight. Hence, states that are just beginning the development of an independent nuclear weapons capability might be rendered *especially susceptible* to preemptive strikes.

NUCLEAR WEAPONS AND ALLIANCES IN THE STATE OF NATIONS

To this point we have examined the *direct* effects of nuclear weapons on deterrence postures. The remainder of this chapter will examine some of the *indirect* effects of nuclear weapons on such postures. More specifically, we will now consider how nuclear weapons affect the ability of *alliances* to assist actors in projecting the image of a credible deterrence posture. In so doing, the would-be attacker will be assumed to possess an *independent* nuclear weapons capability. Before beginning this investigation, however, the reader may wish to reconsider chapter eight where it is pointed out that concern for alliance reliability predates the Atomic Age.

At first glance, where an actor is judged incapable of dealing an unacceptably damaging retaliatory blow after receiving a first-strike attack, the existence of a nuclear-armed antagonist brings alliances immediately to mind. Such an actor may need to be protected against nuclear attack, and protection seemingly requires collaborative assistance in the form of commitments by "nuclear" allies. "Indeed," says Stanley Hoffmann, "only a clear commitment [by alliance partners], either to nuclear retaliation, or to the kind of retaliation that poses a credible threat of ultimate escalation to nuclear weapons, seems capable of deterrence.[39]

But *is* such an alliance commitment capable of providing a vulnerable actor with a credible deterrence posture? Is a prospective attacker likely to believe that a nuclear attack on an actor will be considered a *casus nuclear belli* by that actor's "nuclear" alliance partner? Even where it is assumed that the assistance-promising partners are believed *capable* of delivering unacceptably damaging reprisals on behalf of the vulnerable actor, does their promise of nuclear retaliatory support necessarily imply success in terms of deterrence? Clearly, as such success must also depend on appropriate perceptions of the protecting ally's *willingness* to carry out its commitment, there may be persuasive reasons for favoring a negative reply to these questions.

Unless alliance guarantees promising nuclear retaliation are characterized by an appropriate degree of *automaticity*, they may have little or no deterrent effect. So long as we choose to conceptualize the process of commitment as one of *surrendering options*, it is clear that short of demonstrations of automaticity via "doomsday" type devices an actor will *never* effectively destroy the option not to honor its alliance obligations. No matter how high the value an actor places on protection of an ally, it can never be as high as that which it places on its own security. No level of commitment which involves the risk of nuclear strike on its territory (short of doomsday machinery) will be perceived as irrevocable. Thus, where honoring a commitment may offer the prospect of overwhelmingly destructive nuclear counter-retaliation, the would-be attacker may doubt the would-be deterrer's intention to willingly jeopardize its survival for another actor. "Closeness" of alliance partnership notwithstanding, no actor is believed likely to respond to aggression on another by means of nuclear retaliation where it judges such a response to be suicidal or self-destructive.

This is, of course, the principal thrust of the so-called Gallois Thesis (after the French general of the same name).[40] Implicit in this thesis is the assumption that prospective attackers feel that alliance partners offering the nuclear "shield" are likely to believe that retaliation will be met with unacceptably damaging counter-retaliation. Needless to say, this argument denying successful deterrence of nuclear attack via alliance collaboration may be undercut if we make the following alternative assumption: that the prospective attacker believes that the assisting alliance partner does not believe that nuclear retaliation will be answered with unacceptably damaging nuclear counter-retaliation. The assisting alliance partner might feel this way because (1) for one reason or another, it believes the attacker would lack the *will* to undertake such action, and/or (2) it believes its own retaliatory strike can successfully prevent an unacceptably damaging counter-retaliatory blow.

The advent of nuclear weapons raises yet another important problem in terms of alliance reliability and credible deterrence postures. Not only must we consider the effects of such weapons on the unilateral decisions of actors concerning the honoring of commitments; we must also consider their effects in terms of inducing active *collaboration* or tacit *agreement* with an opposing alliance leader to *deliberately fault* a commitment to protect one's actor partners. Here, the nuclear superpowers, each the leading actor of its respective bloc, would (either because of active and secret collaboration or tacit but unambiguous understanding) permit an attack on their alliance partners to go unpunished. By collaborative design, there would be no honoring of prior commitments to carry out threats of nuclear retaliation. Such collaboration or agreement would derive from the overarching commitment of actors to self-preservation and from the judgment that the dutiful honoring of alliance obligations would *most* seriously jeopardize that preference. In recent history, the possibility of such "counter-collaboration" received prominent and concerned expression in the words of General de Gaulle:

> Who can say that if in the future, the political background having changed completely—that is something that has already happened on earth—the two powers having the nuclear monopoly will not agree to divide the world?
>
> Who can say that if the occasion arises the two, while each deciding not to launch its missiles at the main enemy so that it should itself be spared, will not crush the others? It is possible to imagine that on some awful day Western Europe should be wiped out from Moscow and Central Europe from Washington. And who can say that the two rivals, after I know not what political and social upheaval, will not unite?[41]

In the final analysis, it is the very nature of nuclear weapons which may make the threat of nuclear retaliation by allies difficult to believe. Such weapons are not simply considered to be more modern versions of conventional weaponry. Unlike conventional weapons, nuclear weapons may not be effectively graduated in their use.[42] As Pierre Gallois has suggested, "There is no nuance about its use which determines an exact proportion between the risk taken and the value of the stake coveted."[43]

But what if we broaden our conception of alliance collaboration to permit consideration of multi-actor nuclear forces within the framework of alliance arrangements? Would this not change the nature of some of our conclusions concerning alliances and the achievement of credible deterrence postures? Indeed, if the multi-actor force is conceptualized such that retaliatory strikes might be authorized without the consent of separate and particular contributing members, but rather (1) by some specially created, integrated command structure, or (2) without any discussion at all insofar as automatic response to given provocations has been agreed upon in advance by the constituent units,[44] then several powerful arguments against alliances being of assistance in providing actors with a credible deterrence posture may be overcome. This is the case since the likelihood of nuclear counter-retaliation against any one member of the alliance may be made less likely. If, however, the multi-actor force (MAF) is conceptualized such that all retaliatory strikes require specific authorization from separate and particular contributing members *qua* actors, then MAF may provide little that is new vis-à-vis more orthodox alliance arrangements in terms of deterrence. This is the case because individual actors would suffer the same risk of nuclear counter-retaliation by giving their authorization as they would in conventional alliance agreements where no MAF is created.[45]

If one is firmly convinced that only independent nuclear forces can provide an actor with a credible deterrence posture, however, then *no* conception of alliance collaboration appears satisfactory. Since it is certainly obvious that the value placed on an actor's protection by an alliance partner can never be as high as that which is placed upon such protection by the actor itself, it goes without saying that an actor's commitment to retaliate independently of alliance assistance presents the would-be aggressor with a more credible threat than does the commitment of an alliance partner.[46]

But does it really? Does the proposition that the value assigned to an actor's security by another actor can never be as high as that which is assigned by the actor itself necessarily imply a greater apparent willingness to resort to nuclear retaliation by independent forces? In certain instances, might not an independent nuclear deterrent—even where it appears secure and capable of wreaking unacceptable damage on a potential attacker—yield a similarly incredible deterrent threat? Where actual retaliatory use of a nuclear weapons capability would be *irrational*, i.e., such use would appear very likely to invoke an unacceptably destructive or annihilating counter-response which might otherwise be averted, is there any reason to suppose that an actor possessing an independent nuclear capability would be more likely to retaliate than an assisting ally? Clearly, it might be convincingly argued that the deterrent effectiveness of the independent nuclear capability need not necessarily be greater than that of promised alliance support.[47] This is the case where the retaliatory use of this capability by the would-be deterrer would appear irrational to the would-be attacker.

Of course, where retaliatory use of nuclear weapons would appear irrational, an independent nuclear capability may still provide a credible deterrence posture insofar as the potential aggressor may be persuaded that the would-be deterrer is *not* rational. (Even where *retaliation* is irrational, the *threat to retaliate* may be rational. Such a threat may yield uncertainty about one's own calculations and the rationality of the would-be deterrer.) This does not mean, however, that an independent nuclear capability is necessarily more favorable in terms of deterrence than promised alliance assistance. The same deterrent effectiveness may be achieved by means of alliance collaboration where the potential attacker is persuaded that the assistance-promising ally is not rational.

To this point we have discussed the deterrent effectiveness of alliance assistance *and* independent nuclear capabilities as distinguishable alternatives in terms of several critical factors concerning willingness to retaliate. But in assessing the ability of alliances to assist actors in projecting the image of a credible deterrence posture vis-à-vis "nuclear" actors contemplating attack, is not the proliferation of independent nuclear capabilities *itself* an important factor to be considered? Where alliance collaboration and the development of independent nuclear capabilities coexist within the same system, does not the latter affect the former as far as credibility of deterrent threats is concerned? And if so, *how* does it affect the deterrent effectiveness of alliances?

In the first place, it ought to be pointed out that both the proliferation of independent nuclear capabilities *and* the prevention of such proliferation may weaken alliance commitments. Proliferation of independent nuclear capabilities may weaken alliances where we assume that actors possessing such capabilities may appear less dependent upon the nuclear "shield" of collaborating partners. Efforts to halt the proliferation of independent nuclear capabilities may also tend to weaken alliance commitments. This is the case insofar as we assume (1) that a high degree of cooperation among leading actors of opposing blocs tends to weaken alliance commitments, and (2) that efforts to halt the proliferation of independent nuclear capabilities require a high degree of cooperation among leading actors of opposing blocs.

Proliferation of independent nuclear forces may also strengthen alliance commitments where the actual retaliatory use of such forces is conceived in "trip wire" terms. Here, the prospective attacker would be made to feel that a nuclear strike launched against it in retaliation would more likely commit the victim actor's assisting alliance partners to augment the strike with their own forces than would a non-nuclear retaliation. Ironically, it is doubtful that assisting alliance partners, whose very function it is to augment the deterrence postures of their allies, would view such a tactic with unqualified favor. From the standpoint of the assisting alliance partner, the use of independent nuclear retaliatory forces as a trip wire might appear to make the deterrence postures of its partners *too credible*. That is, the assisting partner may feel that where independent nuclear forces are conceived as a trip wire, there is more to be gained from leaving the alliance than staying.

POSTSCRIPT ON NUCLEAR WEAPONS AND THE RELIABILITY OF COLLECTIVE SECURITY COMMITMENTS

The arguments put forth in the preceding pages concerning nuclear weapons and the ability of alliances to assist actors apply as well to collective security arrangements. This is the case so long as we do not assume that acting in conformity with collective security commitments is believed less likely to evoke nuclear counter-retaliation than acting in compliance with alliance commitments. Such an assumption might be made if (1) there exists some generally shared conviction that collective security measures are necessarily "proper" and that counter-retaliation against any particular actor carrying out such measures is therefore "improper," or if (2) the process of authorizing collective security measures effectively obfuscates separate actor identities, thereby making counter-retaliation against any particular actor meaningless from the point of view of the aggressor. If, however, we do not make either assumption, then there is no reason to suppose that collective security arrangements ought to be more successful than alliances in assisting actors in projecting the image of a credible deterrence posture. Indeed, if we assume that actors will generally be more apt to identify their own specific interests with those of alliance partners than with those of collective security arrangements, then it appears that alliances ought to be more successful in terms of deterrent effectiveness than collective security arrangements.

CONCLUSION

By classifying systems in terms of nuclear weapons, the student of alternative world futures and war avoidance assigns a preeminent position to global *context*. To the extent to which *they* are considered, actor, structure, and process factors are introduced into the models as *intervening* variables. (Just as *context* figures as an *intervening* variable where systems are described in terms of actors, structures, or processes.) This does not imply that these factors are unimportant. But it does suggest that in the individual analyst's calculus of factors relating to power management or war avoidance, the various consequences of a nuclear weapons technology are *uppermost*. From what we have just learned about nuclear weapons and world order, this inclination is easily understood.

NOTES

1. Morton Kaplan, *System and Process in International Politics* (New York: Wiley, 1957), p. 51.

2. Cited in John H. Herz, *International Politics in the Atomic Age* (New York: Columbia University Press, 1959), p. 212.

3. See especially *Conflict and Defense: A General Theory* (New York: 1962) and "The Prevention of World War III," *The Virginia Quarterly Review*, XXXVIII, no. 1, winter 1962, pp. 1-12.

4. See Glenn Snyder, "Balance of Power in the Missile Age," *Journal of International Affairs*, XIV, no. 1, 1960, pp. 21-34. See also Pierre Hassner, "The Nation-State in the Nuclear Age," *Survey*, LXVII, April 1968, pp. 3-27.

5. An actor with a nuclear weapons capability is one which possesses nuclear explosives, associated delivery vehicles, and supporting infrastructure. More specific characterizations of these component factors (e.g., number, yield, velocity, accuracy, type of delivery vehicles) are not built into the definition; rather, they are variable factors in this analysis. Similarly, a nuclear weapons capability is not tied definitionally to an "invulnerable" retaliatory force. Thus, an actor with a nuclear weapons capability may range from absolutely vulnerable to absolutely invulnerable in terms of its nuclear retaliatory system.

6. See Stanley Hoffmann, "Roulette in the Cellar: Notes on Risk in International Relations," *The State of War: Essays on the Theory and Practice of International Politics* (New York: Praeger, 1965), pp. 134-159.

7. See *Peace and War* (New York: Doubleday, 1966), p. 406.

8. See Klaus Knorr, *On the Uses of Military Power in the Nuclear Age* (Princeton, N.J.: Princeton University Press, 1966), p. 82. Where the destructive power of weapons is measured in terms of yield to weight ratio, we may characterize the nuclear revolution in firepower as having produced a million-fold increase in yield for a given weight. On this point see Morton H. Halperin, *Contemporary Military Strategy* (Boston: Little, Brown, 1967), pp. 3-6.

9. See Ciro Zoppo, "Nuclear Technology, Multipolarity, and International Stability," *World Politics*, XVIII, 4, July 1966, pp. 579-606.

10. See Snyder, "Balance of Power in the Missile Age."

11. See Arthur Lee Burns, "From Balance to Deterrence: A Theoretical Analysis," *World Politics*, IX, 4, July 1957, pp. 494-529.

12. Speech in Commons, March 1, 1955, cited in Herz, *International Politics in the Atomic Age*, p. 184.

13. See F. H. Hinsley, *Power and the Pursuit of Peace* (Cambridge: Cambridge University Press, 1963), p. 347.

14. *Ibid.*, pp. 354-355.

15. See Bernard Brodie, "The Anatomy of Deterrence," *World Politics*, XI, 2, January 1959, p. 176.

16. See John Herz, "Balance System and Balance Policies in a Nuclear and Bipolar Age," *Journal of International Affairs*, XIV, 1, 1960, p. 43.

17. In terms of this argument, it is doubtful whether a useful distinction concerning credibility can be made between strategic or large-scale nuclear weapons and tactical ones. It appears that where the threat of strategic nuclear reprisal is deemed unlikely to be executed, the threat of tactical nuclear reprisal will appear unconvincing as well. This is especially the case where the prospective recipient of a tactical reprisal feels that it is believed to possess a strategic second-strike capacity. We derive this argument from the assumption that the critical "threshold" is not between one form of nuclear weapons system and another, but rather between conventional weapons and nuclear weapons.

18. See Herz, "Balance System and Balance Policies in a Nuclear and Bipolar Age."

19. Needless to say, being judged able to survive a first-strike attack is only the first requirement of inflicting unacceptable reprisals. A deterrent force must also be judged capable of penetrating the defenses of the would-be attacker with unacceptable payloads after the enemy first-strike has been survived. (Nuclear weapons capability and invulnerable retaliatory force not-withstanding, an actor is no longer believed to possess a credible deterrence posture when another actor feels that it can initiate a first-strike against it and can successfully halt the retaliatory strike by means of a highly effective system of active defense.) Such a force might lack credibility on this point if it was composed of only a small number of appropriate weapons and/or if the attacker's active defense system was at a sufficiently high level of effectiveness. With the transition from manned bombers to ballistic missiles, however, the difficulties entailed by such active defense make high levels of effectiveness extremely unlikely. So long as active defense lacks an exceptionally high level of effectiveness (a likely prospect indeed) we may say the following: Where the would-be attacker feels unable to count on wreaking sufficient destruction upon his victim's retaliatory capacity in his initial strike to prevent the launching of an "unacceptably destructive" retaliatory payload, he will be deterred.

20.   The importance of a secure retaliatory force has received particularly wide recognition in the literature. Glenn Snyder, for example, has said that a "balance of terror" exists when neither side, in striking first, can destroy enough of the opponent's forces to make the latter's retaliatory strike tolerable. (*Deterrence and Defense*, Princeton, N.J.: Princeton University Press, 1961, p. 97.) Similarly, Robert Osgood describes the essential requirement of deterrence to be a sufficiently invulnerable retaliatory force capable of inflicting unacceptable destruction on the attacker. (See "The Uses of Military Power in the Cold War," in Robert A. Goldwin, ed., *America Armed: Essays on United States Military Policy*, Chicago: Rand McNally, 1963, p. 8.) Albert Wohlstetter (who, incidentally, is the original source of this point) also recognizes that in addition to the magnitude of striking power, successful deterrence depends as well on the invulnerability of the nuclear reprisal arsenal. (See "The Delicate Balance of Terror," *Foreign Affairs*, XXXVII, 2, January 1958, pp. 211-234). J. David Singer tells us that an actor's main deterrent effect derives from his ability to render his retaliatory force invulnerable to a first-strike. (See *Deterrence, Arms Control, and Disarmament*, Columbus: Ohio State University Press, 1962, p. 50.) And Oskar Morgenstern suggests that in order to preserve stability through nuclear deterrence it is essential for all sides to possess invulnerable retaliatory forces. (See *The Question of National Defense*, New York: Random House, 1959.)

21.   There is, of course, no reason to suppose that available alternatives are characterized by exclusivity, i.e., that an actor may choose one means of protecting his retaliatory forces only at the expense of excluding another. The treatment of alternative means of reducing vulnerability as separate and distinct is undertaken herein solely for purposes of analysis. Clearly, an actor may combine several alternative means of assuring retaliatory force survival. As a rule, in fact, a retaliatory force ought to be composed of several different component systems. It should be a "mixed systems" force. This will be discussed below.

22.   Singer, *Deterrence, Arms Control, and Disarmament*, p. 51. If hardening is conceived as a race between the extent of protection which may be offered and the increasing accuracy of missiles, there is little cause for optimism about this method of increasing invulnerability. This is the case because the factor of accuracy is probably rising more rapidly. On this point, see John Strachey, *On the Prevention of War* (London: Macmillan, 1962), p. 61.

23.   See Morgenstern, *The Question of National Defense*, p. 50. In discussing the survivability of retaliatory forces via hardening, Glenn Snyder is more optimistic than Singer and Morgenstern. According to Snyder, "the fixed, dispersed [Snyder does introduce the additional means of *dispersion* into his discussion of hardening], hardened, land-based ICBM gets fairly high marks because of its small size, distance from the enemy's firing points, and ability to survive anything but a direct hit or a very near miss." (*Deterrence and Defense*, p. 86.) In view of the significant technological breakthroughs of the last decade, however, it is certainly doubtful that the writer would stand by these remarks.

24. See Alexander de Volpi, "MIRV—Gorgon Medusa of the Nuclear Age," *Bulletin of the Atomic Scientists*, January 1970, p. 35.

25. See Hans A. Bethe, "Hard Point vs. City Defense," *Bulletin of the Atomic Scientists*, June 1969, p. 25.

26. See Frank E. Bothwell, "Is the ICBM Obsolete?" *Bulletin of the Atomic Scientists*, October 1969, p. 21. Bothwell points out further that where the exchange ratio is well below unity, mere proliferation of retaliatory forces may be insufficient too to redress the balance. This is because increments of retaliatory force may be countered by increments of first-strike force.

27. See Freeman Dyson, "A Case for Missile Defense," *Bulletin of the Atomic Scientists*, April 1969, p. 32. See also Bethe, "Hard Point vs. City Defense," p. 25.

28. Unlike cities, retaliatory forces need not be protected with a nearly 100 percent level of effectiveness. Given a sizeable number of high-yield retaliatory missiles, an effective defense might be one where only a small percentage are rendered invulnerable. This is the case insofar as this small percentage is still deemed capable of striking the prospective attacker with what he considers to be an unacceptably destructive payload.

29. Ordinarily, it is assumed that the accuracy of delivery of multiple independent re-entry vehicles is equal to the accuracy of delivery of single-headed missiles. On this point, see de Volpi, "MIRV—Gorgon Medusa of the Nuclear Age," p. 36.

30. This point has also been made by Oskar Morgenstern (*The Question of National Defense*) and Glenn Snyder (*Deterrence and Defense*).

31. Bothwell, "Is the ICBM Obsolete?" p. 22.

32. See, for example, Glenn Snyder, *Deterrence and Defense*, pp. 88-89. A recent account of the present state of submarine detection technology may be found in John Marriott, "NATO's ASW Potential," *Survival*, September 1970, pp. 298-303. Marriott's conclusion is that presently, at least, submarines certainly have "the edge."

33. On this point, see Raymond Aron, *The Great Debate* (New York: Doubleday, 1965), p. 37.

34. On this matter, see Arthur Waskow, "The Theory and Practice of Deterrence," in Henry A. Kissinger, ed., *Problems of National Strategy* (New York: Praeger, 1965, p. 71). While this problem may develop in a situation characterized exclusively by land-based retaliatory forces as well, it is particularly threatening where sea-basing is widespread.

35. See Waskow, "The Theory and Practice of Deterrence," p. 71.

36. An actor which fears the "mistaken identity" problem associated with sea-basing which we discussed earlier might, however, wish to omit sea-mobile system forces altogether.

37. Although not included in the foregoing discussion, air-borne launch systems might also be included in this "mix." Like land- and sea-based launch systems, air-borne launch systems may be protected by being more or less continually moved about.

38. It should also be pointed out that vulnerability may also depend upon the reaction speed of weapons and on warning systems.

39. See Stanley Hoffmann, "Nuclear Proliferation and World Politics," in Alastair Buchan, ed., *A World of Nuclear Powers*, (Englewood Cliffs, N.J.: Prentice-Hall) p. 110.

40. See especially Pierre M. Gallois, "U.S. Strategy and the Defense of Europe," *Orbis*, VII, 2, summer 1963. See also "Nuclear Strategy: A French View," in Eleanor Lansing Dulles and Robert Dickson Crane, eds., *Detente: Cold War Strategies in Transition* (New York: Praeger, 1965), pp. 215-240.

41. *The New York Times*, December 11, 1969, p. 10. Cited in Herman Kahn, *On Thermonuclear War* (Princeton, N.J.: Princeton University Press, 1960), pp. 30-31.

42. This assumes, of course, that decision-makers perceive the critical threshold to be the conventional nuclear one, and that crossing this threshold necessarily signifies the onset of a "no holds barred" situation. For a different view, see Bernard Brodie, "The 'Firebreak' Theory," Chapter X in *Escalation and the Nuclear Option* (Princeton, N.J.: Princeton University Press, 1966).

43. See Pierre M. Gallois, *The Balance of Terror: Strategy for the Nuclear Age* (Boston: Houghton-Mifflin, 1961), p. 173.

44. It is ironic, perhaps, that increasing the credibility of the threat may involve increasing the levels of danger by mechanical accident or human misinterpretation. Where it is believed that steps 1 and 2 above are advantageous from the standpoint of increased credibility, and where it is also believed that such steps involve increased levels of danger from mechanical accident or human misinterpretation, the decision-makers must compare the consequences of each course of action. As regards step 2, however, it is difficult to sustain the position that actors will feel able to convince other actors that decisions will really be made in fully automatic fashion.

45. An interesting variation to be considered is one where separate and particular actor authorizations *are* required, but where the actual process of authorization is so hidden or obfuscated that nuclear counter-retaliation against any one particular actor becomes meaningless from the point of view of the prospective aggressor.

46. To be convincing, of course, this argument must include the assumption that an independent nuclear capability necessarily appears secure and capable of wreaking damage unacceptable to potential aggressors. Clearly, no matter how enhanced the *willingness* factor becomes as we move from alliance assistance to independent forces, would-be attackers must also be convinced that the means of unacceptably damaging retaliation are present if deterrent threats are to be deemed credible. Indeed, a principal argument against independent nuclear forces in recent diplomatic history derives from the assumption that such forces are less likely to appear *capable* of delivering unacceptably damaging retaliation than are the forces of alliance superpowers. (On this point, see for example Robert S. McNamara, Address at the Commencement Exercises, University of Michigan, Ann Arbor, Michigan, June 16, 1962, *Department of State Bulletin*, XLVII, 1202, July 9, 1962; and

Albert Wohlstetter, "Nuclear Sharing: NATO and the N+1 Country," *Foreign Affairs*, XXXIX, 3, April 1961.) If we accept this assumption, and join it with the additional assumption that *willingness* to retaliate is more credible in the case of independent forces, then an actor forced to choose between the two as alternative means of projecting the image of a credible deterrence posture will have to rank the two components of such a posture in order to reach a decision. If the actor is *not* forced to choose either alliance assistance or independent forces, then it may base what it regards as an appropriate "mix" on its rank order of *means* and *willingness*.

47.   Indeed, it might even be argued that the development of an independent nuclear weapons capability renders an actor *more* susceptible to attack during the transitional phase than it would be if it did not undertake such development.

Chapter 12
Structure

INTRODUCTION

A variety of interesting hypotheses lead to world systems described in terms of *structure* (i.e., the prevailing pattern of global power). The most prominent of these center about the bipolar-multipolar "debate." Here the suggestion is advanced that either bipolarity or multipolarity is the most favorable structure from the standpoint of systemic stability.[1] Occasionally, the plausibility of an hypothesis will be judged to depend upon the status of an important *intervening variable*—context. Those who favor multipolar power systems in the absence of nuclear weapons are likely to reverse the connection when a proliferating nuclear weapons technology is taken into account. The basic contours of these rather well-known arguments will receive our attention in the first part of chapter twelve.

While a great deal has already been written about the relationship of structure (bipolarity, multipolarity) to war avoidance *generally*, nowhere has the "debate" been cast in terms of the *reliability of alliances*. Indeed, although we remember from our discussion in chapter eight that the use of alliances represents a time-honored manner of demonstrating a credible deterrence posture, there has as yet been no attempt to relate the reliability of alliance commitments to *structure*. In short, there has as yet been no systematic effort to determine the extent to which alliance reliability varies in accordance with the number of *conflict axes* in the world system. The second part of this chapter represents such an effort. By critically examining the various assumptions, inferences, and conclusions which are found there, the student of alternative world futures may consider diverse and important implications of structure for world order.

THE BASIC BIPOLAR-MULTIPOLAR DEBATE

In the controversy concerning peacefulness of adjustment in bipolar and multipolar world systems, the principal "debaters" have been Kenneth Waltz (bipolarity) and Karl Deutsch and J. David Singer (multipolarity). The following discussion will examine their respective arguments.[2]

According to Waltz, the classical argument on behalf of multipolarity is ill founded. It is, he claims, an argument that ought to be fully revised. This is because four factors distinctive to bipolar world systems conjoin to more effectively limit the use of force between actors. These factors are the *absence of peripheries*, the *particular range and intensity of competition*, the *persistence of pressure and crisis*, and the *preeminent power position of two major actors*. Waltz contends that these factors combine to create a uniquely stable balance—a bipolar balance. Within this balance, a variety of political, military, and economic changes can allegedly be handled more peacefully than in a multipolar system. Moreover, nuclear weapons can contribute to stability or peacefulness of adjustment only insofar as they may maintain or nurture a condition of bipolarity. We are led to this conclusion because (1) bipolarity preceded two-power nuclear competition; (2) destructive power would still be great in the absence of nuclear weapons; (3) the existence of an increasing number of nuclear states would increase the range of difficult political choices; and (4) nuclear weapons are a *product* of great national capabilities rather than their cause.[3]

Hence, Waltz argues that bipolarity is more favorable than multipolarity *whatever the weapons technology context*. The *classical* position in international relations theory suggests that a multipolar system is more stable than a bipolar one *unless the system is characterized by a proliferating nuclear weapons technology*. This is the position of such prominent international relations theorists as Morton Kaplan (see chapter three) and Hans Morgenthau.[4] With Waltz, however, bipolarity is *always* favored over multipolarity.

In the classical model, then, it is argued that as the system moves away from bipolarity toward multipolarity in the absence of proliferating nuclear weapons, the frequency of war is expected to diminish. This is largely because of the greater flexibility of alignment associated with the latter type of structure. Hans Morgenthau, for example, has argued that the reduction in the number of great powers from eight to two in this century has had a deleterious effect upon the balance of power.

237

While the multipolar position has been widely regarded as self-evident or intuitively reasonable, Karl Deutsch and J. David Singer have presented two distinct but related lines of formal argument as to why the multipolar-stability relationship should turn out "as the theoretician has generally assumed and as the historian has often found to be the case."[5]

Defining stability in terms of large-scale war avoidance, Deutsch and Singer set out to examine the relationship between stability and systemic structure. The resultant analysis has interesting implications for the diffusion of nuclear weapons. It is argued that where principle concern is for rapid de-escalation, multipolar systems may prove more intractable than bipolar ones, but where concern lies in the prevention of any rapid escalation of two-power arms competition, a shift towards multipolarity is preferred.

Moreover, a multipolar world, though often more stable in the short run, allegedly suffers from long-run instability. In the long-run model devised by Deutsch and Singer, even multipolar systems operating under the rules of balance of power policies appear self-destructive. Both in the short- and long-run, however, the instability of "tight" bipolar systems appears to be considerably greater.[6] Hence, the authors conclude that "if the spread of nuclear weapons could be slowed down or controlled, a transition from the bipolar international system of the early 1950s to an increasingly multipolar system in the 1960s might buy mankind some valuable time to seek some more dependable bases for world order."[7]

Nevertheless, there are those (like Waltz) who feel that the stability of bipolar systems—while enhanced by a nuclear weapons technology—in no way *depends* on that technology. To this group, the intervening variable of *weapons technology* cannot be regarded as critical to bipolar stability. Bipolar systems are *by their nature* more stable than multipolar systems. This is because in such systems it is relatively certain that conflict is apt to focus around a single system-wide axis, there exists relative freedom from damaging uncertainties, and there is a probable reduction of complacency which arises from the fear that bipolar conflict is unusually intense.

SOME ALTERNATIVE CONCEPTUALIZATIONS OF STRUCTURE

Despite the intensity of the bipolar-multipolar debate, widespread dissatisfaction with the adequacy of these conceptions characterizes recent writing.

Roger Masters, for example, has defined an abstract model of global structure in terms of a *multiplicity of blocs*.[8] This model is explicitly offered as a supplement to the types presented by Morton Kaplan in *System and Process in International Politics*. And in order that the "multi-bloc" model may serve as a theoretical expression of Kaplan's typology, the system is defined with reference to his work. In brief, the "pure" multi-bloc system is merely Kaplan's "balance of power" model with five or more regional blocs as actors. For purposes of illustration, Masters suggests that these blocs might be the Western Hemisphere, Western Europe, the Soviet Union and Eastern Europe, an Asian region dominated by China, and Africa. Implied in the dynamics of this system is considerable flexibility in alignments, a willingness to limit warfare, and a tendency to absorb uncommitted states into one or another bloc.

As to the stability of the system, Masters seeks to determine whether the stability of the multi-bloc model would be undermined should Kaplan's six rules not apply completely.[9] One of his conclusions suggests that the more numerous the blocs, the more stable the system will be, since the number of "aggressive" actors required to destroy the system increases. This condition is expected to hold so long as all blocs are relatively equal, and so long as systems with odd numbers of actors will be more or less flexible whereas those with an even number of member-blocs will tend toward rigidity. With the introduction of nuclear weapons technology as an intervening explanatory factor, Masters attempts to demonstrate that a multi-bloc model might approximate the only international system in which the diffusion of nuclear weapons does not have catastrophic results.

Wolfram Hanrieder also recommends new conceptualizations of the world system in terms of structure.[10] He claims that while a number of important relationships among nations exhibit patterns which might be labeled *polycentric, bipolarity* is still with us in such respects as nuclear capabilities and the fundamentally tense relationship between the United States and the Soviet Union. What is needed, says Hanrieder, to arrive at a more adequate "abbreviation of reality" is an alternative pattern-image which is more adaptable to the dynamics and complexity of current events because it combines bipolar with polycentric patterns. To call the present international system either bipolar *or* polycentric is thought to be misleading: the terminology of Kaplan's loose bipolar system is too bipolar, while the Masters model goes to the other extreme by neglecting bipolar attributes altogether.

Hanrieder's principal objection, then, is that the language of theorists like Masters and Kaplan fails to permit a "descriptive mix" between bipolar and multi-bloc phenomena. While each concept may be useful on some relational levels—e.g., bipolarity in the case of a nuclear power system or multipolarity in the case of a United Nations voting system—almost all systemic relationships today are characterized by *both* a fundamental bipolar tension *and* a multicentric dimension. Hanrieder's suggestion for a more adequate conceptualization of patterns is as follows:

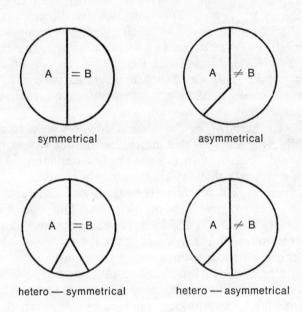

symmetrical   asymmetrical

hetero — symmetrical   hetero — asymmetrical

In effect, Hanrieder creates his four alternative models by subdividing the bipolar universe of cases. This is accomplished by introducing two additional explanatory variables: (1) ratio of power between the two poles, and (2) extent to which secondary actors share in the power. More complete descriptions of these models will be offered later on in this chapter when we explore them in terms of alliance reliability.

For the moment, however, we may note that Hanrieder's attempt to distinguish bipolar systems in terms of the extent to which secondary actors share in the power reflects the constantly changing configuration of global forces. While the disproportionately powerful positions of the Soviet Union and the United States after the Second World War justified analytic use of the bipolar model, this is no longer the case. Today, this model (if it is to be retained at all) must take account of such factors as ideological realignments, the entry into the world system of a significant number of "new" nations, and the increasing proliferation of a uniquely destructive weapons technology.

Oran Young has also argued that the primary distinction between bipolar systems and multipolar ones is inadequate in dealing with developing world political patterns.[11] To remedy this condition, he offers some new ways of conceptualizing world political structures. These involve an alternative model which emphasizes the increasing interpenetration of global axes of conflict with divergent regional or subsystemic ones. Unlike the bipolar model, which emphasizes only a single, system-wide axis of conflict, Young's "discontinuities" model stresses both system-wide and regional factors in various complex patterns of interpenetration. And unlike the multipolar model, which stresses a number of system-wide conflict axes, the discontinuities model stresses differences between system-wide and regional axes and focuses on complex interpenetrations of regional and universal issues.

Finally, we may note the vertically layered system of Richard Rosecrance, which combines elements of bipolarity and multipolarity.[12] Here, the world system is "divided" into bipolar and multipolar realms, and state behavior is characterized in terms of the particular realm (or realms) involved. Moreover, the interests *within* any one realm may be competitive and harmonious at the same time. For example, bipolar actors may be cooperative in restraining conflicts in the multipolar realm but competitive with each other in the bipolar one. Parallel ambivalence characterizes the interests of multipolar states. This means that while there might be certain rivalries between them at the multipolar level, there would also be common interests in resisting hegemonial ambitions of bipolar actors. In terms of war avoidance, Rosecrance favors such a system for the following reasons:

> The probability of war, whether local or general, would be much smaller than in a multipolar system. Conflict would be mitigated on two scores: a multipolar buffer might help prevent the two nuclear giants from coming to blows; and the restraining influence of the bipolar states might in turn prevent extreme conflict among multipolar powers. While simple bipolarity would not exist, the influence of two super-powers would be crucial in limiting the outcomes of the system.[13]

Notwithstanding their awareness of changing patterns of interstate relationships, none of these alternative conceptions come to grips with a profoundly important development in world politics. We refer to the increasing importance of *nonstate* actors. Among these, guerrilla and terrorist organizations are a matter of particular urgency and concern. Although the existing literature has not yet recognized their ability to precipitate sudden and enormously destabilizing conditions throughout the world system, these organizations must soon be accounted for by students of global structure.

To illustrate this point, we may consider the 1972 summer events in Munich and their probable aftermath. With its attack on the Israeli compound at Olympic Village, a small group of Palestinian guerrillas revealed the incredible vulnerability of the world system to "private" acts of terrorism. Such incidents will doubtlessly continue in the years ahead. And their destructive implications may be magnified many times by the growing ease with which nuclear or chemical-biological warfare type weapons may be obtained. For the student concerned with developing models of alternative world futures along a *structural* dimension, these facts present an important challenge. Given the obvious significance of terrorist actors for world order, it is the head of the class for anyone whose models can account for them interestingly.

BIPOLARITY, MULTIPOLARITY, AND THE RELIABILITY OF ALLIANCES

Returning to the basic concepts of global structure, the bipolar-multipolar debate may also be cast in terms of the reliability of alliance commitments.[14] And there are a variety of reasons for arguing that alliance reliability is greater in the bipolar system than in the multipolar one. One of these reasons centers on the difference in the shifting of alignments. As the benefits of collaboration are more evenly distributed in a lasting coalition than in a transient one,[15] actors are more likely to identify their own particular interests with the more permanent coalitions of the bipolar configuration.[16] It follows from what is known of the self-interested manner of actor decision-making that so far as structure is concerned, actors in a bipolar system are more likely to honor their alliance commitments than are their counterparts in a multipolar system.

But why are multipolar alignments considered more susceptible to shift? So long as we do not tie our definitions of bipolarity to the number of independent actors, there appears to be no logical reason why the number of interaction opportunities should be greater in a multipolar setting than in a bipolar one. The number of actors able to enter into alliance agreements with other actors seems to be just as large in the latter setting.

In the bipolar system, however, alignments take place around two fixed points with little or no movement of actors from one point to another. This is because moving between poles in the bipolar system is restricted by the peculiarly intense character of inter-bloc rivalry. Such movement is inhibited even further where this basic polar antagonism is reinforced by an ideological cleavage.

If it is assumed, then, that the shifting of alignments in the bipolar setting takes place around two fixed points with little or no movement of actors from one point to another, the structure of bipolarity *does* tend to limit the number of alignments. A bipolar configuration effectively reduces the number of actors with which any particular actor may align itself. Applying the standard formula for possible pairs, $\frac{N(N-1)}{2}$, and assuming no movement of actors between poles, it can easily be seen that in a bipolar system consisting of the same number of actors as a multipolar system, there are fewer possible alignments. Thus, the multipolar system is characterized by a greater number and diversity of interaction opportunities than the bipolar one. Consequently, actors will be more likely to become subject to a greater variety of cross-loyalties in the multipolar configuration. Such loyalties tend to weaken the reliability of any one particular alliance commitment.

Depending upon one's particular ordering of the conditions believed to minimize the likelihood of inter-actor conflict, an increased variety of cross-loyalties may be regarded as either desirable or undesirable. From the standpoint of classical international relations theory (e.g., Hans Morgenthau, Morton Kaplan), the greater variety of cross-loyalties which characterizes the multipolar configuration represents a *conflict mitigating* factor. Here, no primary connection is assumed between the effectiveness of conflict mitigation and alliance reliability. Quite the contrary! At the same time, the greater variety of cross-loyalties which characterizes the multipolar configuration may be deemed *conflict aggravating*. This is the case where the analyst emphasizes a primary connection between (1) the effectiveness of conflict mitigation and the credibility of particular deterrence postures, and (2) the credibility of particular deterrence postures and the reliability of alliances.

It may also be that the greater diversity of interest which characterizes the multipolar system makes for greater reliability of bipolar alliances for a reason other than the pressure of cross-loyalties. Whether we consider such diversity of interest as the result of the greater number and diversity of interaction opportunities *or* as the outcome of a situation in which there is a larger number of significant actors, its inhibiting effect on alliance reliability may also be in evidence where no contradictory alliance commitments exist. That is, it may be due solely to the increased difficulty for actors to identify their own judgments of self-interest with the interests of their alliance partners. (The wider the range of particular interests, the harder it is for any one actor to reconcile them with its own.) Thus, alliance reliability in the multipolar setting suffers from the increased (vis-à-vis bipolarity) extent of particularity in the world system.

Another reason why alliance reliability is greater in the bipolar system centers on the differences in alliance structure. The shift from multipolarity to bipolarity involves the shift of the "hard shell" from the individual member actor to the entire rim of the alliance region. According to John Herz:

> The chief characteristics of the bipolar system lie in its trend toward an extension of the hard shell, the protective wall which used to surround single territorial units, so as to include (in tendency, if not in actuality) approximately one-half of the world in the case of each of the two blocs. In this way, the unit of defense and protection is being shifted from the nation to the bloc.[17]

Together with this extension of the hard shell, bipolar bloc alliances involve structural changes which go significantly beyond those of multipolar alliances. As the latter type of alliance typically provides only declarations of mutual commitment to assist one another under specified circumstances, individual actors remain separate units of power. Implementation of an integrated military establishment is not undertaken. In a bipolar situation, on the other hand, alliance agreements function under significantly different structural premises. What really matters here is not the alliance agreements as such, but the implementation of the particular system which they foster. This system is founded upon arrangements for integrated defense, bases, stationing of troops, and related matters undertaken by superpower and particular "rim" countries. According to Herz:

> in place of some scattered outposts, bases, and other garrisoned places, all of which were parts of individual defense systems of various powers and which had their guns turned against each other, under bipolarity they are rearranged into one comprehensive hard-shell system opposing

the only other one extant. The guns within each system are now lined up parallel to each other . . . .[18]

A final reason for arguing that alliance reliability is greater in the bipolar system centers on the increased extent of alliance penetration of intra-actor processes of decision-making. While there is no logical reason why such penetration might not also characterize multipolar alliance arrangements, the uniquely powerful position of the leading actors in a bipolar system suggests that such penetration is *more likely* within the bipolar configuration. Moreover, active intervention in the realm of intra-actor affairs by alliance leaders will be all the more likely to the extent that (1) actors represent not only repositories of power to members of the other bloc, but also a particular economic, social, and political system of beliefs, and (2) the superpower at the head of each bloc is interested in preserving and advancing the basic features of this system. To a greater extent than in multipolar systems, then, alliance leaders in a bipolar configuration tamper with processes of decision *within* acting units. Consequently, individual members are more "amenable" to honoring their obligations to the alliance than would ordinarily be the case.

In focusing upon the implications of structure for alliance reliability, we have stressed the number of axes of conflict. Structure, then, has been conceptualized in terms of bipolar and multipolar world systems. We must *now* consider alliance reliability in terms of more complex structural conceptualizations of the world system.

FOUR VARIATIONS OF BIPOLARITY

One interesting set of conceptions is the one provided for us by Wolfram Hanrieder. As we already know, his first configuration or pattern is referred to as a *symmetrical system*. This is a pronounced or "tight" bipolar system, with no actors in the system existing apart from the two blocs, and with a situation of approximate equilibrium existing between the two poles. Moreover, the two poles occupy a position of preponderance within the system. As this pattern represents our own conception of bipolarity as discussed in the preceding pages, we may proceed immediately to the second proposed configuration.

The second model is referred to as an *asymmetrical system*. Here, the two poles still predominate at the expense of the secondary actors, but one pole occupies a position of predominance over the other. What does this suggest for alliance reliability? Is there any reason to believe that the introduction of an inequality of power factor will alter our conclusions concerning bipolar alliance reliability?

Since none of the features of a bipolar configuration which were cited as factors making for greater alliance reliability are changed with the introduction of the inequality of power factor, there is no reason to suppose that such introduction will affect our conclusions concerning bipolar alliance reliability vis-à-vis multipolar alliance reliability. For example, alignments still take place around two fixed points and the rate of alignment shifts is thereby still slowed down. The uniquely powerful position of the leading actor in each bloc vis-à-vis the secondary actors is still preserved. This, too, results in the limiting of alignment shifts. The greater extent of functional integration of facilities which we associate with bipolar alignments and which also inhibits the shifting of alignments (as well as having a more *direct* effect on the credibility of particular deterrence postures) is unaffected as well by imbalance between poles. And the extent of penetration into intra-actor decision-making processes is also unaffected by such imbalance.

But if the introduction of power ratio between blocs as an "intervening variable" has no bearing on our conclusions about bipolar alliances as opposed to multipolar ones, it does make possible an effective difference in alliance reliability between blocs within the same bipolar system. In the first place, if the acknowledged inequality is due to an inferiority of number, we recognize that actors in the bloc with the fewer number of actors have fewer possible interaction opportunities. For reasons discussed earlier, this will tend to make for more permanent alignments and consequently for greater reliability. Fewer interaction opportunities also mean fewer cross-loyalties—loyalties which tend to weaken the reliability of any one particular alliance commitment. Moreover, even where the pressures of cross-loyalties are absent, an increase in the number of actors within a given bloc may inhibit alliance reliability to the extent that the resultant growth of particular interests makes it increasingly difficult for actors to identify their own judgments of self-interest with the interests of their alliance partners. Finally, it ought also to be pointed out that while decreasing the number of actors decreases the number of interaction opportunities, it also increases the ratio of the number of alliances to which any given actor may belong to the total number of possible alliances. In this sense, a decrease in the number of actors may be judged to increase the ability of alliances to assist actors in projecting the image of a credible deterrence posture.

What about differences in alliance reliability between the two blocs where the inequality between them is conceptualized in terms of weapons systems and military hardware? What effect, if any, can we associate with predominance in force level, skill, and systems of delivery? And will our answer to this question depend on the particular manner in which these factors are distributed within each bloc?

If, for example, the state of inequality is due to a more or less significant disparity between the leading actors, with no real difference between the secondary actors of the two blocs, would not the actors contemplating alignments around the less powerful pole be inclined to be less than enthusiastic about the prospects of collective action? So long as we assume that the purpose of alignment is tied to the prospects for *deterrence* and not for victory,[19] and so long as alignment around the inferior pole is judged capable of producing the image of sufficient means for delivering an unacceptably destructive or annihilating response, the answer to this question is certainly "No." There is, then, no reason to suppose that alliance agreements based upon alignment with the inferior leading actor in an asymmetrical bipolar system are less reliable than agreements based upon alignment with the superior actor in this system because of the stated inequality. Similarly, where the situation of inequality between poles is due to a disparity between the secondary actors with no real disparity between the leading actors, or where it is due to a disparity between both the leading actors *and* the secondary actors, there is still no reason to suppose a consequent difference in alliance reliability between the two blocs.

Hanrieder's third and fourth models represent two variants of a bipolar configuration in which a more or less sizeable number of actors exist apart from the membership of the two blocs. Each variant of this configuration resembles the "loose" bipolar system, with the difference between them being the ratio of power between the two blocs (the ratio between them is equal in the hetero-symmetrical system and unequal in the hetero-asymmetrical system). What follows, then, is a look at two forms of loose bipolarity in terms of alliance reliability.

In the loose bipolar configuration there are several changes in the features of bipolarity which were cited as factors making for greater alliance reliability. In the first place, alignments are no longer restricted to taking place around two fixed points in the system. Alignments may now shift around points located apart from the system's two poles and actors may now move from one pole to another in the shifting of alignments. It follows that there exists a greater number of interaction opportunities here than in the "tight" bipolar world and a greater likelihood of shifts in alignment. This increased likelihood is further reinforced by the diminished power position of the leading actors which accompanies the transition from tight to loose bipolarity. And remembering what was said earlier of the connection between "permanence" and reliability, it appears that actors in a tight bipolar system are more likely to honor their alliance commitments than are the actors in a loose bipolar system.

The increased number of interaction opportunities will also tend to weaken the reliability of any one alliance commitment insofar as it produces a greater variety of cross-loyalties in the system. And even in the absence of contradictory alliance commitments that might be engendered by an increase in cross-loyalties, the increased diversity of interest associated with the shift from tight to loose bipolarity may itself make alliance commitments in the latter system less reliable. This is because even where the increased diversity of interest has not produced a conflict of commitments, such an increase still makes it more difficult for actors to identify their own judgments of self-interest with the interests of their alliance partners. Finally, the increased number of alignments may affect the protective character of alliances in ways other than those which are stated in terms of honoring obligations. That is to say, alliances may be less helpful in the loose bipolar system than in the tight bipolar system not only because commitments tend to be more reliable in the latter type of configuration, but also because the increased number of possible alignments in the loose bipolar system tends to decrease the ratio of the number of alliances to which any given actor may belong to the number of possible alliances.

Now, what of an effective difference in alliance reliability *within* the loose bipolar system? First, as our definition of loose bipolarity excludes the situation where nonmember actors constitute a separate bloc (this situation would represent a fundamental transformation of the underlying bipolar structure of the system), our problem becomes one of determining the differences in reliability prevailing between bloc alliances, non-bloc alliances, and alliances between member actors and nonmember actors.[20]

To accomplish this determination, we must first say something about the power position of the leading actor of a non-bloc alliance. Despite the fact that the transition from tight to loose bipolarity diminishes the power position of the leading actors in each bloc, such actors may still be in a more powerful position vis-à-vis their partners than are the leading actors of non-bloc alliances. Where this is the case, despite the fact that in the loose bipolar system member actors may move from one pole to another and from one pole to a nonmember actor in fixing alignments as readily as nonmember actors may move between other non-member actors, it is likely that alignment shifts of the last category would still be the most common. It appears, then, that *within* the loose bipolar system described above, bloc alliances may be characterized by greater reliability than (1) non-bloc alliances, and (2) alliances between member actors and non-member actors.

A VARIATION OF MULTIPOLARITY

One interesting variation of the *multipolar* model is the multi-bloc configuration proposed by Roger Masters. What does this model mean in terms of alliance reliability? Since the multi-bloc system would have fewer actors than the "balance of power" one, alliances would be apt to be considerably more reliable. This is because fewer actors means fewer interaction opportunities and consequently greater value attached to any one particular alignment. Fewer interaction opportunities also means fewer cross-loyalties—loyalties which tend to weaken the reliability of any one particular alliance commitment. Insofar as there is less particularity, fewer actors makes it more likely for any given actor to identify its own judgments of self-interest with the interests of its alliance partners. And fewer actors also means an increased ratio of the number of alliances to which any given actor may belong to the total number of possible alliances.

CONCLUSION

Our concern in the latter part of this discussion has been with the effects of structure on alliance reliability. We are interested in alliance reliability because of its importance to international war avoidance. Needless to say, there are many *other* possible conceptualizations of the world system which might be examined for their alliance reliability features. Whatever set of conceptions is selected for examination, the student of alternative world futures will be focusing upon a particularly crucial relationship concerning effective power management in the world system.

NOTES

1. By *bipolarity* we mean a "duopolistic" arrangement of global power wherein two superpowers effectively control world order. *Multipolarity*, on the other hand, describes an "oligopolistic" arrangement of global power wherein a sizeable number of more or less balanced actors control world order.

2. See Kenneth N. Waltz, "The Stability of a Bipolar World," *Daedalus*, XCIII (summer 1964), 881-907, reprinted in George H. Quester, ed., *Power, Action, and Interaction: Readings on International Politics* (Boston: Little, Brown, 1971), pp. 216-243; and Karl Deutsch and J. David Singer, "Multipolar Power Systems and International Stability," *World Politics*, XVI (April 1964), 390-406.

3. Waltz, "The Stability of a Bipolar World," *Power, Action, and Interaction*, p. 222.

4. See especially Morgenthau's *Politics Among Nations* and Kaplan's *System and Process in International Politics*.

5. Deutsch and Singer, "Multipolar Power Systems and International Stability," p. 390.

6. In the "pure" or "tight" bipolar situation, no actors remain outside of the two blocs.

7. Deutsch and Singer, "Multipolar Power Systems and International Stability," p. 406.

8. See Roger Masters, "A Multi-Bloc Model of the International System," *American Political Science Review*, LV (December 1961), pp. 780-798.

9. As listed in *System and Process*, these rules are as follows:

    1. Act to increase capabilities but negotiate rather than fight.

    2. Fight rather than pass up an opportunity to increase capabilities.

    3. Stop fighting rather than eliminate an essential national actor.

    4. Act to oppose any coalition or single actor which tends to assume a position of predominance with respect to the rest of the system.

    5. Act to constrain actors who subscribe to supranational organizing principles.

    6. Permit defeated or constrained essential national actors to reenter the system as acceptable role partners or act to bring some previously inessential actor within the essential actor classification. Treat all essential actors as acceptable role partners.

10. See Wolfram F. Hanrieder, "The International System: Bipolar or Multi-bloc," *The Journal of Conflict Resolution*, IX (September 1965), pp. 299-308.

11. See Oran R. Young, "Political Discontinuities in the International System," *World Politics*, XX (April 1968), pp. 369-392.

12. See Richard N. Rosecrance, "Bipolarity, Multipolarity, and the Future," *The Journal of Conflict Resolution*, X (September 1966), pp. 314-327, reprinted in James N. Rosenau, ed., *International Politics and Foreign Policy* (New York: Free Press, 1969), pp. 325-335.

13. Rosecrance, "Bipolarity, Multipolarity, and the Future," *International Politics and Foreign Policy*, p. 332.

14. A somewhat more technical discussion of this question may be found in Louis René Beres, "Bipolarity, Multipolarity, and the Reliability of Alliance Commitments," *The Western Political Quarterly*, December 1972, pp. 702-710.

15. As an alliance grows more permanent, actors are likely to feel less and less affected by the relative strength of the other partners. This is the case because as an alliance grows more permanent, the likelihood decreases that today's partner will be tomorrow's foe.

16. Actors are also less likely to fault alliance obligations in the bipolar system because there are fewer places to which defecting allies can turn to create new arrangements. In the bipolar world, not only is there only one other principal point around which defecting allies must look for new arrangements, but the peculiarly intense and antagonistic nature of inter-bloc antagonism characteristic of bipolarity makes it especially difficult to find a welcome around that point. This is all the more so where the polar antagonism is reinforced by an ideological cleavage.

17. John Herz, *International Politics in the Atomic Age* (New York: Columbia University Press, 1959), pp. 115-116.

18. *Ibid.*, p. 121.

19. For a clear discussion of the sharp differences in character between a *deterrence* capability and a *win-the-war* capability, see Bernard Brodie, *Strategy in the Missile Age* (Princeton, N.J.: Princeton University Press, 1959), pp. 274-275.

20. As the ratio of power factor is held constant, there is no reason to suppose a difference in reliability between one bloc alliance and another.

Conclusion to Part II

We have seen that world system models may be described in terms of four principal dimensions: actor, process, context, and structure.[1] Just which of these dimensions is selected depends entirely upon the kinds of hypotheses raised by the individual student. Different kinds of hypotheses lead to the description of world system models along different dimensions. The models provide the context within which particular hypotheses can be examined. This is their purpose. To generate models without the benefit of prior hypotheses is to misunderstand the most elementary logic of scientific discovery. Without hypotheses there exists no way of organizing information about the models. The mode of investigation is "backward."

Recognizing this, the student of alternative world futures must pay close attention to the formation of hypotheses. While there are no given "rules" for this particular stage of inquiry, it should be remembered that one's models are no "better" than one's hypotheses. The latter offer the spark of genesis to the former.

Creative hypotheses are themselves dependent upon the kinds of concepts which they connect. This means that students intent upon developing creative descriptions of alternative world futures must begin to exercise their creative judgments at the level of concept formation. Conceptual creativity is the first step on the way to creative hypotheses and these are the essential foundations of creative analytic models.

But what exactly does it mean to be creative? Unfortunately, this question will not submit to a ready answer. There are no "cookbook" guidelines which offer the student a clear-cut and foolproof step-by-step pattern of assistance. Rather, each individual must decide for himself just what direction of inquiry appears most fruitful, what investigative orientation promises the most original contribution.

Originality, then, is the basic watchword, the guiding precept for students of a peculiarly urgent set of concerns. In order to come to grips with the most comprehensive spectrum of human affairs—the crises of a threatened planet—our minds must be permitted to range freely and imaginatively. They must not be too closely regulated; they must not be too fearful of treading new ground. In short, they must be allowed to go beyond the historically tutored conceptions of world politics to which we have been bound for so long.

At the same time, care must be taken to stay within the limits of *feasibility*. However desirable a particular system of world order might be, its suitability for overcoming the problem which first inspired its creation is tied to its actual prospects for implementation. To be worthy of endorsement and support as an alternative to what now exists, any proposed model of world order must satisfy *two* criteria of evaluation: desirability and feasibility. Unless a system that is judged desirable is also judged attainable, there is no reason to suppose that it will have any bearing on the problem or problems that led to its development.

But this raises yet another problem. After all, what is feasible? How can we actually evaluate the attainability of our "preferred worlds"? Once again, we are left without a specific set of rules or guidelines. Each individual student will have to exercise personal judgment in pinpointing the limits of feasibility. Beyond a number of fairly obvious limitations, the areas of agreement on this matter are likely to be few.

In addition, students may discover to their consternation and dismay that the two criteria their models intend to satisfy—desirability and feasibility—tend to vary inversely. This means that moving to satisfy one criterion is only accomplished at the *expense* of the other, that a *trade-off* of the two criteria must be undertaken. Just *how* this trade-off should be handled is up to the individual student. Once again, it is a decision of uniquely personal proportions.

Indeed, the *entire enterprise* of designing alternative world futures is a uniquely personal activity. One person's "preferred world" may not be another's. As a property of different world systems, *desirability* cannot be defined in terms of some universally agreed upon preference ordering. Rather, it must be evaluated from the standpoint of each individual's *particular* system of values. This system is embodied in the very hypotheses which inform the creation of world order models. The dependent variables (subjects to be explained) in these hypotheses reflect personal judgments of what is most important to global life. Alternative world futures must be designed for an entire planet, but they cannot escape private definition. Their creation is an irremediably personal experience.

NOTE

1. While any of these dimensions may be assigned preeminence in describing an alternative world future, all of them are very closely interrelated. Failure to recognize this interrelatedness leads to defective investigations. Although our discussion has been ordered in terms of each *separate* dimension, such ordering reflects concern for *emphasis* and *clarity of instruction*. There is no hint or suggestion that one dimension may be considered independently in the examination of world order systems.

Conclusion

It is the wisdom of Hermann Hesse to remind the readers of his story of *Siddhartha* that the potential Buddha already lives in the sinner, that the spark of transformation and renewal is touched off in the *passing* form. It is only up to the sinner to *recognize* his hidden potential. So it is with students of alternative world futures. The stuff of a more harmonious arrangement of global life is already present in the extant world system. It is up to us to identify it and to adapt it to our ambitious purposes. How to accomplish this objective has been the subject of our book.

If this book has been ambitiously conceived, there is ample reason. In the Introduction we mentioned that if our subject is to be the whole destiny of man and the entire planet which circumscribes his activity, it is because of the peculiar dangers which now confront him. This represents something of a *substantive* defense of our holistic perspective.

To this can be added yet another defense, one that might be characterized as *epistemological*. This is that there is nothing more inherently pretentious or difficult about tackling a set of problems at its most comprehensive level than at its most specific. It is not necessarily more difficult to challenge the whole of international life than to grapple with any one of its innumerable parts and aspects. The needed intellectual effort is not necessarily more demanding. As H. G. Wells pointed out earlier in this century:

> ... the quality of the work required for making the map of a continent may be less than and inferior to that demanded by the chemical examination of a muscle fibre or the investigation of atomic structure. A man is not pretentious because he works with the theodolite instead of the microscope. Some men work upon the bulkier common issues; some upon finer and subtler questions. To every man his task. There is no hierarchy in human thought.[1]

This idea has been central to our book. Its full meaning must be appreciated by students of alternative world futures.

But there is much more to be appreciated. Having recognized the reasonableness of alternative world future study, students must begin to think self-consciously and inventively about *doing* such study. It is to assist in this activity that our book has been written. In conformity with its principal guidelines, students are urged to range widely and creatively in the search for models of alternative world futures, and to examine these models systematically. This is the overarching "message" of Part I and Part II respectively. *Together*, Parts I and II define the full contours of our subject, the complete pattern of contemplating and designing an improved world order.

This does not mean, however, the *Reordering the Planet* is exhaustive, that its pages contain the entire gamut of ideas that concern its theme. By no means! To use an appropriate metaphor, it is a *guidebook* rather than a map. It distils a variety of starting and stopping points from the whole realm of possibilities, but leaves a large number of additional options open to the traveler. Many of these options may be wondrously exciting. It is up to each individual to judge for himself just which ones best fit into his crowded itinerary.

In terms of Part I, this nonexhaustive nature of the book suggests that students consider a wide spectrum of additional sources for ideas about alternative world futures. These may include a number of science fiction and futurology sources as well as more general literary materials. And from the standpoint of Part II, it suggests that the recommended mode of analysis be extended to still other dimensions of planetary danger. While this second part has been designed with particular reference to the problem of war avoidance, there is no reason to confine future analyses to this problem alone. Indeed, so long as the crisis of world order is defined in terms of a complex of dimensions rather than any single one, students of the subject will necessarily extend their investigations beyond the war problem. More specifically, this means that students of alternative world futures are now encouraged to apply to population pressure, resource shortages, and environmental deterioration the same canons of inquiry that were applied to war in Part II of this book.

This brings us to the *personal imperative* for public action. When all is said and done, when creative thought has prompted careful scholarship and brought it to fruition, students of alternative world futures must make an important decision. They must decide what to do with their findings. This is a critical decision. They can decide to stimulate academic debate and public discussion with their colleagues and fellow citizens or they can decide to do nothing. To opt for the former alternative is to begin the necessary process of creative planetary renewal. It is to submit the question offered by Goethe, foremost titan of German poetry, in *Faust*:

Why have I sought my path with fervent care,
If not in hope to bring my brothers there?

NOTE

1. See *The Open Conspiracy* (London: V. Gollancz Ltd., 1928), p. 7.

Subject Index